W9-BVM-051

PERFORMANCE MANAGEMENT

PERFORMANCE MANAGEMENT

Improving Quality Productivity through Positive Reinforcement

Third Edition, *Revised*

Aubrey C. Daniels, Ph. D.

This book is a rewrite of:
Performance Management: Improving Quality and Productivity through Positive Reinforcement, Second Edition by Daniels & Rosen.

Performance Management Publications
Tucker, Georgia

Original cover art by Bill Morse.
The technique of optically generating graphics was used
to convey R+ as the way of the future.

Published by Performance Management Publications
3531 Habersham at Northlake
Tucker, Georgia 30084
(404) 493-5080

This book was set in Garamond.

Administrative Editors: Brenda Jernigan, Sandy Stewart
Production Coordinators: Sandy Stewart, Brenda Jernigan,
Cover Designer: Judy Doi
Art Coordinators: Michael Kosmas, Sandy Stewart

Copyright ©1989 by Performance Management Publications. All rights reserved. No part of this book may be
reproduced in any form, electronic or mechanical,
including photocopy, recording, or any information
storage and retrieval system, without permission in
writing from the publisher. "Performance Management
Publications" and "PMP" are registered trademarks of
Performance Management Publications.

Library of Congress Catalog Card Number: 82-061868
International Standard Book Number: 0-937100-01-3
Printed in the United States of America
3 4 5 6 7 8 9 – 93 92

This book is dedicated to the memory of my father,
Aubrey O. Daniels, who taught me you can learn
something from everyone and to be curious
and persistent about it.

PREFACE

Several factors led to rewriting the Second Edition of *Performance Management: Improving Quality and Productivity through Positive Reinforcement* by Daniels & Rosen. Although there is only a slight change in the sub-title of the Third Edition, the change reflects the current approach to quality and productivity which is: *that they are one in the same*.

Even though it has only been five years since the last edition was published, the experience base of PM applications has increased dramatically. We have learned a lot about how to make these applications more effective as a result. This book incorporates much of what has been learned.

Second, quality has become the primary concern of managers in the years since the Second Edition. New analytical tools such as Statistical Process Control (SPC) have become popular in the work place to facilitate improvements in products and service. These methods and PM fit together like hand and glove. Although some followers of Deming and Juran may feel there are not enough direct references to the quality technology in this book, the serious student will have little trouble using PM to implement quality technology and make the continuous improvement philosophy a reality.

Third, research in Applied Behavior Analysis also continues to grow. Much has been learned about human behavior in the last five years. Although the basic concepts remain pretty much the same, those who have read the last edition will see many subtle changes in the material that stem from relatively recent research findings that have added to our fund of knowledge of human behavior. Some of the changes in the book have come about not because of recent research findings, but because I now understand the previous research better.

Finally, the last edition was written primarily for managers and supervisors. This book is written to be understood and applied by everyone in the work place. With the current emphasis on teamwork, employee involvement and participation, this edition is oriented more toward anyone wanting to improve the quality of performance at work, whether it is a subordinate, peer, boss, or one's self.

Because of these factors I felt a complete rewrite was necessary. Hopefully you'll find it more readable, more understandable, easier to reference, and an effective antecedent for successful applications of PM at work and at home.

ACKNOWLEDGEMENTS

This is an attempt at positive reinforcement for all those who contributed to the Third Edition of **Performance Management**. An "attempt" because writing a few words about all the effort and hours that people put into the production of this book seems minor. It would be unthinkable not to try because of all the reinforcement and assistance that I received over the course of rewriting this book.

First and foremost, I would like to express my appreciation to Ted Rosen, the co-author of the First Edition. Without Ted's assistance, that book would never have been written. He did a lot of the writing and had a significant impact on the concepts that were included and the way they were expressed. I am most grateful for our association.

Working with Beth Sulzer-Azaroff has been a real treat for me. She is an outstanding researcher, writer and teacher in the field of Applied Behavior Analysis and has provided invaluable technical and grammatical assistance. She not only pointed out problems but offered a better alternative—a writer's dream editor.

Janis Allen established the world's record for quick turnaround of the manuscripts to be edited; her reinforcing comments caused me to look forward to her editorial remarks. She did a thorough job of editing, and often asked if she could help by writing an example, or creating a form or figure for the text—R+ I gladly accepted!

Gail Snyder made a major contribution to my writing style. Her writing skills, command of the English language and PM knowledge allowed her to see problems and suggest changes that made this book much clearer and more readable.

As a naive reader for this particular type manuscript, Betsy Graham made a significant contribution by suggesting changes that improved clarity, readability and understanding. She also made suggestions for the layout and design.

I was fortunate to have the assistance of Michael Kosmas, a recent graduate in Applied Behavior Analysis. Mike's enthusiasm for the subject kept him on task through seemingly endless planning and revisions of the material. I value his input on the subject matter and ideas he shared for the layout.

Jamie Daniels gave valuable feedback on the entire book but particularly on pinpointing and measurement, his specialty.

Susan Cannon graciously agreed to edit the early drafts and gave me much needed feedback from a user's perspective.

As usual Courtney Mills provided much data and many editorial comments. I have been telling "Courtney stories" for over 20 years. He has enriched the book, my speeches, and my life as well.

Wilson Rourk, Tucker Childers and Dick Beers gave me feedback and words of wisdom on the entire text and provided numerous examples from the real world, where they are helping clients apply PM every day. Their examples and comments improved the book considerably.

Mark Nunnelee, Andy Morency, and John Cochran made suggestions and offered examples from their consulting experience.

John O'Connell provided numerous data examples and John Davis was particularly helpful in editing Chapter Four.

Dave Fluharty read the manuscript at the eleventh hour and made numerous helpful suggestions from the perspective of a quality management professional.

Few things would get done in our office without the assistance of Brenda Jernigan and Sandy Stewart. Having been through the task of finalizing the first two editions, they knew what to do and did it with meticulous attention to detail. Their dedication to quality would provide comfort to any author and certainly made my job a lot easier. Many thanks as well go to their assistants Debbie Farquhar and Sharon Braman.

It seems trite to thank one's family, but this revision has been two years in the making. That is a long time to ask family to tolerate my anti-social behavior, do things without me, and take on my responsibilities while I sat at the computer working on the book nights and weekends. Becky, Laura Lee and Joanna were great through it all and I am especially thankful for each of them.

Although Dr. B. F. Skinner's contribution to the field is acknowledged in the text, something should be said here as well. His writings contributed significantly to the quality of my life and I hope by extending the principles he discovered to the work place that he will be pleased.

ACD
Tucker, Georgia

CONTENTS

5

6

7

8

9

10

1
Introduction to Performance Management

Imagine you work in a manufacturing facility where your job is to prepare ceramic vases for packaging. The vases come down a conveyor belt in groups of ten, each vase in a box, standing upright. Your job is to lay them on their sides before they go on to be automatically shrink-wrapped and placed on pallets for shipping. The vases come by quickly and it requires some skill to do the job efficiently.

Your productivity is nothing to write home about but it is enough to keep you out of trouble. You have had this job for several years, and although the pay is good, you don't particularly like the work and often complain of boredom and a lack of challenge.

Your performance is reviewed in quarterly appraisals. The sessions are predictable unless there is a problem; but in any event, they are not particularly satisfying. If performance is below standard you are asked what you are going to do about it. If performance is above average your supervisor's attitude is "that's what you are paid for."

You get very little feedback during the course of your shift. When there is a problem, the boss assembles the group and talks about the need for higher performance or improved quality. He may even mention the consequences of failing to improve. But most of the time, one day is pretty much like the next.

Now let's consider another task in a different setting that is very similar to the one just described, but one which the performers look forward to doing and always enjoy immensely. Let's call it Task 2. These employees also have to put ten objects at a time on their sides. Task 2 is more difficult than the vase-packaging task because the objects are 30 feet away. The employees use a special tool to accomplish this task. They get two attempts to put the objects on their sides, but after that an automatic device removes any remaining objects and puts a new set of ten in place. In spite of the potential pressure to put all the objects on their sides in only two tries, the performers do not feel stressed. Instead, they really enjoy the task and over a period of time become quite proficient at it.

Why is Task 2 so much more productive and more enjoyable than Task 1? Let's look at the amount of feedback and positive reinforcement provided by each activity. In Task 2 the performers have a form on which they record the results of each trial. They also keep a running total of their daily performance. Totals for the entire group are publicly posted so everyone can see how the group is doing. They like this and would hate to work at a job in which they did not receive such prompt feedback on performance. In addition their boss and co-workers come over from time to time to watch them work and to look at the record of their performance. They don't resent the fact that others look at their performance data because when they are doing well they pat each other on the back and laugh and joke. When one of the group has a problem he either asks for, or others offer, feedback on what they observe him doing wrong; and they give him advice on how to correct the problem. The boss also recognizes the performers with plaques, trophies, and patches for their shirts or jackets. He distributes them frequently— sometimes weekly. Each group of performers is organized into a team and each team picks a name.

In Task 2 all the performers know how much they are expected to do. They set group and individual goals. The individual goals differ for each person. The boss notices even small improvements and is quick to give praise. Since the performers know their improvement will be appreciated, the team continuously sets higher goals. As a result, most people consistently improve.

Task 2 has one unique attribute—people aren't paid to do it! They pay to do it. What is this task? Bowling. You might say, "Of course, a sport is more fun than work!"

But just what is so enjoyable about bowling? All you do in bowling is take a sixteen-pound ball and roll it down a long alley toward ten large pins over and over and over again—a very repetitive task. Even so, millions of Americans bowl as often as they can. You may think that a sport is fun because of the activity itself. In fact, it is not what you do that determines whether you have fun; it is what happens to you when you do it. For example, what would we need to do to bowling to take the fun out of it? First, we could give the bowlers a "boss." Then, we could make the bowlers take the game seriously. That is, we would keep conversation and distracting activity to a minimum. Idle talk and chatter would not only distract those who are bowling but would take the other bowlers' minds off the game. Therefore, no loud talking, joking, or horseplay would be allowed during the game.

Then, since bowlers are there to bowl, and bowl only, let's not load them up with paperwork. Rather than have them keep their own score, we will keep score for them. Since we don't want them hanging around the alley after the match is over to see their score, we will mail it to them. And again in

order to cut down on paperwork we will send scores only once a month. That way we not only save on processing time and paperwork, but we also save on postage.

When we send the reports we will circle the poor or problem performances in red and write a comment on the report such as "What happened here?" or "See me about this!" We will never express satisfaction with the level of performance because we think if we do, the bowlers would not do their best. In order to prevent this we will set high goals for everyone and use the best bowler's performance to show the others what is possible. We will, of course, compare teams in the same way. If someone bowls above average, we take the position "that is what you are paid for" and no other consequences from management are necessary.

We will rank the bowlers—not only by score but also on such things as attitude and initiative. We will threaten the ones on the bottom with loss of team membership if their performance does not rise above average by the end of the next reporting period. This discouraging scenario could go on and on. No doubt you could think of some other things to take the fun out of the game and make it something we would have to pay people top dollar for, in order to get enough people to keep the roster full.

If we can take a sport and make it something people don't want to do, can we take work and make it something people want to do with the same energy and enthusiasm they typically put into sports? The answer is an unqualified YES! But to accomplish this, we must first examine the elements in sports that, in most cases, are absent at work.

SOME CHARACTERISTICS OF TEAM SPORTS

1. Specific job responsibilities

In team sports individual assignments are clearly defined. Even in sandlot games players know their responsibilities.

2. *Teamwork*

Because individual assignments are well defined it is easy to know when and how to help your teammates. Since individual success is affected by how well the team performs, team members help each other.

3. *Measurable results*

It's hard to think of sports without measurement. Imagine bowling without keeping score or football without yard markers.

4. *Challenging but attainable goals*

Although the goal is to win, sub-goals are an exciting part of every game: getting a hit in baseball, getting a first down in football, or landing on the green in two in golf.

5. *Immediate feedback*

In sports you know where you stand at all times. You can see your progress on every play, frame, or time at bat. Not only do you know how well you are doing, you also know what you need to do to improve.

6. *Positive reinforcement from peers, fans, and coaches*

This is the most prominent element in sports and the one that is usually missing at work. It is natural in sports to congratulate, applaud, pat on the back, cheer, and otherwise celebrate the accomplishments of teammates. Unfortunately in many work places these things are considered unnatural.

7. *Emphasis on behaviors*

Nowhere are results more important than in sports, but in sports more than in business, it is common to praise the good swing, good form, or the good follow-through. The best coaches are those who applaud not only the good result but all the right behaviors along the way.

Should we copy sports characteristics in business?

If we use these elements at work we can get the same interest, energy, enthusiasm, and teamwork that we witness in sports. However, it's not as easy as it seems. Some things that work very well in sports will not succeed at work. For example, the competitive methods used in sports are effective, but used the same way in the work place, these methods bring disastrous results. We cannot mimic sports in the work place any more than we can simply copy Japanese management techniques such as Quality Circles. A great many companies have learned this lesson the hard way.

Of course, competition and Japanese management techniques can be used effectively. But the ways these motivational methods are used in the average business in the U.S. create more problems than they solve.

How can we profit from the successful methods of others? When can we adopt a technique directly from another activity, country, or company and when can we not? The only way we can learn the answers to these questions is to understand all the variables that affect the outcome. We do this in much the same way a researcher would as she seeks to find what variables control a physical process in manufacturing or in the lab. To stay competitive, we must learn to manage human performance precisely.

Thomas Gilbert (1978), in his book *Human Competence*, has estimated that the performance improvement potential of the average plant and store management is greater than 300 percent. The range of effectiveness of individual managers varies dramatically. Therefore the company that is able to isolate effective management processes and procedures and implement them efficiently will have a significant competitive advantage over those who cannot. Separating management myth from reality, specifically as it relates to the motivation of people at work, is what this book is all about. The following chapters give you a precise system for managing performance. The system, based on scientific knowledge of human behavior, is called Performance Management.

WHAT IS PERFORMANCE MANAGEMENT?

Performance Management is a systematic, data-oriented approach to managing people at work that relies on positive reinforcement as the major way to maximizing performance. The essential words in this definition are systematic and data-oriented. Systematic means that in order to determine if any particular management procedure is effective, you must specify the behaviors and results to be affected. Furthermore, you must develop a way to measure these behaviors and results and determine the methods for changing current performance. The final steps are to use those methods and evaluate the results. Figure 1.1 is an example of this procedure as used to evaluate the effectiveness of a Performance Management intervention to improve the job performance of a game room attendant.

Although this process is familiar to business people for evaluating a change in a product or service, it is rarely used when making decisions about the way we deal with people. This book will show you how to do this in a practical way that is both time- and cost-effective.

Data-oriented means that we use data to evaluate the effectiveness of motivational strategies. This assumes that all performance can be measured. Indeed, whether one is trying to improve on the quality or efficiency of an existing product or service, or to develop a new product or service, critical behaviors and results can be measured. In other words, contrary to popular belief, every job can be measured.

Many of you will recognize from the above description of Performance Management that the approach is basically one of scientific problem solving. In fact, the techniques and practices of Performance Management (PM) are derived from the field study called Applied Behavior Analysis, the term applied to the scientific study of behavior. The field was clearly defined by Baer, Wolf and Risley (1968). Its subject matter is human behavior: why we act as we do, how we acquire habits, and how we lose them; in other words, why we do the things we do and how we can change them, if change is needed.

In order to understand behavior, applied behavior analysts use the same scientific methods that the physical sciences employ: precise definition of the behavior under study, experimentation, and consistent replication of the experimental findings. Basic research in this area has been con-

Figure 1.1

Illustrates two main points. The first is the game room attendant spends well under 60% of his time actually working on the job according to the employer's job description. This three-week measure taken before PM is called the Baseline. After the first PM intervention, performance increased to 95% proficiency in two weeks. The second point of interest is once PM techniques are stopped, performance drops to below 60% again. Lastly, when PM is reintroduced, performance again rises to above the 95% efficiency level. Each point indicates separate recorded observations. *(From "Alternative Evaluation Strategies in Work Settings: Reversal and Multiple Baseline Designs" by Judi Komaki, 1977, Journal of Organizational Behavior Management, 1-1, pp. 53-57. Copyright 1977 by Behavioral Systems, Inc. Reprinted by permission.)*

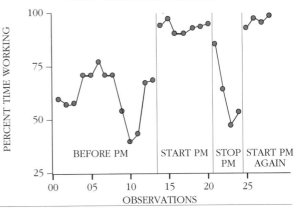

EXAMPLE OF A PROCEDURE FOR EVALUATING PERFORMANCE CHANGE

ducted for nearly a century. However, applied research has been conducted for only about 40 years. Business, industrial, and government applications began in the late 1960s. Compared with most of the established sciences, Applied Behavior Analysis is very young, but much has been learned in a short period of time. Many of the principles of learning are relatively well understood at this point. Although much remains to be learned, what is currently known has been used to solve thousands of business problems in the last 20 years. Many of these problems had plagued organizations for a long time and in some cases had been thought to be unsolvable.

We now know enough about these principles to know that the kind and level of performance that the organization achieves is a direct reflection of how management applies the principles. In order to change performance we must change the way we apply these principles. Because many manag-

ers do not have a thorough understanding of these principles, they are unable to apply this knowledge systematically to produce either the kinds of performance or the consistency of performance that will best serve their organization.

WHY AREN'T ALL COMPANIES USING PERFORMANCE MANAGEMENT?

Many dramatic results in practically every area of business have come from the deliberate and systematic use of PM. See Figure 1.2. Because of this you might ask, "Why don't all companies use PM?" There are at least four reasons:

1. Although successful applications have been documented since the late 1960s, most managers have still never heard of PM;
2. Most people superficially acquainted

Figure 1.2

CLAIMS ADJUDICATED PER DAY

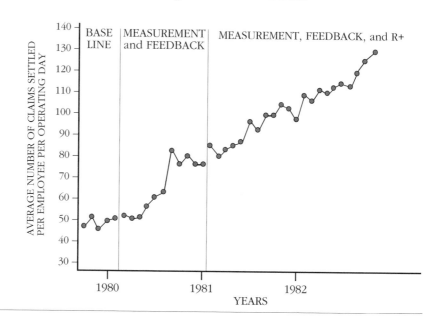

An example of how the deliberate, systematic use of PM, which included Measurement, Feedback and Positive Reinforcement (R+) increased performance from an average of 45 claims settled per day to over 130. *(From "Alabama Blues: Don't Sing the Blues Anymore" by Richard Dowis, 1983,* Performance Management Magazine, *1-2, pp. 3-5. Copyright 1983 by Performance Management Publications. Reprinted by permission.)*

with it think they are already doing it;

3. Others think that something so "simple" could not solve their serious or important problems;

4. It often requires major changes in the interaction at all levels of the organization and requires continuous effort at maintaining these changes.

Although thousands of people in hundreds of companies have been trained and have successfully applied PM since the early 1960s, most companies have still not heard about this technology. Many companies have programs called performance management, but these are usually performance appraisal programs and not Performance Management as defined by the principles of Applied Behavior Analysis.

When many people hear the terms feedback and positive reinforcement, two key concepts involved in PM, they often think not only that they know about them; they believe they're already using them. It's true that all organizations, with the advent of computers, have dramatically increased the amount of performance data available at all levels, but they do not use the information wisely.

It is a rare company that is not doing some positive things for employees these days. However, the availability of data and the existence of positives in the work place do not mean that PM is being used effectively. Indeed, in many companies there are mountains of data but little feedback, and, believe it or not, the way many employee benefits and human relations programs operate, they actually decrease quality and productivity, while increasing operational costs.

Relative to the third issue, when many people hear that positive reinforcement includes things like a pat on the back or other common ways of showing appreciation, they automatically think that this system can't affect the larger problems of the organization such as quality, cost, labor relations, and profit. But PM works on all problems, simple and complex.

Finally, using PM effectively requires time and effort. Managers consistently underestimate what it takes to bring about lasting change. It requires more than training. It requires more than verbal support. In order to realize the potential of this technology, managers must do things daily, not just monthly, quarterly, or annually. It is hard work but it is worth it, not only because it brings about bottom-line results but because it elevates the quality of life of all involved.

THE VALUE OF PM TO ORGANIZATIONS

There are many reasons that organizations use PM. However, there are seven that highlight the value of PM to business, industry, and government:

1. PM works

It is practical. It is not a generalized abstract theory that suggests ways to think about problems; it is a set of specific actions for increasing desired performance and decreasing undesired performance. Firms using PM have reported returns on investment ranging from 4 to 1 to 60 to 1 in the first year. Successful applications have occurred in a wide range of organizations, from manufacturing and service to research and development. Applications range from sales and safety to customer service and vendor performance. In a survey of the research literature, Duncan (1989) reports the average improvement in PM applications is 69 percent. Figure 1.3 lists some general areas of PM applications and some specific topics of successful interventions within them.

2. PM produces short-term as well as long-term results

Mitchell Fein (1981), the creator of a gainsharing system called Improshare, says that if you go onto the production floor, into the office, or into the lab and do the right things, you will see a performance change in fifteen minutes. He's not entirely correct. If you do

Figure 1.3   **AREAS OF SUCCESSFUL PM INTERVENTION**

Manufacturing
- Increased units produced per hour
- Increased maintenance work orders completed per hour
- Increased total outgoing quality
- Improved housekeeping
- Increased yield
- Increased start-up efficiency
- Increased changeover efficiency
- Increased amount error-free lines typed per hour
- Increased number implemented suggestions
- Improved on-schedule performance
- Improved inventory control
- Improved budget performance
- Increased conformance to process control standards
- Increased safety (lower insurance costs)

Engineering
- Increased percentage products delivered on time and within budget
- Increased engineering efficiency
- Improved teamwork
- Increased percentage of error-free drawings
- Increased internal and external customer satisfaction
- Increased requests for engineering service
- Increased percentage of current process standards
- Increased quality of total job performance
- Increased percentage of milestones met on time
- Increased percentage work completed on CAD/CAM

Sales
- Increased sales dollars
- Increased referrals
- Increased number of presentations
- Increased number of qualified leads
- Increased number of closes attempted
- Increased percentage of quality presentations
- Increased in-person contacts (prospecting)
- Increased paperwork accuracy and timeliness
- Increased number proposals written
- Improved conversion rate (leads to sales)
- Decreased cost of sales
- Increased profit margins

Vendor Performance
- Increased percentage on-time deliveries
- Increased quality
- Increased economic recovery of defective parts
- Increased number acceptable products
- Increased response time replacing defective parts
- Improved invoice accuracy
- Increased percentage complete shipments received
- Increased orders within specifications

Customer Service
- Improved customer service ratings
- Increased on-time shipments
- Improved customer response time
- Decreased complaints per thousand orders
- Improved quality of correspondence
- Increased customer problems solved within target times
- Increased percent phone inquiries answered promptly and politely
- Improved scores on customer satisfaction surveys

Research and Development
- Increased number new products
- Increased idea sharing
- Increased number quality tests completed
- Decreased design revisions per accepted design
- Increased number of design phases completed on or ahead of schedule
- Increased percentage release dates met
- Increased percentage commitments met
- Improved budget performance

Information Management
- Increased number programs delivered on time and within budget
- Increased percentage first-time runs
- Improved programmer efficiency
- Decreased number deadlines rescheduled
- Decreased computer costs
- Improved information accuracy
- Decreased paper costs
- Improved internal customer satisfaction
- Increased number technical assistance requests closed

Safety
- Increased number employees working according to safety standards
- Decreased insurance costs
- Decreased number OSHA recordables
- Increased proper use of safety equipment
- Proper labeling of hazardous materials
- Increased number people using proper lifting procedures
- Decreased workman compensation claims
- Improved scores on safety audits
- Increased quality of accident investigations completed

Distribution and Transportation
- Increased load average
- Improved engine rebuild quality/cost
- Increased fuel efficiency (MPG)
- Increased space utilization efficiency
- Increased percentage cargo loaded properly
- Improved turnaround time: warehouse response
- Increased miles per recap
- Increased percentage trailer space
- Improved stock storage accuracy

the right things, you will, in many cases, see the effect immediately.

Many programs make no claim that results can be expected quickly. In fact, their presenters warn that changes will not be noticeable for several years. Few managers can stick to any motivational program or system that takes several years to show results. The truth is that in some cases the manager may not be around that long.

If you try to solve a problem using the procedures and techniques described in this book and do not see changes in performance within the first ten data points, you can bet you are doing something wrong. The good thing about this approach is you will know what steps to take to correct the problem. To sustain commitment and enthusiasm, people must see both short- and long-term results. See Figure 1.4 A-D.

3. PM requires no psychological background

Performance Management is supported by more than 50 years of experimental and applied research in laboratories, universities, schools, clinics, hospitals, homes, and, since the late sixties, in business and industry. (See O'Brien, 1982; Fredrickson, 1982; Martin and Hrycaiko, 1983; Sulzer-Azaroff and Mayer, 1977; Millenson and Leslie, 1979; Cooper, Heron and Heward, 1987; Kazdin, 1975.) This research is based on the pioneering work of the American psychologist, B. F. Skinner (1938, 1953, 1972, 1976).

Dr. Skinner rejects the belief that in order to work effectively with people you must first understand their deep-seated anxieties, feelings, and motives. He takes the position that the only way you can know people is by observing how they behave (what they do or say). We do not need to know how people were potty trained, that they hate their fathers, or that they are middle children.

PM accepts people as they are, not as they were. Because it deals with the here and now, managers do not need to pry into people's private lives or their history in order to manage them effectively. Because it deals

with the present, everybody can learn the techniques of PM. In other words you do not need to be a psychologist, psychiatrist, or a mind reader. As a matter of fact everyone makes use of the laws of behavior and is influenced by them. Unfortunately in many cases, they are using them ineffectively.

The principles of behavior are so simple that infants learn to use them to gain control over their parents in a very short period of time. Notice how quickly people respond when a baby cries or smiles. However, the paradox is that even though the basics are very simple, they are not obvious. Subsequently we often inadvertently end up teaching people to do what we don't want rather than what we do want. You can avoid this mistake by learning how such situations occur and how to avoid them.

4. PM is a system for measuring all kinds of performance

Because PM is based on knowledge acquired through a scientific study of behavior, the principles are applicable to behavior wherever it occurs. This means that PM applies to people, wherever they work and no matter what they do. The applicability of PM to routine and easily measured jobs is apparent with a basic understanding of the principles. However, it may be easier to see how PM applies to production jobs than to jobs where the main outcome is creativity, such as in research or engineering, or to complex organizational problems such as bringing about a cultural change or creating autonomous work groups.

Be assured that if one or more people are involved in any activity, PM can enable them to work consistently at their full potential. These principles work whether the performer is the president of the company or the janitor; whether the target is an R&D group working on telecommunications systems for the next century, or a group of textile employees producing a product that the company has been making for fifty years; and also, whether the company has five employees or fifty thousand.

Figure 1.4

EXAMPLES OF RAPID IMPROVEMENT WITH PM

A.

Illustrates improved performance within the first ten days of PM. The application was a sanding process in which units finished per shift rose from an average of 2500 to an impressive 4200 per shift.

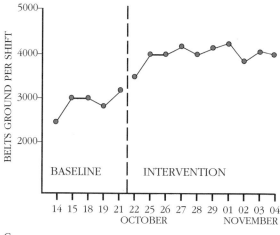

B.

PM shows an immediate and consistent effect on a project intended to increase the percentage of time employees used their ear protectors. Points represent two observations per day.

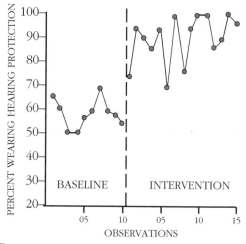

C.

From a two-year baseline of 83%, performance on the assembly of electrical circuit breakers rose to over 100% of standard in four days.

D.

In many cases you may see the effect of PM immediately upon intervention. The ascending axis indicates units produced per labor hour.

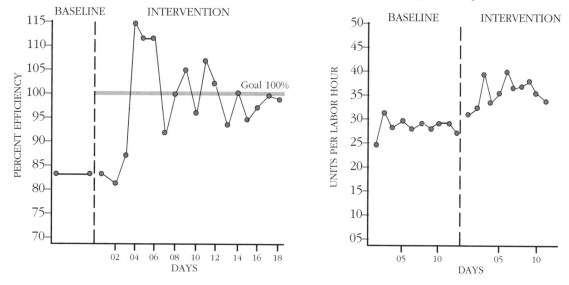

(1.4D From "A Performance Feedback Intervention to Reduce Waste; Performance Data and Participant Responses" by Eldridge, Lemasters, Szypot, 1978, Journal of Organizational Behavior Management, *I, pp. 258-266. Copyright 1978 by Behavioral Systems, Inc. Reprinted by permission.)*

5. PM creates an enjoyable place in which to work

Most people agree that if you are doing something you enjoy, you are more likely to perform well than if you don't like what you are doing.

Unfortunately some managers have the notion that fun and work don't mix. Indeed, in many cases they think the way people have fun at work is at the expense of the work rather than through it.

It's true that the only way many people have any fun at work is through off-task behavior such as horseplay, practical jokes, or other forms of goofing off.

If, however, the fun comes from doing the work, then management should be preoccupied with how to increase fun rather than eliminate it. A manufacturing executive recently said, "Sales and marketing folks know how to have fun at work. In manufacturing we haven't had much fun—no, we haven't had any fun. We've got to change that."

Fun and work are so antithetical to some managers that even this subject may turn them off. But, research is clear; when you have fun that is directly related to your job mission—quality, productivity, cost and customer service can be dramatically improved.

6. PM can be used to enhance relationships at home and in the community

While this book focuses on the work place, we use many examples from everyday life because not only are they easy to relate to in order to teach a principle or a technique, but they illustrate very well the universality of the approach. Indeed, many managers have been convinced of the power of the approach by applying PM to a difficult problem at home.

7. PM is an open system

PM includes no motivational tricks. There is nothing you will learn in this book that you would not want everybody in your organization to know. You will learn nothing that is illegal, immoral, or unethical (although it may be fattening in some cases). Because of the sizable number of positive reinforcers needed to sustain high levels of performance, high-performance organizations teach these principles to everyone so that employees at all levels can facilitate each other's performance.

Just as managers influence the performance of the people they supervise, employees influence the performance of managers by the same process. There is nothing about the principles that says reinforcement only works down the organization. Reinforcement works on people. Therefore PM works equally well up and across the organization. Performance Management suggests nothing about changing another person's performance that you would not want done to you in the same circumstance. Therefore, there is no need for secret plans to improve performance. On the contrary, every reason exists to be open and honest in all relationships at work. In the final analysis, changing performance with PM will result in everybody getting more of what they want from work. Who could complain about that?

NOTES

2

Antecedents

In order to change performance (the combination of behaviors and their accomplishments) you must first change what people do (their behavior). **Behavior** is any observable and measurable act. For purposes of this book it is defined, simply, as anything that you can see a person do.

Most of the time we think of a **performance** as composed of a number, or series, of behaviors directed toward some outcome or goal. A musical performance on the piano may be composed of several behaviors repeated many times, such as striking the keys and pressing the pedals. The goal might be to please the listener or to execute a passage without error. At work, performance may consist of the behaviors of picking up a sheet of plastic, placing it on a machine, pressing a button, removing a molded part, and stacking it neatly on a pile. The goal might be to mold a certain number within a given time and within certain quality specifications. A change in any of the behaviors changes the performance.

Technical readers probably know the term "performance" as it refers to the effectiveness or efficiency of a machine or work system. In this book the word performance refers to human performance. In order for a machine to "perform" as it was designed, someone may have to monitor it, turn knobs, check gauges, flip switches and enter data into a computer. Such human performance is the subject of this book: How do we design a work place in which people know what to do and do it consistently?

THE ABC MODEL OF BEHAVIOR CHANGE

Behavior can be changed in two main ways—by what comes before it and by what comes after it. When you try to influence behavior before it occurs you are using antecedents. When you attempt to influence behavior by doing something after it occurs you are using consequences. Performance Management involves the systematic use of antecedents and consequences to improve work-related performance.

The three elements—**Antecedents, Behavior, Consequences**—combine to form the ABC model of behavior change. An *antecedent* prompts a *behavior* which is followed by a *consequence.* An understanding of the way these elements interact allows us to analyze performance problems, take corrective actions, and design work environments and management systems in which high performance will occur.

WHAT ARE ANTECEDENTS?

An **antecedent** is a person, place, thing, or event coming before a behavior that encourages you to perform that behavior. Figure 2.1 shows some antecedents and the performances they influence.

Although in Applied Behavior Analysis the word antecedent has a very precise meaning, there are many similar words in everyday language. The words stimulate, signal, cue, prompt, trigger, and encourage are all similar to the concept of antecedent.

The word antecedent, chosen by Dr. Skinner, is not in common usage and many people wonder why we don't use a "better" word. Dr. Skinner wanted a word to describe a precise relationship between behavior and the environment. All of the more common words had connotations that did not communicate the precision he wanted. Although we could use another word, the word antecedent allows us to remain consistent with the research on which the approach is based.

Examples of antecedents in business and industry

Almost every behavior has an antecedent. Therefore, antecedents surround us all the time. In businesses we design the work place to prompt the correct or desirable responses and performances. Some of the more common antecedents used in business are such things as goals, objectives, priorities, accountabilities, job descriptions, policies, procedures, standards, and rules. All of these are intended to communicate what is expected of employees; and of course, we use

**EXAMPLES OF ANTECEDENTS
AND THEIR EFFECTS**

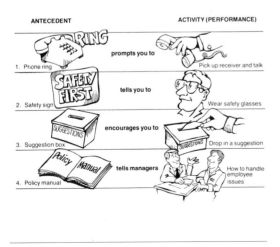

ANTECEDENT		ACTIVITY (PERFORMANCE)
1. Phone ring	prompts you to	Pick up receiver and talk
2. Safety sign	tells you to	Wear safety glasses
3. Suggestion box	encourages you to	Drop in a suggestion
4. Policy manual	tells managers	How to handle employee issues

one of the most common antecedents of all to communicate those listed—meetings.

All resources provided to help you do your job are antecedents. Tools, raw materials, and conditions of the work place such as temperature, lighting, and housekeeping affect the way you work. All of these "set the stage" for a work behavior or performance to take place, but they do not guarantee that it will occur.

Training and education are probably the most common antecedents used by business to change or improve performance. Indeed, businesses spend billions of dollars every year on these activities. Seminars, workshops, motivational speeches, films, videotapes, audiotapes, and textbooks are all designed to prompt performance of one kind or another.

Advertising uses antecedents to influence behavior. Packaging, commercials, and direct mail campaigns all directly manipulate antecedents to influence purchasing behavior.

Instructions and directions are very popular antecedents used by managers. When managers tell employees to do something and to do it in a particular way, they are using antecedents. Managers may give this direction or instruction face-to-face, by phone, or in writing. In these cases, the information being given is an attempt to influence some performance and is given prior to the performance.

Sometimes written directions or instructions appear in checklists, directories, flowcharts, labels on equipment, or operating manuals. Signs and color coding are frequently used. Such antecedents are referred to as "job aids."

Much effort is expended in the work place providing the proper job aids; indeed it has become a science. Human factors researchers study the proper design of machinery and equipment and how to arrange it in order to facilitate performance. Control panels are designed so that switches are easy to reach, easy to see, and easy to operate. Computers and computer programs are designed to be "user friendly." Such job aids can be a very cost-effective alternative to training. All of this work attempts to control work performance through antecedents.

The behavior of other people is also an antecedent. This is a special class of antecedent called **modeling**. The actions of fellow employees and the boss influence the actions of other employees. If older employees complain, new employees may soon start complaining. If the boss comes to work early and leaves late, aspiring young managers tend to do the same. Thankfully, people do not model all behavior they see in the work place. Behaviors which others see positively reinforced are most likely to be modeled.

The conditions under which people will and will not imitate what they see others do have been the subject of considerable research by Dr. Albert Bandura (1969).

Cognitive antecedents

Things you say to yourself that prompt behavior are called **cognitive antecedents**. These include words or phrases we say to ourselves such as "I can do it," "I'm hungry," "This is hard," "I'm tired of this," "That reminds me," and so on. Feelings of hunger, stress, frustration, happiness, and accomplishment may be antecedents to behavior. The positive-thinking approach of authors like Norman Vincent Peale, Og Mandigo, Clement Stone, Dale Carnegie, and Albert Ellis use cognitive antecedents to change behavior.

CHARACTERISTICS OF ANTECEDENTS

1. Antecedents always come before the behavior they influence

2. Antecedents communicate information

The primary function of an antecedent is to communicate information about behavior and its consequences. Antecedents may tell someone what to do, when to do it, and often, how to do it. A sign saying "Persons in this area must wear safety glasses at all times" states the desired behavior.

Another sign may say "Ring bell for service." This antecedent communicates information about both the desired behavior and its consequences. An automobile gas gauge with the needle pointing to the "E" tells us that continuing to drive without getting gasoline will result in negative consequences.

3. Antecedents work because they have been paired with consequences

The reason antecedents influence behavior at all is that they have been associated with certain past consequences. The most influential antecedents are those that are always paired with a particular consequence (a hot stove always burns). The less consistently they are paired, the less effective the antecedent will be in prompting the behavior. The TV weather forecast may not cause you to carry an umbrella because your history with the forecaster is such that you will take a chance that it won't rain. When people learn to discriminate which element/stimuli in their environment predicts desired consequences, they are using what is known in Applied Behavior Analysis as a **discriminative stimulus (S^D)**.

Consider the case where a new manager walks out on the shop floor and notices that the employees do not look at him as he approaches and talk to him only when he asks a question. This is disturbing to the new manager because he feels that a friendly and relaxed atmosphere where employees are free to question and make suggestions is associated with high quality performance.

The answer to why they act as they do may be found in the fact that the previous manager, a stern and no-nonsense person, had on many occasions chewed out employees for goofing off when he saw them talking or laughing. His presence was an antecedent for "being busy." It may take some time before the employees will be comfortable around the new boss. In other words it will take a number of pairings of his presence with consequences different from those given by the previous supervisor.

The effectiveness of an antecedent may be measured by the degree of correlation between the antecedent and the behavioral consequence that is associated with it. When the correlation is high, the behavior reliably occurs in the presence of the antecedent; when the correlation is low, the behavior will often appear to be unaffected by that particular antecedent. A "danger–high voltage" sign practically always prompts the desired response from everyone who can read and has been shocked by electricity. But a "Speed Limit - 55 MPH" sign has a low compliance rate because most people have had no immediate positive consequences for obeying the speed limit and no negative consequences for going faster.

Trust is measured behaviorally by the correlation between antecedents and consequences. In other words, those who always do what they say are trusted; those who do not are not trusted. This is why carefully choosing the antecedents that you want to use to prompt performance is important. An unkept promise by a manager causes the person not only to distrust the manager but the company as well.

4. Consequences may also be antecedents

A consequence to one person may be an antecedent to another. For example, when we see someone do something that leads to a positive consequence, this may increase the likelihood that we will behave similarly under the same or similar circumstances. Advertising, of course, tries to take advantage of this by showing successful people using a particular product, hoping that it will be an effective antecedent for the behavior of purchasing the product.

Employee performance is constantly affected by what people see being rewarded and punished at work. If they see hard work pay off, there probably will be more hard work; if one employee is continually late to meetings with no negative consequences, others will tend to be less punctual. If they see risk-taking being punished, they will take

few risks.

Consequences of one's own behavior also act as an antecedent for additional behaviors. This effect is probably best illustrated by a once popular potato chip commercial with the tag line, "Betcha can't eat just one!" The taste of each chip (a consequence of eating) was an antecedent for the behavior of eating another one.

5. Antecedents without consequences have short-term effects

When an antecedent prompts a behavior and the anticipated consequence does not occur, the antecedent will quickly lose its power to prompt the behavior. Antecedents get a behavior started, but only consequences maintain behavior.

Job descriptions are notorious for their short-lived effect on what people actually do on the job. Many employees learn very quickly that what the job description says and what gets the desired consequences are very different.

How many of us have seen cars at the airport filling all available parking spaces when right by every car is a sign saying "Parking for loading and unloading of passengers only—Unattended cars will be towed"? The experience of these drivers is that, despite the sign's message, they have never been towed. So, they ignore the sign.

Some advertisers have solved this problem by frequently changing antecedents. In other words, if an antecedent has a short life or effect, then by using several different ones, each with short effects, you can achieve a longer effect.

When Soap-O starts lagging in sales, we see *New* Soap-O. When New Soap-O sales begin to decline then we see New*Blue* Soap-O. Then we get *Improved* NewBlue Soap-O. This continues until the adjectives run out or customers realize that, from their standpoint, in spite of all the improvements, the new Soap-O cleans pretty much like old Soap-O no matter what they call it. While advertising is an important antecedent to getting a customer to try the product, in the end no amount of clever advertising can save a product that does not provide reinforcement for the buyer.

For the reason stated above, novel antecedents get responses where the usual signs, signals, and rhetoric get none. The first-time visitor to Pennsylvania may be

the consequences associated with it.

OVERRELIANCE ON ANTECEDENTS BY MANAGERS

To most managers, management responsi-

(Reprinted with special permission of King Features Syndicate, Inc.)

slowed by the speed-limit signs because they state the amount of the fine, such as: 60-65 MPH $75, 65-70 MPH $90 and so on. At a South Carolina resort the speed limit signs have unusual speeds, like 34 and 46 MPH. Chili's restaurant recently had a sign at the entrance to the parking area that said "Cars illegally parked will be crushed and melted."

The television show, Candid Camera, capitalized on the fact that you can get people to do strange things when they are confronted with a situation where they do not know the consequences. However, as novel and clever as some antecedents are, they still are only as effective as the consequences that are associated with them. (Would you believe that people still park in the "no parking" places at Chili's, even at the risk of having their cars crushed and melted?)

The fact that antecedents have short-term effects does not make them bad or a waste of time. Remember, practically every behavior has antecedents. In the work place, if an antecedent gets a behavior to occur one time it has done its job. That is all that can be expected of it. Whether the behavior occurs again will be determined for the most part by

bilities include such things as planning, organizing, directing, controlling, and delegating. Four of the five are clearly antecedents. The other, controlling, may also include antecedent activities. Data collected a number of years ago when installing PM programs indicated that managers spent, on average, approximately 85 percent of their time either telling people what to do, figuring out what to tell them to do, or figuring out what to do because people didn't do what they told them to do.

Although planning, organizing, etc., are important, managers spend far too much time doing these activities and far too little time delivering consequences. While the research is not available on the ideal balance between the amount of time spent on antecedents and consequences, our experience is that if you don't spend at least as much time planning and delivering consequences as you do planning and delivering antecedents, then your effort will most certainly be inefficient and only minimally effective.

For example, objective setting is a major management activity in most organizations. Organizations are not considered to be sophisticated at all if they do not have some kind of Management By Objectives program (MBO). However, there are few activities engaged in by managers that are more dreaded than MBO programs. Why? Because most managers have not experienced MBO as a way to be more successful, have an easier job, get more done, or get more recognition. As a matter of fact, the experience is more often just the opposite. The program probably increases the likelihood that managers will get punished—punished for not choosing the right objectives; punished for not setting the right goals, and punished because they put a lot of time and energy into developing the objectives—while those not involved in MBO fared just as well as they did. Thus they know that their MBO efforts will make little difference in what they do, how they do it, or what happens in the organization.

MBO can be very consonant with the PM system. However, since most MBO programs neglect consequences, their real value to the organization is considerably reduced.

In reality most people participate in these programs, not because they want to, but because they must to stay out of trouble. In the end many organizations spend enormous amounts of time and energy in activities that have a dubious payback. If you have an objective- or goal-setting program in your organization in which consequences for achievement are not specifically spelled out, then almost certainly your program is not producing maximum results.

The classic error people make regarding antecedents is that if other people don't do what they are told the first time, they tell them again. But the second time they tell them louder, longer, or meaner. In other words, they intensify the antecedent. If people ignore a small sign, we put up a large one. If a large one is ignored, we put up two.

Most quality, safety, and productivity programs used in industry are heavy on antecedents and light on consequences. Attempts at problem solving place heavy emphasis on things like "understanding the importance of

...," "accepting the challenge," "being committed to...," " being aware of...." We want employees who are committed to quality, aware of safety, and dedicated to increasing productivity. Commitment, awareness, and dedication are all antecedents. We can get people to make a public commitment and not live up to it; we can have increased awareness of safety procedures and practices and still have people engaging in unsafe procedures and practices.

If we get people to commit to "doing it right the first time," then we must plan and deliver positive consequences to them when they do. If we teach people what safe work practices are, then we must make sure that people who follow these practices receive positive consequences for doing so.

"Hey, guys, can I come in?"

(Reprinted by permission: Tribune Media Services.)

SELECTING THE RIGHT ANTECEDENT

As stated before, behaviors usually follow particular antecedents. However, even if an antecedent is specific and paired with a consequence, it may not be the best antecedent to produce the desired performance. For example, if procedure manuals are not kept current, performers may use outdated procedures; if tools are worn, specifications may not be met; if supplies are not readily available, performers may wait for them or try to do the job without them.

In order to help you plan the right antecedent it may be helpful to consider the three most powerful classes of antecedents.

1. Those that clearly describe expectations and desired performance (for example, objectives, job descriptions, job specifications, standards, and priorities);

2. Those that have a history of being associated with a specific consequence (for example, hot stoves, traffic stoplights, or police cars);

3. Behaviors occurring *just prior to the desired performance* (for example, a customer in a grocery store asking to be helped, someone asking for directions, or turning on your machine).

Your planning may also be facilitated by the following list of the six most common types of antecedents used in business to prompt work behavior. They are:

1. Providing job aids (instructions, directions, flow diagrams, checklists, color codes);

2. Training (speakers, films, books, tapes);

3. Providing tools and materials;

4. Providing policies and procedures;

5. Arranging the work environment (for example, temperature, lighting, noise level);

6. Holding meetings.

For any activity, several of the types may be required. The types of antecedents used will of course depend on the particular situation. In order to determine which ones will be most effective, you may find it helpful to answer the following questions:

1. Are *current* expectations described clearly and precisely? Examine objectives, job descriptions, standards, and priorities and make sure the performance you want is clearly specified in all such documents.

2. What has the individual's past experience been with the performance? What antecedents now signal a positive consequence for the performance and what antecedents now signal a negative consequence for the performance?

3. What does the person or you and your peers do just prior to the performance that may serve as an effective antecedent?

4. Are job aids adequate? Could wordy manuals and instructions be simplified and rewritten? Can flowcharts or checklists be developed? Would better labeling or color-coding help?

5. Are the performers able to do the job? Have they ever done it? Could they perform if their lives depended on it? Is retraining necessary?

6. Are the correct tools available and in good repair? Are the materials necessary to do the job adequately supplied and in the proper condition?

7. Is the general work environment conducive to the desired performance? Are there obstacles to performance such as cramped working space or difficulty in getting supplies? Are temperature, lighting, and noise levels satisfactory?

ANTECEDENT VS. REINFORCEMENT CONTROL

Johnson (1975) conducted a study to examine the relative effect of antecedents and reinforcement in producing stable performance change. In the initial part of the study, he reinforced 108 business college students for high-speed performance on a keypunch task. All subjects were subsequently subjected to a variety of experimental conditions.

To test the effectiveness of antecedents on performance, he exposed half the students to persuasive influences such as a plea for increases in quality and an announcement that their pay would be heavily influenced by quality. The other half received none. To test the effectiveness of the reinforcement he varied the conditions under which they were paid. During different phases of the experiment, all of the students were paid for either quality (accuracy of their work) or quantity (speed with which they keypunched cards).

The results were that the announcements and the plea for quality had no effect on the level of quality. On the other hand, their performance changed as the reinforcement changed. When they asked for quality but paid for quantity, they got an increase in quantity and a decrease in quality. When they paid for quality they got an increase in quality but no corresponding increase in productivity. In other words, the experimenters got what they paid for, not what they asked for.

Johnson concludes:

> ...from the current experiment it appears that stimulus control procedures such as announcements (publicity campaigns) or verbal attitude influences (Zero Defect lectures and workshops) are relatively ineffective in achieving changes in performance quality unless they are backed up by appropriate environmental changes. Apparently it takes new environmental outcomes to overcome old habits at the work place.
>
> This, of course, suggests that organizations might prudently forego the expenditure of time and money that typically attends the initiation of a new ZD program and concentrate instead on making meaningful changes in the outcomes associated with work in order to encourage high quality performance.

Consistent with the material in this chapter, the results indicate that antecedents are relatively ineffective if they oppose a previous reinforcement history or if they conflict with an active reinforcer. They are also consistent with other research in demonstrating that reinforcement control is necessary for stable performance change to occur. Finally, the study indicates that, under some circumstances, reinforcement alone may be sufficient to produce stable performance change.

NOTES

3

Consequences

The last chapter introduced the concept that consequences are the reason for antecedent effectiveness. In this book, the word consequences refers to behavioral consequences. **Behavioral consequences** are events that follow behaviors and change the probability that they will recur in the future.

Consequences are the single most effective tool a manager has for increasing employee performance and improving morale. As amazing as it may sound, there is one straightforward answer to the problems of poor quality, low productivity, high costs, and disgruntled employees—consequences.

In hundreds of plants and offices, as well as hospitals, hotels, restaurants, and other kinds of organizations, the ineffective use of consequences has created and maintained poor performance and low morale. But providing *appropriate* consequences has produced dramatic increases in the bottom line and employee satisfaction.

This chapter will describe the various consequences and how they operate in the everyday work environment. As with all concepts in Performance Management, you will see that consequences affect performance whether you attempt to manage them or not. If you don't manage them they will simply operate unsystematically and often in ways that are counterproductive.

We will describe and compare the two basic types of consequences: those that increase performance and those that decrease it. This chapter will provide background for a detailed discussion of positive reinforcement,

the least used consequence in business. Yet it is the most effective tool for increasing performance on the job.

THE EFFECTS OF CONSEQUENCES

Some consequences increase or maintain the probability that a desired behavior will occur and some decrease it. We can illustrate consequences by expanding our example of antecedents from the last chapter. Figure 3.1 presents some of the same antecedents and performance displayed in Chapter Two.

Behavior followed by consequences—this pattern repeats itself many, many times throughout every day. It is so obvious, so commonplace, we have learned to ignore it. For example, put money in a candy machine and pull the lever. Usually, the candy comes tumbling out. But what if no candy comes out? Will you use the machine again? You might try the machine another day, but if it still failed to work, you'd probably stop. The behavior of putting money in that machine depends on the consequence—receiving a candy bar. Remove that consequence and behavior changes. You will seek another machine that works—one that produces the consequence you want.

Every behavior has a consequence. In fact, behavior can be viewed as a function of its consequences. That is, consequences do not simply influence what someone does; they *control* it. In order to understand why people do what they do, instead of asking,

Figure 3.1

EXAMPLES OF THE ABC RELATIONSHIP

ANTECEDENT	BEHAVIOR ⇨	CONSEQUENCE
• Phone rings	Pick up receiver and talk	Caller gives you information you requested
• Safety sign	Put on safety glasses	Your ears hurt because the glasses are too tight
• Suggestion box	Drop in a suggestion	Receive call from your boss saying she'll give your suggestion a try

"Why did they do that?" ask, "What happens to them when they do that?" When you understand the consequences, you are able to understand the behavior.

Consequences come in many forms and endless varieties. What people do, what they say, what they give us, and even what they don't give us can all be consequences that will affect our behavior.

Take a look at the examples in Figure 3.2. In each of the examples, something has happened to the individuals after their performance. We cannot say how these consequences will affect other performers in similar situations because different people often respond differently to the same consequence.

If Bill likes to travel, the consequence of being sent on the road for turning in reports on time will increase the likelihood of his continuing to be punctual in submitting his reports. If he doesn't like to travel, he may decrease his efficiency in the future. The point is that whether a consequence has a positive or negative effect on behavior depends on the person receiving it.

The need for understanding consequences

Four basic reasons explain why people don't do what we want them to do on the job: 1) they don't know what to do; 2) they

Figure 3.2

WORK PERFORMANCES AND THEIR CONSEQUENCES

PERFORMANCE ⇨	CONSEQUENCE
• Bill completes and turns in budget.	Bill sent out of town immediately on assignment. He's the only man available, everyone else is working on the budget.
• Tom makes two large sales on Monday.	On Tuesday, the boss congratulated him.
• Third shift generates excessive waste.	Shift is switched to easier process.
• Second shift is below production goal.	Employees are given overtime.

don't know how to do it; 3) obstacles in the environment discourage or prevent them from doing it; or 4) they don't want to do it.

Not knowing what to do or how to do it, or being hampered by obstacles in the environment are problems of antecedents. Not wanting to do it is a problem of consequences. Our earlier discussion of antecedents pointed out that even if people know what to do and how to do it, they still might not do it.

Consequences provide the key to performance. When people don't do what we want them to do, we say things like, "They should do it; they ought to do it; that's what they're paid to do; it's their job." In other words, to use a phrase from Robert Mager (1970), "They really oughta wanna." Unfortunately all too often people don't do all that they could or should. The difference between those who "wanna" and those who "don't wanna" is *consequences*.

People do what they do because the consequences support it. A plant manager works hard to get the plant to increase productivity because his pay increases, bonuses, and promotions may be contingent on it. In fact, his job may be in jeopardy if he does not keep productivity at an acceptable level. In other words, there are many consequences for him for increasing productivity.

Organizational levels beneath the plant manager, however, may experience negative consequences for increasing productivity. Increased productivity usually involves more work which may increase both stress and fatigue. More pressure may be put on the maintenance department to keep equipment running and to repair it quickly when it is down. Design engineers may have to come up with modifications and new designs at a higher rate, meaning working around the clock. The shipping department will have to work faster, causing more fatigue and higher chance of errors. The immediate consequences to almost all employees in the plant for increasing productivity are frequently negative.

Once we understand the consequences people experience when they do or don't do something, motivation becomes clearer. For example, consider the case of the "rate-buster." When she first came to work in the plant she produced at a much higher rate than her fellow employees. Over time, however, her performance decreased to that of her peers. An analysis of the consequences that she experienced is helpful in figuring out why.

First, her peers criticized her, ostracized her from the peer group, and generally provided unpleasant consequences for her high level of performance. Once she dropped to the average rate, they were more friendly to her and began to ask her to go on breaks with them, to eat lunch with them, and to join them in social activities after work. In other words, they provided positive consequences for her mediocrity and negative ones for her high performance.

In addition, she never received any positive consequences from management for her above-average production because their attitude was "that's what she is paid for." She also saw that peers were doing much less but were treated the same (pay, benefits, etc.). She soon realized that the common sense thing to do was to slow down and put her energy elsewhere.

The "oughta wanna" view goes under various names. But in all forms it denies the basic fact that people do those things for which they receive positive consequences or avoid negative consequences. When someone is not performing as we would like, we often say it is a "motivation problem" explained as "She doesn't care," "He's got a bad attitude," "He's lazy." All these explanations are used when the real problem is consequences.

How we experience consequences determines their effect

The expression "different strokes for different folks" expresses the fact that consequences affect people differently. The likes and dislikes of every individual determine the particular consequence that will be effective in changing his behavior. In order to be effective in working with other people, you must know how they experience various consequences. A consequence that you desire or like very much may be one that the other person cares nothing about or even dislikes.

For example, a frequent management practice is to give employees who have perfect attendance for various periods of time some sort of special recognition. In one service organization, the "recognition" had the opposite effect of what was intended. The consequence for one year's perfect attendance was to be invited to an awards banquet. One employee offered her perception of this consequence when she told one of her friends, "I'll miss one day so I won't have to sit down front with the big wheels." The awards banquet was a consequence that decreased her attendance—certainly not what management wanted. What management thought employees would experience as a positive was, at least in this case, a negative.

Or, consider the case of a top-performing mechanic who was promoted to a supervisory job. When he was a mechanic, his most positive consequence was "beating out" his fellow employees. Competing with them caused him to finish jobs quicker and to show that he could solve problems that the others could not solve. Unfortunately, as a supervisor, he still liked to show subordinates that he was faster, better, and smarter than they were. Believe it or not, their success was punishing to him. As a mechanic, competition with the mechanics made him do his job better; as a supervisor, it destroyed his effectiveness.

Nevertheless, his actions made sense to him. He had a long history of experiencing positive consequences for "beating out" the people he worked with, whether they were co-workers or subordinates. Although we may say this shouldn't occur, it is more common than one might think. Practically everyone has known of a father who could not stand to be beaten in a game by his children. The movie "The Great Santini" provides a dramatic example of this phenomenon.

What is positive to one can be negative to another. It is a common problem for managers to look at consequences from the perspective of the organization, not of the performer. In management, or in life in general, to be effective with others we must know how they experience consequences—not just how we experience them.

DOING NOTHING IS DOING SOMETHING

Consequences occur for every behavior. This means that if a manager provides no consequence for a particular behavior, even his lack of action will have an effect on the employee.

For example, suppose an employee does not follow a difficult and time-consuming safety procedure. If someone does not provide a negative consequence, the safety violation will continue to occur because the employee saves time and trouble—a positive consequence for him.

On the other hand, sometimes doing nothing will cause a behavior to stop. If an employee goes to a lot of extra trouble to solve problems for the boss and the boss says or does nothing to acknowledge it or to show his appreciation, then we can expect that the extra effort will soon stop.

Every behavior has a consequence that affects its future occurrence. Many times the consequences that are causing a behavior to occur, or not occur, are not obvious, but on closer inspection they can usually be discovered. Once we discover what consequences people are experiencing, it is usually easy to understand why they do the things they do. This perspective is illustrated by the old saying that before you criticize another person you should "walk a mile in his shoes."

DELIVERING CONSEQUENCES

Behavior is affected by the consequences which follow it. Consequences either strengthen or weaken behavior. Because a consequence affects the behavior that precedes it, it is critical that the consequence be timed to follow the behavior we want to be affected. The necessity of paying attention to the consequence that follows a behavior is illustrated by the example below.

A supervisor in a manufacturing plant complained that one of his employees was "driving him crazy." Every time he went out of his office, she would call him over to where she was working and proceed to complain to him about everything from the condition of the restrooms to the work load. The complaining was chronic. She was well known to all the managers because she had been doing it for years. Most of her complaints were about things the supervisor could do nothing about, but when he could satisfy a complaint she quickly found another. He spent a lot of time with this employee, but it was always centered around a complaint of some kind. Unfortunately, his attention rewarded an undesirable action.

A simple change in the supervisor's behavior solved the problem. He decided to talk and listen to her only when she was working.

The moment she started complaining about the "same old things," he would politely excuse himself and leave.

Complaining decreased to practically zero and productivity increased to maximum efficiency (Figure 3.3). In addition, their working relationship improved dramatically.

Such interactions occur at all levels of an organization. We're all familiar with the adage, "the squeaky wheel gets the grease," and with crisis-oriented management. We often don't have time to spend with people until there is a problem. Since the "squeaky wheels" get the grease, many times there is none left for the ones that are running well. Before you know it you have many more "squeaky wheels." All too often the people who say things like "I can't...," "I don't like...," "It's too hard," get more attention than those who say, "I can do...," "I like...," or "No problem, I'll handle it."

If managers devote the majority of their time to problems, they will never run out of work. Management attention is a major positive consequence to the vast majority of the work force. When it goes only to problems, then problems increase. This does not mean

Figure 3.3

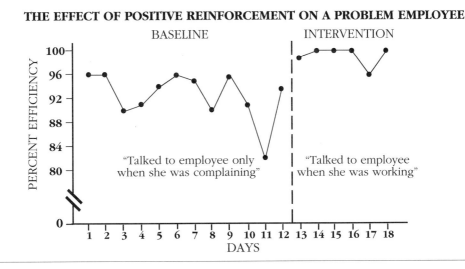

THE EFFECT OF POSITIVE REINFORCEMENT ON A PROBLEM EMPLOYEE

that people are consciously creating problems to get attention, but that's just the way it happens. This effect has been demonstrated in the widest possible range of settings—from home, to school, to work.

Closely related to the above example is the issue of showing concern for subordinates. Managers should certainly listen to and show concern for employees. However, this is a case where the frequency of the behavior is a good indicator of whether your concern is constructive. If an employee who rarely ever complains or has a negative thing to say starts complaining or talking negatively, it will probably be constructive to listen—even at the risk of increasing the wrong behavior.

On the other hand, if the person complains all the time, then responding to the complaining may be counterproductive. It is not "showing concern" that is the problem, but when and for what you show concern. Indeed, in many work places a more common problem is that managers show little concern for either the good or the bad.

Immediate consequences are most effective

Consequences have their greatest impact on behavior when they are immediate. Even the slightest delay between the behavior and its consequence weakens the association, thereby reducing effectiveness. The most immediate consequences are those that occur *while* the person is working. Even consequences that occur at the end of the work day lose some of their effectiveness on behavior that happened earlier in the day.

The annual performance review is a good example of the effect produced by delayed consequences. The good and bad comments made at the review represent positive and negative consequences. Unfortunately, the behaviors they are intended to affect often occurred months earlier. A project completed on time needs to be complimented when it is completed, not several months later during a performance review. The consequences de-

livered during annual, semi-annual, or quarterly performance reviews have little effect on performance. Since the behaviors they are intended to influence are by that time only remotely related to the consequences, those behaviors are only remotely affected.

Consequence certainty affects behavior

The more certain a consequence is, the more influence it has. Certainty refers to the probability that the consequence will follow the behavior. Generally speaking, the higher the probability of the consequence, the greater the impact.

A red-hot stove provides a clear example of a *certain* consequence. The consequence of touching a hot stove is pain. The pain will *always* happen; it is *certain* (100 percent probability). The pain also meets the other criteria for an effective consequence that is mentioned above: it follows a behavior (touching the stove) and it is very immediate. This is why we don't have a lot of trouble getting people, even the very young, not to touch hot stoves.

Cooking that always tastes good is harder to resist than cooking that is inconsistent. A drug that practically always makes you feel better when you have a cold is more likely to be taken than one that only works occasionally. For most people the uncertainty of winning a magazine contest is not even worth the behavior of filling out the entry form and mailing it. (In some contests the probability of winning may be as low as one in fifty million.)

TYPES OF CONSEQUENCES

Consequences affect behavior in one of two ways. They either increase it or decrease it. There are four behavioral consequences: two *increase* behavior and two *decrease* behavior. See Figure 3.4.

Figure 3.4

THE FOUR BEHAVIORAL CONSEQUENCES

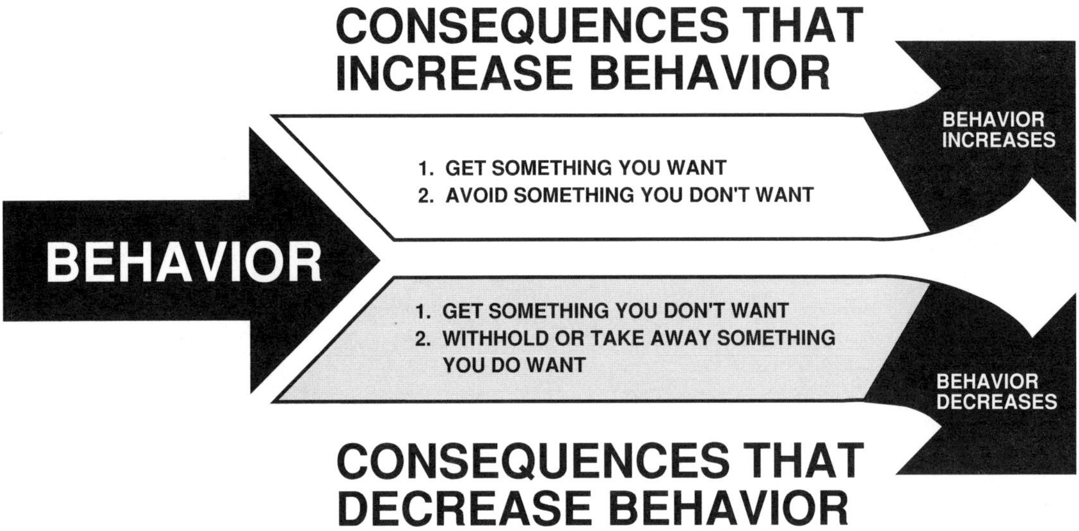

CONSEQUENCES THAT INCREASE BEHAVIOR

BEHAVIOR INCREASES

1. GET SOMETHING YOU WANT
2. AVOID SOMETHING YOU DON'T WANT

BEHAVIOR

1. GET SOMETHING YOU DON'T WANT
2. WITHHOLD OR TAKE AWAY SOMETHING YOU DO WANT

BEHAVIOR DECREASES

CONSEQUENCES THAT DECREASE BEHAVIOR

Positive and negative reinforcement—consequences that increase behavior

The phrases "increasing behavior" and "decreasing behavior" will be used frequently. They refer to either increasing or decreasing the *frequency* of recurrence of a particular thing people do or say, or to increasing or decreasing the *intensity* with which someone does something. Thus the focus of PM is to provide positive consequences for desired behavior for the purpose of increasing its frequency or intensity. This is called **positive reinforcement**. Positive reinforcement is such an essential part of PM that many equate the two. Although Performance Management is much more than positive reinforcement, it is a major tool for bringing about desirable performance change. Because of its significance, it will be examined later in more detail.

Behavior is reinforced in two ways. We will continue to do something if the action enables us to get something we want. Or we will continue to do something if the action enables us to *avoid* something we *don't* want.

As we describe consequences we will sometimes use the terms wants, likes, or needs. A person's wants, likes, or needs are measured by what the person will "work" or "behave" for.

Getting something you want (positive reinforcement). A **positive reinforcer** (abbreviated **R+**) is technically defined as any consequence that increases the probability that the behavior that preceded it will occur more often in the future. For example, in a meeting the group is asked for ideas to solve a problem and someone volunteers one. If the boss says, "Great idea," it will more than likely increase the number of ideas or suggestions that person will make. If it does, we would say that the boss's response was a positive reinforcer. If the person makes no more suggestions as a result of that comment, then we would not be able to claim that saying "Great idea" was a positive reinforcer.

It is important to know that a reinforcer is defined by its effects. If you respond to something someone does in a way that you think is very positive yet it does not increase the behavior in question, then it was not a positive reinforcer for that individual.

Fortunately, there are many things we do that most people find positively reinforcing. Attention in the form of a conversation, a "thank you," a smile, or individual recognition for some accomplishment are all *potential* positive reinforcers. Whether they *are* reinforcers can only be determined by the data.

Escaping or avoiding something you don't want (negative reinforcement).

There are some consequences that people will work hard to avoid. If we have a toothache, we will go to the dentist to get rid of (escape) the pain; we go for a dental check-up to avoid the pain. In both instances we are motivated by **negative reinforcement** (abbreviated **R-**). Much of our behavior is under the control of negative reinforcement. Think of all the things people will do to avoid or eliminate tension, anxiety, discomfort or the displeasure of others. Figure 3.5 lists some examples of things people will do to escape or avoid certain consequences.

In looking at the variety of examples, you can probably think of many others. In a work environment that is managed primarily by negative reinforcement, people will do what they must to avoid negative consequences—even lie, cheat, and steal—if there is no alternative.

An auto rental company made national news when it was discovered that one of their managers had overcharged customers by more than $13 million. His motivation was not to get rich, because he took none of the money. The news account said he did it in order to meet his budget every month. In reality, he probably did it to avoid the consequences of *not* meeting the budget. One can only wonder what those consequences might have been. We all know of cases where people will falsify reports, tell a white lie, cheat a customer, or in some other way deceive another, not for monetary gain, but to avoid some unpleasant consequence.

Negative reinforcement is not always bad. There are times when it is the most appropriate consequence to use. There are other times when it is clearly the wrong consequence for strengthening the performance that we want. (When to use positive reinforcement and when to use negative reinforcement will be discussed in more detail in Chapter Five.) For the present it is sufficient

Figure 3.5

EXAMPLES OF NEGATIVE REINFORCEMENT	
BEHAVIOR ⇨	**CONSEQUENCES**
•Putting on your top coat	Avoid getting cold
•Putting on safety glasses when you see a supervisor coming	Avoid getting chewed out
•Give an employee a better performance appraisal than he deserved	Avoid confronting employee with poor performance
•Give in to whining child	Stop whining or tantrums temporarily
•Working to get performance up to standard	Avoid losing job

to know that even though the processes of positive and negative reinforcement are different, they both *increase* behavior. See Figure 3.6.

Punishment and extinction– consequences that decrease behavior

Getting something you don't want (punishment). Sometimes we do something and get a consequence we don't want. When we do, we are less likely to do it again. Getting something we don't like is called **punishment** (abbreviated **P+**). As with positive reinforcement, punishment is defined by its effects. If a person does something and receives a consequence that results in his doing it less often in the future, he has been punished even though we might not consider it to be punishing. A **punisher** is anything that happens to people that decreases their behavior.

For example, someone may say something

we don't like or they may simply state it in a way we don't like. They may do something to us that we don't like. There are a number of consequences we might experience from the environment that are undesirable.

Take the example of a department manager who, in a weekly meeting with other managers, brought up the problem of a corporate support group's poor responsiveness. The plant manager immediately assigned the department manager the task of researching whether the other plants were having the same problem and if so how they were handling it—and of presenting a written report of his findings at the weekly meeting. After the meeting the department manager said, "I wish I hadn't brought that up."

A similar situation occurred in a large manufacturing plant where problems were arising with the quality of one of their products. Management decided to have shift meetings to get suggestions on how to solve the problem. One shift produced 50 suggestions and the other only produced six. The difference was caused by unintentional punishment.

Figure 3.6

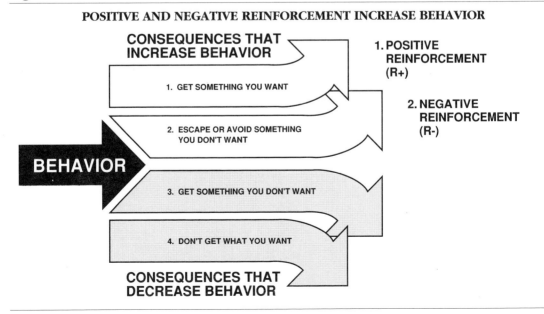

POSITIVE AND NEGATIVE REINFORCEMENT INCREASE BEHAVIOR

CONSEQUENCES THAT INCREASE BEHAVIOR

1. POSITIVE REINFORCEMENT (R+)

2. NEGATIVE REINFORCEMENT (R-)

1. GET SOMETHING YOU WANT

2. ESCAPE OR AVOID SOMETHING YOU DON'T WANT

BEHAVIOR

3. GET SOMETHING YOU DON'T WANT

4. DON'T GET WHAT YOU WANT

CONSEQUENCES THAT DECREASE BEHAVIOR

On the shift that produced six, when employees made suggestions, one of the managers, who was reputed to be a world authority on the product, would go to the board and say something like, "Let me show you why that won't work." Interestingly, he was practically always right. His intention was to teach them something about the process; however, it stopped suggestions.

In the other meeting, when employees made a suggestion, the supervisor listened intently, wrote down the suggestion, asked questions about the details, and told them he would check it out. He then asked for more ideas and, of course, got many.

Unfortunately, many managers are unaware how often they punish the very behavior they want to encourage. But even when unintentional, punishment still decreases behavior. Figure 3.7 provides some examples of behavior followed by punishing consequences.

Although there are occasions where we inadvertently decrease behavior we want, there are other occasions where we want to decrease some undesirable behavior. See Figure 3.8 for some examples.

In general, any time people do things that are unsafe, unhealthy, or unfair, delivering a punishing consequence may be the most appropriate thing to do. However, in general we should use punishment sparingly because if it is not done appropriately it may create more problems than it solves. Punishment has several negative side effects and in order to use this consequence effectively, you must know how to deal with the ripples that follow in its wake. These techniques will be discussed in detail in Chapter Eight.

Remember any time people do something and get something they don't want, they will be less likely to repeat that behavior under similar circumstances in the future. This means that in order to be effective in working with people, you must know both their reinforcers and their punishers.

Failure to get something you want (extinction). When people do something and as a result get no reinforcement, they will be less likely to repeat that behavior in the future. Reducing or eliminating behavior in this way is called extinction. Technically, **extinction** (abbreviated **P-**) is defined as the withholding, or non-delivery, of reinforce-

Figure 3.7

EXAMPLES OF INADVERTENT PUNISHING CONSEQUENCES AND THEIR EFFECTS

BEHAVIOR	CONSEQUENCE (PUNISHER)	FUTURE BEHAVIOR
•Submits reports on time	Is assigned more reports	Turns in reports late
•Takes initiative on a project	Is criticized for minor error	Shows less initiative
•Wears safety equipment	Is uncomfortable	Doesn't wear equipment
•Boss gives one hour off	Employee takes two hours off	Boss won't give time off in future
•Makes suggestion for improvement	Boss makes sarcastic comment	Suggestions stop

Figure 3.8

EXAMPLES OF PUNISHING CONSEQUENCES THAT DECREASED UNDESIRABLE BEHAVIOR

BEHAVIOR	CONSEQUENCE (PUNISHER)	FUTURE BEHAVIOR
•Frequent use of telephone for personal calls	Reprimanded by manager	Reduced personal calls
•Leaves work early	Pay is docked	Did not leave early
•Makes typing errors	Is given the errors to correct	Made fewer errors
•Drives forklift recklessly	Has serious accident	No more reckless driving

ment for previously reinforced behavior.

In cases where one's attention is the reinforcer, ignoring behavior is a very effective method of decreasing it. Ignoring involves withholding social reinforcement. For example, suppose someone tells a joke and no one laughs. Joke telling, to that group at least, will probably decrease. One extinction trial may not eliminate the behavior but after several times with the same response, the joke telling will probably stop altogether.

Another example occurs when people put money in a vending machine and nothing falls out. We may try it again, but if the item fails to be delivered, we will probably stop trying that machine. Few people would continue to put money in the machine over and over when they don't get what they want.

A frequent problem in many work places is that productive behavior is ignored. The people who work the hardest and do the best are ignored because the supervisors are spending all their time dealing with the problem performers. It's no wonder that over a period of time performance falls to a level necessary only to avoid punishment. Since the failure to reinforce productive performance constitutes extinction, one can see that this is a common consequence in business and that many performance problems may be created, not by what we do, but by what we *don't* do.

WHY POSITIVE REINFORCEMENT IS THE PREFERRED CONSEQUENCE

While all consequences have their use, positive reinforcement is the most effective means of helping people achieve work-related goals. Positive reinforcement is the only consequence that maximizes performance; negative reinforcement only produces a level of performance necessary to escape or avoid punishment. Punishment and extinction may be useful at times, but they have numerous disadvantages. For the present, it is probably sufficient to point out that punishment and extinction *weaken* behavior. The mission in most organizations is to strengthen work-related behaviors—not weaken them.

Although punishment and extinction may occasionally seem to increase behavior, they don't. On close analysis one will discover that the increases are generated by negative reinforcement—not punishment. In fact, stopping one behavior by using punishment may lead to decreases in other behaviors you don't want to stop.

Positive reinforcers are readily available to everyone in the work place and usually cost little in time or money. Praise, attention, and various forms of recognition are only a few examples. Socially (or ethically) acceptable punishers are few and they are difficult to use effectively.

Finally, the impact of PM is positive, not negative. While negative reinforcement, punishment, and extinction have negative side effects, positive reinforcement not only produces higher performance levels but also has positive side effects (Epstein, 1985). It is easy to see why those who understand and apply positive reinforcement effectively are able to create a high-performance culture where excellence is the norm and improvement is constant.

CONCLUDING REMARKS

Figure 3.9 is a summary of the four behavioral consequences and their effects.

Whether we are aware of it, performance is strengthened or weakened every day. Everything that people do at work is the result of reinforcement—positive or negative. Reinforcement may be provided by management, peers, or in some cases by the work itself, but if the behavior persists, it is receiving reinforcement from some source.

Performances that stop occurring or decline over time are being punished or extinguished. To solve performance problems it is helpful to analyze the consequences that occur when people do what we want and the consequences that occur when people don't do what we want. A formal method for doing this is called an ABC analysis—the subject of the next chapter.

Figure 3.9

SUMMARY OF THE FOUR BEHAVIORAL CONSEQUENCES AND THEIR EFFECTS

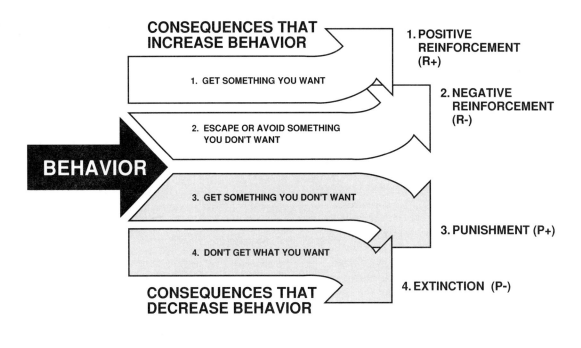

NOTES

4

ABC Analysis

In the previous chapters the concepts of antecedents, behavior, and consequences were introduced. Behaviors have both antecedents and consequences. Some behaviors may have many antecedents that prompt them and many consequences that are associated with their occurrence. Because of this, it is sometimes difficult to understand the relationships that exist between the three elements. In other words, it is often difficult to understand why people do what they do because a casual examination of the consequences may seem to favor behavior other than that which occurs.

By looking, in a systematic way, at all the antecedents and consequences associated with a given behavior or performance, we are usually able to gain a useful perspective on why people do what they do. The formal

process for doing this is called an ABC analysis. An **ABC analysis** is a problem-solving process in which the antecedents and consequences currently operating for both the problem and the correct behaviors are identified and classified.

The relationship of antecedents, behavior, and consequences was illustrated in the last chapter. A modification of that illustration is presented in Figure 4.1. An ABC analysis involves much more than finding an antecedent or consequence for a specific behavior. Because it is very difficult to discover exactly which antecedent prompts a given behavior, or which consequence maintains it, the ABC analysis helps us discover patterns among the many possible antecedents and consequences that are associated with the behavior.

Figure 4.1

COMPONENTS OF AN ABC ANALYSIS		
A **ANTECEDENT**	**B** **BEHAVIOR**	**C** **CONSEQUENCES**
1. Phone rings (prompts you to)	Pick up receiver and talk	Caller gives you information you requested
2. Safety sign (tells you to)	Wear safety glasses	Your ears hurt; glasses too tight
3. New policy manual (encourages you to)	Tell employees what is expected of them	Employees argue with you

OVERVIEW OF AN ABC ANALYSIS

To complete an ABC analysis you must determine the following:

1. the behavior or performance of interest;
2. the antecedents and consequences that currently operate for that behavior or performance.

Study the examples in Figure 4.2. The antecedents and consequences for each behavior have been identified. A useful way

problem" will get us nowhere. But, if we specify the "safety problem" as "employees not wearing protective glasses while at their machines," we have a much easier task.

Assume in spite of a policy that all employees *must* wear safety glasses, a few consistently do not. First, let's examine the antecedents for *wearing glasses*.

The policy manual states that glasses will be worn in the manufacturing area and that failure to do so is grounds for immediate dis-

Figure 4.2

DISPLAYING THE ABC RELATIONSHIP

Problem Behavior: Child *not* cleaning his room

Antecedents	Consequences
Doesn't have the time	Less of a "work load"
Friends come over or call	Gets yelled at
Watching favorite TV show	Gets to watch TV
It will just get messy again	Spends time playing with friends

Desired Behavior: Child *cleaning* his room

Antecedents	Consequences
Threaten to take away privileges (knows that threat will be carried out)	May get fussed at if not done properly
Company coming over	The cleaning is a lot of *work*
Can't find things	Less time for fun activities
Child is buttering-up for something	Might get praise
	Company will mess it up again

of displaying an ABC analysis is in a chart called an **ABC grid** as in Figure 4.2.

The first step in an ABC analysis is to clearly describe the behavior or performance that is creating a problem or the behavior we want to influence. The behaviors in Figure 4.2 are precisely defined and easily described.

In organizations, however, describing what we want people to do is not always easy. Take a look at the examples in Figure 4.3. As the list indicates, it is easier to do an ABC analysis when the behaviors are stated specifically.

Let's do an ABC analysis of a safety problem. Now, a definition as vague as "safety

missal. Several signs in the work area declare "Safety Glasses Must Be Worn In This Area." Employees have been taught the importance of wearing protective equipment through training which included viewing slides of many gruesome accidents resulting from failure to wear proper safety equipment. While all employees wear glasses when they see a member of management in the area, some are known to take them off when the manager or supervisor leaves. Figure 4.4 shows how these antecedents would appear on an ABC analysis form.

What are the consequences for the employees when they wear the glasses as

Figure 4.3

EXAMPLES OF ABC ANALYSIS DESCRIPTIONS

Poor descriptions for an ABC analysis	Good descriptions for an ABC analysis	
Problem Performance	Problem Performance	Correct Performance
• Poor morale • Bad attitude • Sloppy work • No loyalty • Has no pride	• Absenteeism • Works without following proper safety procedures • Overspending budget • Keeps excessive inventory levels • Turnover • Continues to use old methods	• Attendance • Follows safety rules • Stays within budget • Reduces inventory/ maintains service levels • Retention • Implements new methods quickly and efficiently

required in the policy? Let's look at it from one employee's perspective—a man who often doesn't wear the glasses.

The glasses hurt his ears; he cannot see as clearly with the glasses on; the glasses constantly slide down on his nose; and they always seem to be dirty and he can't clean them easily. Now look at the consequences section of Figure 4.4.

Our analysis suggests why some employees don't wear safety glasses. However, in order to complete the analysis, we need to look at the antecedents and consequences the person experiences when he doesn't wear them. Some of the antecedents are: he sees other employees not wearing their glasses; he often forgets his glasses and is embarrassed to keep checking out additional pairs from the plant nurse; and he remembers how the glasses hurt his ears. Some of the consequences of not wearing his glasses are: his ears don't hurt; he doesn't have to keep pushing the glasses up on his nose; he doesn't have to clean them; he can see better; he doesn't have to keep up with them; and, even though he doesn't wear them, he has never

Figure 4.4

ABC ANALYSIS

Pinpointed Behavior: Wearing safety glasses while operating machinery

Possible Antecedents	Consequences
Safety signs	Ears hurt
Policy manual statement	Can't see clearly
Training	Constantly slide down face
	Must clean dirty lenses frequently

Figure 4.5

ABC ANALYSIS

Pinpointed Behavior: *Not* wearing safety glasses while operating machinery

Possible Antecedents	Possible Consequences
•Some peers don't wear them •Leaves glasses at home •Embarrassed to ask for spare pair •Thinking of how they hurt the ears •Never been caught *not* wearing them •Never been injured *not* wearing them	•Ears don't hurt •Less trouble •Can see better •No injuries

even had a near miss, let alone an eye injury. See Figure 4.5.

The reader can possibly think of other antecedents and consequences because this is not an exhaustive list, but it presents enough to illustrate how a pattern becomes apparent when problems are analyzed this way. In this case, it is relatively clear that unless positive consequences for wearing the glasses are added or negative ones removed, the employee will probably continue to ignore the rule.

ABC AS A DIAGNOSTIC AND PROBLEM-SOLVING TOOL

An ABC analysis should be done when: 1) what you want to happen isn't occurring

often enough, and 2) what you don't want to happen is occurring too often. Let's look at the safety glasses problem again. This time let's do a more extensive listing of the antecedents and consequences associated with the problem. Notice in Figure 4.6 that the consequences list includes some negative consequences as well as the positive ones listed in Figure 4.5. The possibility of an injury, or getting chewed out, or even getting fired seems significant enough to correct the problem. If there were only positives for not wearing the glasses, understanding the problem would be easy. But if there are also negatives, why would they not cause the person to wear them? To understand this, further analysis is needed.

In an ABC analysis, it's necessary to examine each consequence and classify it in the

Figure 4.6

ABC ANALYSIS

Problem	Antecedents	Consequences
Not wearing safety glasses	•Forgot to put them on •Doesn't have them, left them somewhere •Doesn't believe accident will occur •Sees others not wearing them •They are a lot of trouble •Thinks he won't get caught	•Sees better without them •Less trouble •More comfortable •Doesn't have to keep track of them •Might have injury •Boss may chew him out •Might get suspended, fired

following three ways:

1. **P/N** (Positive/Negative)—Determine whether the consequence is likely to be experienced as positive or negative by the person(s) involved, *not* by the boss or organization.

2. **I/F** (Immediate/Future)—Determine whether the consequence occurs *while* the behavior is happening (**I**mmediate) or some time later (**F**uture). This will be examined in more detail in a later chapter, but for now all you need to know is that the more immediate the consequence, the more impact it has on the behavior.

3. **C/U** (Certain/Uncertain)—Determine whether the consequence is certain or uncertain to happen. The Certain/Uncertain dimension refers to probability. If the consequence *always* follows the behavior, then the consequence would be classified as **C**ertain.

For purposes of an ABC analysis we may classify a consequence as Certain if it does not have a perfect correlation but has a very high one. For a smoker, every cigarette may not taste good, but the correlation is high enough that we would classify the consequence "tastes good" as a PIC, or a **P**ositive, **I**mmediate, **C**ertain. People who eat too much, don't always like everything they eat; but for our purposes, we would also call eating a PIC or Positive, Immediate, and Certain consequence. The anticipation of a Certain consequence will reliably produce the behavior associated with it.

Some behavior-consequence connections, for example, are *almost certain.* If you touch a live wire you will always get shocked; sugar always tastes sweet, etc.

Figure 4.7 shows a completed consequence analysis for our safety glass problem. Notice that even though the positives and negatives are roughly equal, the I/Cs (Immediate/Certains) are all associated with the Positives/ and the F/Us (Future/Uncertains) and I/Us (Immediate/Uncertains) are associated with the Negatives. If you look at a similar analysis for "wearing safety glasses" (Figure 4.8), you will see that in this case, the I/Cs are associated with the Negatives rather than the Positives, and the F/Us and I/Us occur for both Positives and Negatives. What this tells us is that the problem performers are receiving PICs (Positive/Immediate/Certain consequences) for "not wearing" and NICs (Negative/Immediate/Certain consequences) for "wearing." In other words, the current consequences *reinforce* not wearing and *punish* wearing safety glasses.

It usually occurs to people at about this point in the analysis that most people wear their safety glasses as they are supposed to do. Remember, the consequences for them are different. An analysis of those who wear their glasses would be quite different from the one in Figure 4.7.

As you learn more about PM, the ABC

Figure 4.7

ABC ANALYSIS

Problem	Antecedents	Consequences	P/N	I/F	C/U
Not wearing safety glasses	•Forgot to put them on	•Sees better without them	P	I	C
	•Doesn't have them, left them somewhere	•Less trouble	P	I	C
		•More comfortable	P	I	C
	•Doesn't believe accident will occur	•Doesn't have to keep track of them	P	I	C
	•Sees others not wearing them	•Might have injury	N	I	U
	•They are a lot of trouble	•Boss may chew him out	N	I	U
	•Thinks he won't get caught	•Might get suspended, fired	N	F	U

analysis will not only give you a better understanding of performance problems, but will also suggest solutions to those problems.

THE 7-STEP ABC ANALYSIS

There are seven steps for completing an ABC analysis. Figure 4.9 summarizes them. Detailed descriptions of each step follow.

Step 1: Describe the problem performance and the performer(s)

First, select a problem and describe it in terms of the behaviors that are occurring or not occurring. While the consequences might seem the same for a group of people who are all engaging in the same behavior, an ABC analysis is only accurate when done from the perspective of the *individual.*

A common difficulty in completing an ABC analysis is that the problems are described too generally. Statements such as "low morale," "bad attitude," "sloppy work habits," and "poor motivation" are too vague for completing useful analyses. As a matter of fact, if you are having trouble completing the remaining steps, it's usually because you've stated the problem non-specifically, or that you pinpointed the wrong problem.

One way to specifically describe a problem, and especially the behaviors that cause the problem, is to ask the question, "What did I see the person do, (or hear that he did) that led me to conclude that he is lazy, has a bad attitude, or has poor morale?"

For example, you might say such a person:
• is often absent or late,
• takes too many breaks,
• was caught not wearing safety equipment,
• does not volunteer to help others,
• argues when requested to make changes in the work, or
• says negative things about the company, management, and co-workers.

A person who is said to have a "bad

Figure 4.8

Correct Performance	ABC ANALYSIS				
	Antecedents	Consequences	P/N	I/F	C/U
Wearing safety glasses	• Recently saw an accident	• Won't stay in place	N	I	C
	• Just had a "near-miss"	• Hurt ears and nose	N	I	C
	• Just chewed out for not wearing them	• Can't see as well	N	I	C
		• Get dirty	N	I	U
	• Just been trained	• Fog up occasionally	N	I	U
	• Everyone else is wearing theirs	• May get harassed by peers	N	I	U
		• Won't get an eye injury	P	I	U
		• May get praise from supervisor	P	I	U
		• Decreased company insurance premiums	P	F	U

Figure 4.9

STEPS IN AN ABC ANALYSIS

STEP 1 Describe the performance you don't want and who is doing it (the problem).

STEP 2 Describe what this person should be doing (correct or desired performance).

STEP 3 Determine the severity of the problem. If the problem occurs frequently, complete Steps 4-7.

STEP 4 Complete an ABC analysis for the problem performance.
a. Write person's name and problem performance on form.
b. List all possible antecedents and consequences.
c. Cross out any consequence not relevant to the performer.
d. Indicate whether each remaining consequence is: P/N, I/F, C/U.

STEP 5 Complete an ABC analysis for correct performance.
a. Write the correct performance for the performer.
b. Complete as in Step 4.

STEP 6 The Diagnosis: Summarize the antecedents and consequences which are presently occurring.

STEP 7 The Solution: Add "Positives/Immediates" and antecedents for the correct performance.

attitude" or "morale problem" may engage in one or all of the preceding. Finding the behaviors that precisely define the problem is called **pinpointing**. The most effective ABC analyses are those in which the behaviors and/or the performance have been pinpointed.

Step 2: Describe the correct or desired performance

The problem behavior was described in Step 1. In Step 2 we specify what we want the person to do differently from the behavior described in the first step. The question asked here is: "If the person were not doing the problem behaviors, what would I want him to be doing?" Believe it or not, it is often harder to pinpoint what we *do* want rather than what we *don't* want. Defining the "right" pinpoint will be considered in detail in Chapter Twelve.

A list of examples of problem behaviors and frequently desired alternatives is pre-sented in Figure 4.10. You will see that many of the "correct or desired" behaviors are easily defined because they are the opposite of the problem behaviors. For example, "submitting reports on time" is the opposite of "submitting reports late." However, it may not be obvious to some that for the problem behavior—"excessive errors"—the correct behavior is not "making no errors," but "increasing error-free work." While this appears to be a trivial difference, it often makes the difference between success and failure. The best way to "make *no* errors" is to do nothing—definitely not what you want.

Step 3: Determine the severity of the problem

In most cases the severity of a problem is determined by its frequency. Obvious exceptions, such as crimes of violence, are serious even if they occur only once in a lifetime. However, for most of the things we deal with daily, frequency determines severity. For

Figure 4.10

PROBLEM AND CORRECT BEHAVIORS FOR AN ABC ANALYSIS

Problem Behavior	Correct Behavior
1. Submitting reports late	1. Submitting reports on time
2. Only making calls on hot leads or very likely prospects	2. Making cold calls
3. Let work area become or remain dirty or cluttered	3. Cleaning up work area
4. Calling in to boss or home office less than once a week	4. Calling in to boss or home office daily
5. Working without safety equipment	5. Working with safety equipment
6. Excessive sales expenses	6. Managing sales expenses to stay within budget guideline
7. Delivering meals too slowly (get cold)	7. Delivering meals while hot (hospitals)
8. Generating excessive waste	8. Monitoring and inspecting machine more frequently

example, a person who gets angry at a customer once in ten years would probably not be accused of having a problem with anger. In most cases, people who knew the employee would probably think the customer had the problem. However, somebody who gets angry at a customer at least once a day would be considered as having a serious problem and would probably be fired, or at the least moved to a job where he did not come in contact with the public.

An ABC analysis is most appropriate when the behavior you don't want occurs frequently. Don't do an analysis on someone who submits one late report, but if she is always late, the analysis will be helpful.

If you are not sure how big a problem a particular behavior or performance is, you will need to collect some data on it. For example, you may think that a subordinate makes too many errors in reports. Before you start working on "reducing reporting errors," you should collect some data on the frequency of errors. You may discover, as many people do when they get the facts, that what made you think there was a problem was that the error was in an important report but that, overall, the person had the best record in the department for producing error-

free reports. Once you pinpoint the problem, be sure that it is a recurring one and that it warrants the time and energy required to solve it. To illustrate the remaining steps in the ABC analysis, a single example will be used. The problem behavior is *not learning to use the computer.*

Step 4: Complete an ABC analysis for problem performance

Step 4a: Write the problem performance and the name of the performer on the form.

Step 4b: List all the antecedents and consequences you can think of for the problem behavior.

This list is the backbone of the ABC analysis, so attempt to identify as many in each category as possible. Put down anything that comes to mind.

Figure 4.11 shows the completed portion of the ABC analysis form for the problem performance, "not learning to use the computer." For purposes of this illustration, assume you have a highly skilled person who resists learning new technology. She is very effective using the old technology, but as her supervisor, you know that with advancing technology, those who do not move into the computer age will eventually not be able to compete.

Step 4c: Cross out any antecedents and consequences that are not relevant to the performer.

Many people make mistakes in this step. Review each consequence that you have listed on the form and ask: "Does this consequence have a payoff for the employee?" Determine whether the employee personally considers this consequence important. Initially, many people list consequences that have a payoff for the organization, but not for the employee. Examine the list of consequences below:

• Increased costs
• Increased waste
• Decreased quality of goods or services
• Loss of business
• Dissatisfied customers

These consequences are usually unimportant to problem performers, however significant they may be to the organization or the manager. In other words, *consequences that are significant to management are often not significant to the problem employees.*

Now cross out any consequence considered unimportant to the employee. Figure 4.12 shows the list in Figure 4.11 with two consequences crossed out—consequences the employee in our illustration would probably find unimportant.

Step 4d: For each remaining consequence indicate whether it is **P/N, I/F, C/U**. This is the last step in completing the ABC grid for the problem behavior. The consequences are categorized according to three criteria: type of consequence, its immediacy, and the probability of occurrence. The combination of these criteria will determine whether the behavior will or will not occur. Keep in mind that the consequences are categorized from the perspective of the

Figure 4.11

ABC ANALYSIS

Performer(s) _Brenda_

Problem Performance	Antecedents	Consequences	P/N	I/F	C/U
Not learning to use the computer	•Doesn't have the time •Doesn't like the confusing nature of computers •Afraid won't learn as quickly as others (look dumb) •Others haven't learned either •Hears the others complain that it's difficult •Sees the others struggling •Sees the others working late to catch up to normal work load	•Comfort with present way	P	I	C
		•Can't take advantage of new technology	N	I	U
		•Avoids failing task at hand	P	I	C
		•Lack of consistency with other offices	N	I	C
		•Avoids hassles of training	P	I	C
		•More time to do other things	P	I	C
		•Might get reprimanded	N	F	U
		•Might get fired	N	F	U
		•Peers may ridicule	N	F	U
		•Peers may support not learning the new material, stick by you	P	F	U
		•Will have limited skills for future employment	N	F	C

Figure 4.12

Problem Performance	Antecedents	Consequences	P/N	I/F	C/U
Not learning to use the computer	• Doesn't have the time • Doesn't like the confusing nature of computers • Afraid won't learn as quickly as others (look dumb) • Others haven't learned either • Hears the others complain it's difficult • Sees the others struggling • Sees the others working late to catch up to normal work load	• Comfortable with present way	P	I	C
		• ~~Can't take advantage of technology~~	~~N~~	~~I~~	~~U~~
		• Avoids failing task at hand	P	I	C
		• ~~Lack of consistency with other offices~~	~~N~~	~~I~~	~~C~~
		• Avoids hassles of training	P	I	C
		• More time to do other things	P	I	C
		• Might get reprimanded	N	F	U
		• Might get fired	N	F	U
		• Peers may ridicule	N	F	U
		• Peers may support not learning the new material, stick by you	P	F	U
		• Will have limited skills for future employment	N	F	C

ABC ANALYSIS

person in question.

• **Positive or Negative.** To categorize on this dimension, you simply need to determine if this is something the person wants or doesn't want.

In Figure 4.12, there are five positives and six negatives; however, two of the six negative consequences for not learning the computer have been crossed out as unimportant to the performer. There is no simple rule for deciding whether the impact of a particular consequence will be positive or negative. As you get to know people, the ability to correctly classify the P/N dimension improves.

• **Immediate or Future.** Immediate consequences are those that occur during a behavior or on its completion. All other consequences would technically be considered Future. Many consequences in business occur weeks or months after the performance has occurred. Remember that generally speaking, the longer the delay between the behavior and the consequence

the less effect the consequence will have on the behavior in question.

• **Certain or Uncertain.** The final criterion for evaluating the effectiveness of a consequence is the likelihood, or probability, that it will actually occur. Again, we must take the perspective of the problem performer. The question to ask is: "Has the person experienced the consequence as certain to happen, or not very likely to happen?"

A manager may warn an employee that he will be suspended if he violates a particular rule again. The employee, however, knows many people who violate the rule and has never seen anyone suspended for it. Therefore, the employee may regard this consequence as uncertain. The manager believes she will suspend people, even though she rarely does and, accordingly, thinks she has promised a "certain" consequence. Despite this, her warning will have little effect because in the employee's experience the consequence is uncertain.

Step 5: Complete an ABC analysis for the correct or desired performance

Step 5a: Write the correct performance on the form. In Figure 4.13, the behavior in our example has been typed in the correct space.

Steps 5b, 5c, and 5d are the same as those in Step 4. Simply ask the same questions about the correct behavior that were asked about the problem behavior. For example:
1. What is the payoff to the *problem* employee for learning to use the computer?
2. What consequences have value to her?
3. Does the performer experience the consequences as P/N, I/F, C/U?

Still, some additional guidelines need to be considered when doing an ABC analysis on correct behavior.

Step 5b: Training is usually an antecedent for the correct or desired behavior. This is significant because the first thing most managers do to improve performance is to give the employee more training. But an ABC analysis often demonstrates that training has been adequate. The employee already knows what he should do and how to do it—but the consequences don't favor it. The basic question to answer concerning training is: "Could the employee perform the correct behavior if his life depended on it?" If your answer is yes, then training will not solve the problem. The solution is a change of consequences.

Step 5c: In examining the consequences in Figure 4.13 you will see two with little significance to the problem employee. Her supervisor and top management may be reinforced or punished by the consequences that have been crossed out, but they do not represent a payoff for the employee.

When identifying consequences for the correct performance, people sometimes make the mistake of switching from the "problem" employee to the "good" employee. In other words, to make a valid analysis you would not want to look at the consequences from the perspective of those people who love to learn new things and always seek new ways to do things. This part of the analysis starts with the question: "If the person who resists

new technology started to learn, what antecedents would cause her to start and what would the consequences be if she did?"

One test to make to see if you have maintained the perspective of the same person through both parts of the analysis is to check for PICs on this part. Although you will occasionally find one or two PICs, they should be infrequent because PICs for good performance suggest that you don't have a problem. If there are several PICs, you have probably unconsciously changed performers.

Step 5d: Positive/Negative. There are four positive consequences listed for learning to use the computer. However, they are all Future and Uncertain and as such will have limited effect on the problem behavior.

Everyone who has ever tried to learn anything as complicated as using a computer knows that it requires considerable effort—psychological as well as physical. You are sure to make mistakes, and in the case of the person who does not want to do this in the first place, there are many other things that she would rather do. These are all classified as NICs.

Step 6: The diagnosis: Summarize the antecedents and consequences that are occurring now

Having identified the antecedents and consequences causing the performance problem, we need to summarize and review this information. This process results in five conclusions.

- **Antecedents.** The first conclusion is that the problem behavior will have many antecedents and the correct behavior will have few. This shows that for most of our problems, many things in the environment are prompting the problem behavior while there are usually few prompting the correct behavior.

- **Positives and Negatives.** The second conclusion is that the number of positives and negatives are roughly equal for both the problem behavior and the correct behavior. Based solely on this part of the analysis, it

Figure 4.13

EXAMPLE OF ABC ANALYSIS "NOT LEARNING TO USE THE COMPUTER"

Problem Performance	Antecedents	Consequences	P/N	I/F	C/U
Not learning to use the computer	• Doesn't have the time • Doesn't like the confusing nature of computers • Afraid won't learn as quickly as others (look dumb) • Others haven't learned either • Hear the others complain it's difficult • Sees the others struggling • Sees the others working late to catch up to normal work load	• Comfortable with present way	P	I	C
		• ~~Can't take advantage of technology~~	N	I	U
		• Avoids failing task at hand	P	I	C
		• ~~Lack of consistency with other offices~~	N	I	C
		• Avoids hassles of training	P	I	C
		• More time to do other things	P	I	C
		• Might get reprimanded	N	F	U
		• Might get fired	N	F	U
		• Peers may ridicule	N	F	U
		• Peers may support not learning the new material, stick by you	P	F	U
		• Will have limited skills for future employment	N	F	C

Desired Performance	Antecedents	Consequences	P/N	I/F	C/U
Learning to use the computer	• Pressure from management • Seeing others learn • Last one to learn • Enjoy a challenge • See as an opportunity to increase your own market value	• Takes time from other things	N	I	C
		• Hard going (difficult)	N	I	C
		• Makes mistakes	N	I	C
		• Gets behind in regular work	N	I	U
		• Could set self up for failure	N	F	U
		• May make job easier	P	F	U
		• May get raise or promoted	P	F	U
		• May get a good performance appraisal	P	F	U
		• May get praise from superior	P	F	U

would be difficult to predict what the person would do. This is not unusual; therefore, further analysis is necessary.

• **Impact of Positives and Negatives.** It may occur to you that even though the positives and negatives are about the same for the undesired behavior, the negatives appear to be quite powerful in relation to the positives. Getting fired or reprimanded seem to be rather "heavy" negatives while having more time to do other things or avoiding the hassle of training seem to be rather "light" positives. The answer lies in the fact that even though the negatives are quite serious, they are future and uncertain (NFU). Even though the positives don't seem to be significant in the long haul, they tend to be immediate and certain (PIC).

Of course, it is the immediacy and certainty that have the most impact. NICs may be considered to be as powerful as PICs, but NFUs are no more powerful than PFUs.

• **PICs.** The fourth conclusion is perhaps the most important one. The problem behavior has more PICs than the desired behavior. While it is true that NICs are as powerful as PICs, you must remember that NICs stop behavior rather than keep it going. Therefore, PICs are the most effective consequence for maintaining or increasing performance.

• **Future/Uncertain Consequences.** Consequences that are uncertain and delayed have limited impact on performance. Generally speaking, the more delayed the consequence, the less impact it will have on the behavior or performance. In addition, the fewer times a consequence is associated with a behavior, the weaker effect it has on the behavior. An ABC analysis usually reveals that for the problem performance, the future/uncertain consequences tend to be negative. The opposite is typically true for the desired behavior. The future/uncertain (F/U) consequences tend to be positive. This means that the positive consequences for the *desired* behavior are weak. Also, the negative conse-

quences for the *undesired*, or problem behavior, are weak. To repeat: consequences— either negative or positive—that are uncertain or delayed have limited impact on performance.

Step 7: The solution

The completed ABC analysis suggests two possible ways to increase the correct or desired behavior.

1. Add Positive/Immediate consequences for the correct or desired behavior.

2. Add antecedents for the correct or desired behavior.

The best way to evoke productive behavior is to make sure the individual gets a payoff for doing it—the more immediate the better. The payoff may be as simple as a pat on the back, or it may be something more tangible. Most managers underestimate the power of their praise and recognition. It is clearly one of the most underutilized consequences in business.

As an aid to increasing this type of positive/immediate consequence, managers should monitor performance and record it on a graph. Each day they can plot the number of calls answered, letters typed, or items produced. By showing the performer his activities on the graph, the managers have something specific to point to as they praise improvement. If the graph has a daily goal on it and goal attainment has been paired consistently with praise, the graph will become an effective antecedent for improved performance.

The most obvious way for managers to provide positive/immediate consequences is to spend time in the area where the work goes on. In this way it is easy to "catch somebody doing something good." If performance is being graphed, managers can write comments on the team or unit graphs. They can talk to the employees about the things they did to improve their performance. By being in the work area, managers can easily observe proper work habits, cooperative behavior, and other desirable actions. These can be commented on or otherwise reinforced as they happen. Also, by developing a reinforcement system where everybody knows precisely what is expected of the team, the team members can participate in providing reinforcement (P/I) for each other.

Although positive/immediates are usually in the shortest supply, positive/future consequences usually need to be increased also. One way to do this is to get the team together at the beginning or end of the shift and review accomplishments. Another is to plan celebrations when they reach specified goals. Numerous examples of how to choose and deliver positive reinforcement are presented in Chapters Five and Six.

In addition to adding positives for the desired behavior, the ABC analysis also indicates that there are usually too few antecedents. The few that are present have been consistently associated with the undesired behavior or inconsistently with the desired behavior. In any event, add new antecedents.

Although the analysis showed no NICs for the undesired behavior, it is not recommended that they be included in the initial solution. Sometimes adding negatives for the undesirable behavior will increase the desirable behavior. However, this often creates unwanted side effects. The job may become unpleasant, morale may decline, and employee sabotage may increase. For these and other reasons, NICs are not recommended for the problem behavior unless no other approach has worked. Adding positives for the desired behavior will produce the desired results in most cases.

THE VALUE OF AN ABC ANALYSIS

The ABC analysis of someone who doesn't want to learn to use the computer could easily be applied to any problem involving "resistance to change." For example, see the sidebar which illustrates the problem of a boss whose employees don't keep him informed of potential problems.

If you have any problem performance that you don't understand, the ABC analysis will be helpful. The ABC analysis can be applied to any behavior or performance problem. The analysis shows that there are logical reasons why people do what they do. More important, it usually suggests a solution. Over the years many people have solved serious and long-standing problems at work and at home by analyzing them with ABC analyses.

The ABC analysis assists us in arranging the environment to promote those behaviors that will benefit the individual and the group in both the short- and long-term.

The analysis almost invariably shows that when problems exist, there are practically never any PICs for the desired performance. The solution almost always involves adding several positive/immediates for the desired behavior. Because of this people often ask, "Why do an analysis if the results are always the same?" There are several reasons. One is that doing ABC analyses helps you develop the discipline of looking at problems from the perspective of the other person. This is a healthy perspective for any problem at any level of society.

Second, it is often helpful to do an ABC analysis when we are planning for a new performance. This allows us to see what antecedents and consequences might exist in the environment that might interfere with the new performance.

Third, the process often generates ideas for an effective solution because it may reveal powerful reinforcers for the person or group.

And finally, it helps people "think" PM. "Thinking" PM involves using the terms antecedents, consequences, reinforcers and punishers and applying them in everyday situations.

Although the discussion in this chapter has been directed primarily toward analyzing "problem performers," the ABC analysis can be used just as effectively in understanding the barriers that prevent good or high performers from doing even better. The ABC analysis is a very useful tool in planning any performance change. To use it effectively, an in-depth understanding of reinforcement, the subject of the next chapter, is essential.

ABC Analysis: "Informing the Boss"

Frank is a manager with a problem. He complains his people never talk to him. This makes it difficult for him to run his department because he is surprised often when his department fails to meet its commitments to other divisions in the company.

Frank's employees complain they can't talk to him without him jumping down their throats with negative responses to any problems that may arise. When a problem does occur, they must waste time and energy avoiding Frank, and then try to solve the problem themselves.

One of Frank's employees, Nancy, related an ordeal she suffered through with Frank when she did, in fact, try to talk to him about a potential problem. A situation had arisen where Nancy's staff might not meet their deadline on a quality assessment report that was to be delivered to Frank's supervisor. As she began to describe the problem, Frank rose from his desk infuriated, "I don't want to hear any of your flimsy excuses," deliberately pounding his fist—"do what you have to do to get it done and do it—now!" He stamped out leaving Nancy sitting there.

Another employee, Jerry, spoke about the time he tried to inform Frank that a mistake in his production area caused a problem for an internal customer. Before Jerry could start telling him what he'd done to start solving the problem, Frank burst out and began yelling at Jerry for allowing one of his employees to delegate some important decisions within his area. The result was an altercation in which Jerry was protecting his employee from Frank's command to fire him. In the following ABC analysis, we'll address Frank's problem.

ABC Analysis

Correct Behavior: Informing the boss of problems   **Performer:** Frank's staff members

Antecedents	Consequences	
Doesn't want boss to be surprised	Boss gets angry at me	NIC
Wants boss's help with problems	Offers no advice or solutions	NIC
Always informed previous bosses	Makes demands	NIC
Wants up-front work relationship with boss	Slams fist on desk	NIU
	Gives ultimatums	NIU
	Storms out of office	NIU
	Degrades subordinate's decisions	NIU
	Threatens to fire someone	NIU
	You are covered if problem arises	PFU

Incorrect Behavior: Not informing the boss of problems

Antecedents	Consequences	
Doesn't want boss's negative reactions	Won't have to defend himself	PIC
Doesn't have time	Avoids boss's temper	PIC
Thinks he may solve problem without boss knowing there was one	Spends time working on solution	PIU
Wants to maintain pleasant daily interaction without an altercation	Boss will get angry later if he hears about it after the fact	NFU
Thinks he may jeopardize subordinate's job	Boss may never know there was a problem	PFU

5

Reinforcers

A **reinforcer** is typically thought of as an object or event. The process whereby a person receives a reinforcer is called **reinforcement**. Since reinforcement increases behavior, reinforcers and reinforcement are the most important concepts to understand in managing performance.

There are times when we want to decrease or stop a behavior or decrease its frequency. However, even when we do that, it is practically always to facilitate an increase in the frequency of appropriate or productive behavior. Before examining reinforcers in detail, let's consider why positive reinforcement should be a primary concern for managers of organizations.

THE VALUE OF POSITIVE REINFORCEMENT IN MANAGING ORGANIZATIONS

The research of the last fifty years proves that positive reinforcement works. People need it and like it. For those reasons alone it should certainly be of interest to managers. However, there are other equally compelling reasons for organizations to try to use this approach effectively.

1. Positive reinforcement has positive side effects

In business we find that positive reinforcement improves the supervisor-employee relationship: when it takes place they like each other more. It improves job satisfaction:

the job is liked more. It improves morale and increases employee loyalty to the organization: the company is liked more. These benefits are documented by the experiences of thousands of managers and other employees. Positive reinforcement produces long-lasting, measurable change.

2. Most performance problems in organizations are motivational

As stated in the previous chapter, Mager (1970) identified two kinds of performance problems. They are "can't do" and "won't do." "Can't do" problems require some antecedent intervention such as training. "Won't do" problems require a change in consequences. "Won't do" problems are motivational. In order to identify a motivational problem, ask the question: "Could the individual do this job if his life depended on it?" If the answer is yes, it is a motivational problem.

Most employees admit they could do more if they "wanted to." In "A Public Agenda Report on Restoring America's Competitive Vitality," Yankelovich and Immerwhar (1983) reported that fewer than one of four (23%) say they are performing to their full capacity and are being as effective as they are capable of being. The majority say they could increase their effectiveness significantly. Nearly half of the work force (44%) say they do not put more effort into their jobs than is required.

It is management's job, then, to create the conditions under which people "want to."

Positive reinforcement is clearly the most effective way to produce that kind of motivation.

3. People need positive reinforcement

Both daily experience and psychological research tell us that everyone seeks positive reinforcement, and people will do many things to get it. Some of those things are socially acceptable and some are not. The thief and the drug pusher are positively reinforced by quick and easy money. The hardworking music student practices more and more as her recitals draw applause and praise. As the young athlete begins to win, he works harder and harder. Although we see examples every day where someone has been positively reinforced for inappropriate behavior, most of the positive reinforcement we get is for productive, socially acceptable behavior.

Some of the reinforcement people work for is obvious and some is not. An obvious example is the child who does something "to get attention." However, the person who works hard to get a promotion, a raise, or approval from the boss or her peers is also working for positive reinforcement even though her actions may not be as obvious.

A very popular theory of motivation taught in most business schools is Abraham Maslow's "Hierarchy of Needs." Maslow (1943) describes a range of needs from food, shelter, and clothing to esteem and self-actualization. It is useful to look at these needs as a general description of reinforcers. Just as people need food, air, and water—the most basic needs—they also need social recognition, praise, and challenge—the higher needs.

People's need for positive reinforcement can be seen as similar to the need a business has for profit. The income statement must show a profit for the business to survive. And profit must not be too long in coming since the business cannot survive for an indefinite period without it. The same is true for the individual for whom positive reinforcement is the profit. In many cases it only takes days, or a few weeks, without positive

reinforcement to lead to decreases in performance.

It's hard for some managers to understand that money doesn't provide enough "profit" to keep people performing to their potential. We have all heard people say things like "You couldn't pay me enough to work for him." Money is necessary, but not sufficient, to produce outstanding performance, especially over a long period of time.

The best job you will ever have is one that you leave every day, feeling that you not only made a financial profit but a psychological one as well. Interestingly enough, having received some simple sign of appreciation for your work such as a telephone call to say, "You did a quality job on the Rourk project," or a note of appreciation for some extra effort, may be enough "profit" to excite you about coming back and doing the same thing again tomorrow.

Individuals will find reinforcement at work whether it is provided by the manager or not. If reinforcement is not provided by the manager, it may be found in ways that are not beneficial to the organization, such as in off-task behaviors and, in some cases, even stealing. After over twenty years of applying PM in business, it's clear that managers who systematically provide positive reinforcement for desirable performance outperform those who don't.

4. Positive reinforcement creates a positive climate for positive accountability

Positive reinforcement produces good feelings in an organization. People who receive positive reinforcement begin to think more positively about the person delivering it to them. This increase in morale improves the quality of work life and creates a positive climate for accountability.

Traditionally, people have feared and resented measurement and accountability because more often than not it provided a better way to deliver negative consequences. Surprisingly, in an environment in which positive reinforcement is used effectively, people seek both measurement and accountability. Employees who have been given consistent and sincere reinforcement for their accomplishments are more receptive to change and less defensive about suggestions for improving performance. In such an environment the relationship between management and labor invariably becomes more cooperative and less adversarial. All these factors lead to the creation of an organization that is receptive to change—a must in today's business environment.

WHAT IS A REINFORCER?

There are two kinds of reinforcers: positive and negative. The focus of most of this book is on the use of positive reinforcers and positive reinforcement in business. For ease of reading throughout the remainder of the book, the word reinforcement will refer to positive reinforcement—not negative—and the word reinforcer will refer to a positive reinforcer unless specifically stated otherwise. Negative reinforcement and negative reinforcer will be specifically denoted.

A reinforcer is anything that follows a behavior and causes it either to increase or maintain a maximum level. The abbreviation R+ will be used for positive reinforcer and positive reinforcement. The context will let you know to which it refers. It should be pointed out that in some of the research by applied behavior analysts you will see the abbreviation S^r rather than R+.

Reinforcers have at least three distinguishing features:

1. A reinforcer follows behavior
A reinforcer can only follow behavior, it can never precede it. As stated in Chapter Two, anything that comes before a behavior (or prompts it) is called an antecedent. Although this seems a simple concept, it is sometimes difficult to recognize in practice.

For example, giving children candy if they promise to study is not a reinforcer for studying but for "promising to study." A reinforcer for studying would only be given *after* the

studying had actually occurred. In analyzing behavior, you must first determine the behavior you are concerned with and look at what follows it. This is the only way you will discover reinforcers.

2. Reinforcers increase the frequency of a behavior
Something is a reinforcer only if it increases the frequency of a behavior. If a behavior is consistently followed by a particular consequence but the frequency of the behavior does not increase, then we cannot say that the consequence is a reinforcer. If behavior increases for a period of time but decreases later, the consequence may no longer be reinforcing. This is an important point to remember. Reinforcers change.

Things we enjoy now may lose their appeal later. As we grow older, some things lose their reinforcing value. Activities we enjoyed when we were younger are no longer engaging. Our tastes for certain foods change over time. What we like to wear changes—sometimes seasonally. What we like to talk about can change almost daily.

The frequency with which one receives a reinforcer also affects its reinforcing value. We tend to tire of some things simply because of repeated exposure to them. Seeing your name on the bulletin board or in the company paper for some accomplishment may be quite reinforcing the first time it appears, but after seeing it for many months in a row, it may not matter.

Remember that things that were reinforcing at one time or place may not be reinforcing at another time or place. This means that managers must constantly monitor performance to ensure the consequences are still effective.

3. A reinforcer can be tangible or social
The definition states that a reinforcer can be "anything." There are several ways to classify reinforcers but the most useful seems to be tangible and social. Tangible reinforcers are usually thought of as objects or activities, whereas social reinforcers are usually thought

of as interactions between people. Tangible reinforcers are material items such as meals, gift certificates, or prizes. Social reinforcers are interactions such as a pat on the back, giving someone a thank-you note, or talking to someone about a subject of interest to her.

A balance between the tangible and social reinforcement people receive is important. The balance is heavily weighted, however, in favor of the social. Social reinforcement is the mainstay of a PM environment; that is, it is by far the most common. In order to have the most effective work place, some combination of social and tangible reinforcement is usually necessary.

FINDING EFFECTIVE REINFORCERS

To help you discover the kinds of things that are reinforcing to individuals and groups, it is important to know about primary and secondary reinforcers. A **primary reinforcer** is one that is biologically important, such as food, water, warmth, and sexual stimulation. Primary reinforcers do not have to be learned. In contrast, **secondary reinforcers** are neutral stimuli that do not have biological importance but have been paired with primary reinforcers or other established secondary reinforcers. In other words, they are acquired or learned.

Because other things associated with reinforcers—both primary and secondary—can themselves become secondary reinforcers, it is easy to understand how each person comes to have a unique set of reinforcers. What we see, hear, touch, taste, and smell during reinforcement has the potential of becoming a new secondary reinforcer.

Smoking and drinking alcohol, though initially aversive to many, may become a highly potent reinforcer through association with peer approval, anxiety reduction, and other reinforcers. Acquired tastes in food, drink, music, and art all have a history of being paired with other established reinforcers.

People's varied likes and dislikes complicate the problem of finding effective reinforcers. No two people are exactly alike in this regard. Fortunately, many of us have reinforcers that are similar. This is what allows us to reinforce groups of people. However, the larger the group, the lower the probability that any single reinforcer you choose will be a reinforcer for everyone.

How then do you find the reinforcers for the individuals and groups that you work with? This section will give you some ways to simplify the task.

Wants, desires, values, and reinforcers

In attempting to find an effective reinforcer, it is helpful to think in terms of what the person or group wants, desires, or values. However, people's wants, desires, and values are not identical to reinforcers. You may say you want, desire, or value something but not be willing to increase a particular behavior or performance to get it.

Even though wants, desires, and values are not the equivalent of reinforcers, they are helpful to know in trying to discover reinforcers. If the wants, desires, and values of other people are the same as ours, we will probably have many reinforcers in common. But in the final analysis, no matter what we call it, if it doesn't increase the behavior it isn't a reinforcer.

One of the most common errors made in choosing reinforcers for others is that we assume they want what we want, even when there are large differences in age, education, social status, and culture. Many plant managers have offered to take a top performer and spouse to dinner at a fancy restaurant when that was the last thing that particular couple wanted. They may well have preferred beer and pizza or dinner alone! Of course, the opposite mistake is also made when we assume that because of certain background factors they would prefer beer and pizza when in fact they want to go to a fancy restaurant.

This brings up a strong feature of the PM process. We cannot be successful in working with others if we treat them stereotypically. The variety of people's wants and needs is tremendous. To further complicate the matter, no two people are the same. Because of this, PM will not work effectively unless the individual's reinforcers are used.

At first glance it appears that choosing effective reinforcers for one person is difficult and for a group, impossible. Fortunately, there are some things that seem to transcend all the differences mentioned above. For example, most people of all ages, education, social status, and culture respond favorably to expressions of appreciation for good performance. There are other reinforcers but the question is, "How do we find them?"

Three methods of identifying reinforcers are: asking, observing, and testing.

Asking people what they like

One way to identify effective reinforcers for people is by talking to them. Ask them what non-work activities they spend their time and money pursuing. Do they hunt, jog, ski, read, or play a musical instrument? The simple act of talking to people about something they are interested in is practically always a reinforcer. For example, spending some time talking to someone about her family or her hobby is usually reinforcing.

Asking people what they like about work is also helpful. Some may like overtime; others may want more time off. Some may want to work alone; others as part of a group. An example of asking people what they like and using it as a reinforcer is provided by Dr. Thomas K. Connellan. Connellan (1978) is a pioneer in the application of Performance Management techniques. He relates the following incident:

A young manager at one of the major automobile manufacturers...was put in charge of a line that assembled rear-end units for trucks and buses...and discovered that although the standard was 72 units an

hour, workers were lucky if they completed 45 units. Being fairly new with the company, the young manager asked the people working that particular line what it would take for them to bring their output up to standard. After talking it over, they decided that if they were permitted to get in an extra break once in a while, that would justify an increased effort on their part. The final deal was that once they had completed 72 units within a given hour, the rest of that hour was theirs for a break. It took only a week before the workers produced up to standard within 35 minutes; they took the remaining 25 minutes for their break. Both the manager and the workers were aware that such a long break was impractical, so they renegotiated the agreement. This time the standard was raised to 92 units per hour, which they were able to produce and still get a ten-minute break.

Note that their beginning performance was typically in the range of 37 percent below standard (below 45 units per hour). They eventually performed 28 percent above standard (more than 92 units per hour) which was more than double their starting performance. While this is an outstanding improvement, it is not rare. When we add reinforcement where it previously did not exist, significant improvement is the rule.

Unfortunately, our example doesn't end happily. An upper manager, Dr. Connellan says, intervened:

Everything was fine until one of the divisional vice presidents, hearing of the improved production, came down to see what was going on. As luck would have it, he showed up in the middle of a break and raised the roof; increased production notwithstanding, those workers were paid to work eight hours a day, and that was exactly what they were going to do.

Needless to say, the employees went back to "working" eight hours a day, and production dropped to below the original standard. The new supervisor's unorthodox reinforcer was visible and accessible, and there was no doubt that it was effective. The real question revolved around the choice of having a labor force that produces or one that merely puts in time.

This example brings up an important point about asking people what they like. The reinforcer must be under the control of the person delivering it. In this case the supervisor thought he had control when he did not. Make certain that you won't be overruled after you have set up a contingency.

Personally asking what people's interests are can be supplemented by a questionnaire. Sometimes referred to as **reinforcer surveys**, these forms list items covering a wide range of possible interests, and people check the ones they like. A survey is helpful because if you ask people to tell you about their interests and hobbies, they may not remember them all at that time or may not think you would be interested in some of the things they do. The survey provides a memory jogger and gives you specific information.

A sample survey is provided in Figure 5.1. Use it as a guide only. Modify it to the local interests of the people taking it. See the Appendix for two versions of a Reinforcer Survey that may be copied or modified to suit your needs.

A reinforcer survey is best used to help you get to know the person better. Do not send it in the office mail or leave it on a person's desk with a note to fill it out and return to you. This invites disaster. Sit down with the person or group and explain what you want and why you want it. Introduce it simply as a way to get to know them better. Refer to, "Using the R+ Survey," for some administrative guidelines.

After they fill it out, spend some time talking about it with them so that you understand precisely what they mean. One man wrote on his R+ Survey that he'd like "tickets to cultural events." His boss gave him tickets to the symphony. The man later told the PM consultant that what he wanted

was tickets to a wrestling match. It pays to ask people to be very specific.

The "cafeteria" benefit approach is a kind of reinforcer survey. These are compensation plans designed to tailor benefit programs to individual desires. The total cash value of the package is determined and the employees are able to choose more of one benefit, e.g., life insurance, and less of another, e.g., health insurance, up to the limit of the plan amount. Note, however, that cafeteria plans typically violate one of the most basic characteristics of reinforcement: they are not contingent on performance. In most cases as long as people are employed, they receive all the customized benefits regardless of their performance.

Before asking people what they want, you should be aware of some potential problems. The three that are encountered most often are:

1. They don't know.
2. They won't tell you.
3. They tell you things you can't deliver.

Sometimes people aren't aware of their reinforcers. For example, most people know that they want more money but may fail to realize, or be unwilling to admit, the importance of recognition from their boss. Someone may list in a reinforcer survey that they love to attend symphony concerts. But when asked how often they attend, they may say they haven't been to one in years. After administering a reinforcer survey, you may want to ask the individuals when was the last time they actually did the various things they listed.

Occasionally managers may use something that a particular group or individual told them was a reinforcer only to discover that performance didn't increase when that reinforcer was delivered. This does not happen because people are dishonest but because they simply thought it was more important to them than it turned out to be.

Most people are not accustomed to listing the things they like, either verbally or on paper. In the past when PM class participants have been asked to make a reinforcer list, the average list contained only eight items. In reality everybody has hundreds. In the beginning, performers' lists may be short, but as you work with them the lists will grow. Although making a list may be difficult at first, most of the time just asking for a list is reinforcing to people. Most people are reinforced just to know that someone is interested in them.

Many times when bosses ask subordinates for a reinforcer list, they tend to tell them things they think are acceptable to the boss, or organization, rather than things they really want. In work environments where there is a low level of trust, performers may only tell others those things they consider "safe"; that is, only those things that they are sure they will not be punished for revealing. If people are afraid they will be ridiculed, or in any way made to feel uncomfortable about something that they like, they will not tell it.

Sometimes when you ask people to tell you what they want or like, you may set up false expectations. When you ask the question, be sure to say you are trying to get to know the types of things they like or enjoy. Tell them you may not be able to arrange for every particular thing they mention, but don't be afraid to at least ask. Who knows, you may be able to arrange something they wouldn't think you could ordinarily do for them.

Observing people

Even though common sense seems to indicate that "asking" would be the best way to find reinforcers, for the reasons mentioned above, it is not. When you begin to reinforce, it is usually best to start with one of the other methods. Then, once people have experienced reinforcement at work or are trained in the approach, "asking" is a very

---

Well Known Reinforcer Surveys...

My Favorite Things

Raindrops on roses and whiskers on kittens,
Bright copper kettles and warm woolen mittens,
Brown paper packages tied up with strings,
These are a few of my favorite things.
Cream colored ponies and crisp apple strudels,
Doorbells and sleighbells and schnitzel with noodles,
Wild geese that fly with the moon on their wings,
These are a few of my favorite things.
Girls in white dresses with blue satin sashes,
Snowflakes that stay on my nose and eyelashes,
Silver white winters that melt into spring,
These are a few of my favorite things.
When the dog bites, when the bee stings,
When I'm feeling sad,
I simply remember my favorite things
And then I don't feel so bad.

(Reprinted with permission, Chappell & Co., Inc. 1956 by Alan Jay Lerner and Frederick Loewe)

I Love

I love little baby ducks, old pick-up trucks, slow movin' trains, and rain

I love little country streams, sleep without dreams, Sunday school in May—and hay.

I love leaves in the wind, pictures of my friends, birds in the world, and squirrels.

I love coffee in a cup, little fuzzy pups, bourbon in a glass, and grass.

I love open honest smiles, kisses from a child, tomatoes on a vine, and onions.

I love winners when they cry, losers when they try, music when it's good—and life.

And I love you, too.

(Reprinted with permission, Ryckman Music Publishing Co. 1974, Tom T. Hall Hallnote Music)

CHAPTER FIVE

Figure 5.1

REINFORCER SURVEY

Name:_____   Company:_____

The items in this survey refer to things and experiences that may make you feel good. Check each item in the column which describes how much pleasure you receive from it.

	None at all	A little	A fair amount	Much	Very much
1. Spending time on hobbies (list specific hobbies)					
Surfing					✓
Water skiing					✓
Sailing competitively					✓
2. Listening to music (list specific kind)					
Reggae					✓
Jazz				✓	
English progressive			✓		
3. Attending concerts					
Reggae					✓
Outdoor Reggae concerts					✓
4. Watching sports					
College football					✓
Great moments in sports films				✓	
5. Playing sports					
Softball games for the company					✓
Touch football games for the company					✓
Any water sports					✓
6. Reading					
Performance Management books/articles					✓
"Far Side" comic books					✓
Sports car magazines				✓	

	None at all	A little	A fair amount	Much	Very much
7. Watching movies					
Tom Hanks, Eddie Murphy, Comedy specials					✔
Vietnam themes				✔	
Science fiction (like "Alien" but not "Star Wars")			✔		
8. Watching TV					
CNN News					✔
Nature specials				✔	
9. Attending parties					
Casual outdoor					✔
Black tie (every now and then)			✔		
10. Solving problems					
Artistic layout questions					✔
Ask my opinion on a presentation before submitting					✔
11. Completing a difficult job					✔
12. Singing		✔			
13. Dancing	✔				
14. Playing a musical instrument		✔			
15. Shopping		✔			
16. Playing cards		✔			
17. Being around people					✔
18. Involvement in church/temple			✔		
19. Writing					✔
20. Organizing a program or refreshments for a meeting				✔	
21. Cooking					✔
22. Painting					✔
23. Other					

effective way to increase the potential number of reinforcers for both the group and the individual.

Simply stated: Be sensitive to people. Pay attention to their interests as indicated by what they talk about, what they wear, and what they spend their time doing. The effective manager is one who develops an interest in the things in which her employees are interested. Many reinforcers can be discovered just by talking to people, or better yet, by listening to them. Unfortunately, we are so busy telling people what *we* want that we have little time left to listen to what *they* want.

What people *do* may be a clue to what is reinforcing to them. Under certain conditions, something that a person chooses to do frequently may be used as a reinforcer. This is the Premack Principle, named for its discoverer, Dr. David Premack (1959).

More precisely, the **Premack Principle** states that a high probability behavior may serve as a reinforcer for a low probability behavior. Some people know this informally as Grandma's law: "If you eat your spinach (low frequency choice), you can have dessert (high frequency choice)."

The Premack Principle allows managers to find reinforcers that occur naturally in the work place. It takes some practice to find them, but once you begin to see them, it will open up a new dimension of reinforcement for you. As one of the great manipulators of the English language, Yogi Berra, once said, "You can see a lot by observing." He was right. For example, if employees consistently refuse overtime, we might conclude that time off is more reinforcing than extra money. If a mechanic spends most of his unassigned time repairing electric motors when he could be doing something else, we would assume that repairing electric motors is a reinforcer to him. When given a choice of leads, if a salesperson always chooses to call on large companies rather than small ones, that would tell us that calling on large clients could be used as a reinforcer for that salesperson. If a

---

The Premack Principle in a Small Business

A young psychology student working in a local drugstore after classes took the opportunity to observe some of the laws of behavior operating in her work place.

She noticed she seldom completed a task in the same amount of time from one day to the next. The quality was very consistent and thorough, yet the manager never seemed to pay attention to how rapidly the tasks were completed. To find if the variations in task-completion time were due to the Premack Principle, she questioned other employees about their preferences for different tasks. She collected data and found that sometimes employees were told which tasks would follow a particular job, but sometimes they were not informed.

Over three weeks, she timed how long it took employees to perform tasks under three conditions: 1) When they knew a more preferred task would follow; 2) When they knew a less preferred task would follow; 3) When they were unaware of the task which would follow.

The results were clear. For each task and all the tasks combined, considerable time was saved when employees knew a desirable task would follow an undesirable one. In other words, a high probability assignment followed a low probability assignment.

In the second phase of her project, she tried to improve work performance. Whenever possible, she traded jobs with others to ensure that a high probability assignment would follow a low probability assignment. A problem previous to her project was the typical shift problem: the night shift never finished their tasks before they went home, leaving more work for the morning shift. When the employees started getting tasks they desired after completing an undesired one, all work was finished by the end of the evening with time left over.

(Adapted from "An Application of Contingent Management" by T. Lyons, 1973. An unpublished term paper.)

data-processing supervisor always volunteers for a certain type project, then we might say those types of projects might be used as reinforcers for doing other types of projects.

The use of the Premack Principle relies on a contingency contract, explicit or implied: If you do X, then you can do Y. On first reading, a contractual arrangement may appear less than reinforcing. However, in practice people most often feel freer under this arrangement. In the first place, they enter into the arrangement by choice. Second, the preferred activity is sanctioned. The mechanic who knows that he spends too much time on electric motors may feel guilty about it but still does it because he likes it so much more than the other tasks. But when the contingency is set up (when you do X, then you can spend the rest of the afternoon on electric motors), he will feel relaxed, comfortable, and guilt free working on them.

The Premack Principle supplies us with one of the best time-management techniques. Take all the things you have to do and rank them in order of the thing you most like to do, to the thing you least like to do. Then start with the one on the bottom. A curious thing happens as you work. Every time you complete a task, the next one is more reinforcing! If you do this, not only will you be more efficient at your tasks, you will also have more fun doing them.

Trial and error: testing a consequence to see if it's a reinforcer

Probably the most frequently used method for finding reinforcers is to try something and see if it works. Usually this is not pure trial and error because what people try works an amazingly high percentage of the time. This method is really a combination of the first two. Before trying something, people often do some observing, talking, and listening. They also usually talk to those who have used reinforcers before, or they may try something they have read about.

When using this approach don't be discour-aged if something you try doesn't work. People will typically forgive you if you are trying to increase positive consequences in the work place.

Also, you may get some negative reactions when you first start to use R+. People may "pooh-pooh" your efforts. Most of the time this is because they are not accustomed to reinforcement in the work place. This is not a frequent occurrence and usually is short-lived. Believe it or not, sometimes when people protest that they don't need reinforcement, their performance increases after they get it. This is why it is important you monitor performance carefully to determine by the data whether you have a reinforcer.

CHARACTERISTICS OF EFFECTIVE REINFORCERS

Readily available. The best reinforcers are those that are always available to you. A readily available reinforcer is a **WHIP—W**hat you **H**ave **I**n your **P**ossession. Social reinforcers are the ones that are most available. You don't have to ask permission or have a budget to pat someone on the back, write a note to her on her performance, or praise her in some other way. There are a multitude of ways that one can show appreciation for effort and accomplishment. The more you do it, the more ways you will find.

Tangibles, on the other hand, require advanced planning and approval. Many organizations require considerable paperwork for any cash expenditure. Since increased paperwork is punishing to most people, this tends to reduce the use of tangibles. Also, because tangibles are not always readily available, you cannot rely on them as the primary way to reinforce.

Can be used frequently. The second characteristic of an effective reinforcer is that it can be used repeatedly. It must be something that doesn't lose its appeal to the recipient through repeated use. Obviously, promotions, raises, job transfers, and trips

Using the R+ Survey

1. Give a copy to performers as part of a discussion on how it will be used—never mail out asking people to complete and return.

2. Points to make in the discussion:

   a. This will be kept in a file so I may select a reinforcer which will be meaningful to you. It's not automatic you'll receive everything on the list.

   b. Reinforcers can be given for achieving pre-set goal performances, or for the things you do. Some will be connected to performance improvement, some will not.

   c. Tangibles: think of small items which can be given often. Your favorite at-work snack, a cassette tape, a plant for your desk, a book, golf balls, tickets to events, etc. Be specific: popcorn or a Snickers bar? Decaf or regular? Wrestling match or the symphony? Avoid items I simply cannot deliver, such as raises or promotions.

   d. Social: be specific on how you'd like to receive it. A marginal note on a report? A phone call to talk about the things you did well? A private discussion about a project you're currently working on? Ask your opinion on a problem? Your name on a bulletin board? Recognition in a meeting? Avoid generalities such as "praise, recognition, attaboys, high rating on appraisal, pats on the back."

   e. Work-related reinforcers: think of activities you enjoy doing at work. Informal discussions with co-workers? Opportunity to train in a different part of the business, a new piece of equipment, software? A chance to talk to others about your pet project? Working in a project you're very interested in? Working with people whose expertise you'd gain by observing? Solving a technical problem?

3. Some people have difficulties thinking of their own reinforcers when faced with a blank sheet. Help them overcome "writer's block" by:

   a. Holding a group brainstorming session on reinforcers. Use three sheets: social, tangible, and work related.

   b. Complete a survey for yourself. Give copies to everyone on your team. The open attitude on your part will help break the ice, give them ideas, and, as a bonus, let them in on what would be reinforcing to you! Do one survey for your team, another for your boss.

4. Suggest to your team you create an open file of reinforcers, so everyone will have access to information on how to reinforce co-workers. This should be voluntary, of course.

J. Allen

cannot be handed out often, but social reinforcers can. And there are other groups of reinforcers that can be used frequently, such as food and celebrations (parties), badges, pins, T-shirts, and other symbols of accomplishment.

Cost effective. It goes without saying that the cost of the reinforcer should not exceed the value of the accomplishment. There are certainly exceptions, but an organization could not survive long if its reinforcers were not cost effective. Social reinforcers are the least expensive. They often cost nothing, and their effectiveness is increased by occasional pairing with some form of tangible appreciation or recognition.

Some organizations spend large amounts of money on tangible reinforcers. They do not look on it as an expense because they are able to demonstrate a return in excess of the cost. The return on investment for reinforcing employee performance is likely to be higher than any capital improvement, personnel change, training, or other traditional solutions to performance problems.

Controllable. Managers should never plan or promise reinforcers that are not under their control. Some obviously effective reinforcers are not under the direct control of most managers. Wages, promotions, and raises, for example, are all influenced by managers, but they rarely have complete control over them.

There are few things that cause more grief to those who are trying to reinforce others than to set expectations that a particular reinforcer is forthcoming only to have it denied at the last minute because of budget cuts, policy issues, or other cultural factors. Cultural factors include such things as objection by a union, the "we've never done that before" reason, and even things that go against the community culture. For example, buying beer may be quite acceptable in some settings, but taboo in others. A lottery may be great fun in some places, but considered gambling in others. This simply means that

even though a particular reinforcer is under your control and is reinforcing to the people involved, others outside the area may object. Experience tells us that in most cases, it is easier to find another reinforcer than to use something that has the potential for creating additional problems.

Specific reinforcers

Examine the list of potential reinforcers in Figure 5.2. Check those available to you in your work setting. Which ones meet the characteristics of effective reinforcers?

You can use this list to generate ideas. You may be able to use a number of them in your work. Others may be inappropriate.

CLASSES OF REINFORCERS

Social reinforcers

The most likely candidates to fit the four criteria for effective reinforcers are social reinforcers: attention, gestures, words or symbols of recognition, and appreciation.

A **social reinforcer** is any interaction between people that increases behavior or performance. During our daily activities we usually have many interactions with fellow employees. The extent to which these interactions are reinforcers for some behavior is consistently underestimated.

Time or attention from the boss can be a powerful reinforcer. In analyzing how we spend our time, we often discover that we focus most of our time and attention on the marginal or poor performer, leaving little time for the good performers. While poor or problem performers require some supervisory time, if it is at the expense of spending time with the good performers, you may get an increasing number of problem performers. Also, effective managers must find time to reinforce not only the good performers but all who are improving.

Obvious social reinforcers are direct expressions of praise such as, "I appreciate

Figure 5.2

A SAMPLE OF REINFORCERS USED IN PM APPLICATIONS

Social

Spending time with the boss (one-on-one)

Receiving letters from customers

Presenting results to upper management

Well-known person (outside the plant) to give out reinforcers

Letters from upper management on achievement

Letters to spouse or employee's family on achievements

Letters from supervisors, managers on employee's performance

Memos from other department managers

Verbal praise

Plant or corporate write-up with photo in newsletter

"Brag-sheet" (flipchart at plant entrance noting individual or team performance)

Spend time asking about home activities, events (birthdays, graduations, softball team win, etc.).

Asking for opinion

Work-related

Working as a team leader

Running lab tests

Trouble-shooting problems/projects with/ without manager

Training for different jobs within the plant, advanced training

Assignment of new duties

Seeing a job through to the end

Promotions

Flexibility with scheduling

Move to newer equipment, machinery

Assignment to preferred duties

Exempt from "close" supervision

Include employee in a management presentation of a project or results of project to upper management

Leading a meeting in the place of a manager

Opportunity to help set/decide goals

Assisting in implementing suggestions

Let subordinates be a boss for the day

Asking employees for advice and suggestions

Quick follow-up on requests, problems, etc.

Assisting manager in some of her duties

Job rotation

Visits to customers, suppliers; plant tours

Tangibles

Dinner for two at restaurant of their choice

Seniors serve cafeteria meals

Time-off for sports-related activities

Sporting goods/equipment (golf/tennis balls, rod and reel, croquet or hobby materials)

T-shirts with special logo, delivered at special R+ meeting

Items with company logo (pens, pencils, balls)

Certificates designed for special ceremony

Progressive R+ notation for performance (bronze, silver, gold medals, ribbons, etc.)

Photo, symbolic of the company, with president's thank-you written on it

Items engraved with company name (no-skid mugs, pens, lighters)

Breakfast cooked and served by managers

"Free-Vend" vending machines for a day/week

Products the company produces

Contingent holiday foods (Thanksgiving turkey)

Record-setting plaques

Patches for clothing with catch phrases

Time off

Increased length of a holiday based on plant performance

BBQ by the managers for the entire plant

Opportunity to travel on company business (when not normally a part of that trip)

Photo of employee by her graph, framed and signed

Pizza and beer parties

Status-model car rental for a weekend

Lunch tickets

Watermelon party

Give out humorous T-shirts at lunches

"Wish-Book" (item from a catalogue)

Get-away weekends

Shopping certificates

Goody-drawer or Grab-bag.

"BINGO" spaces filled for improvement

Contingent fringe benefits

Company stock

Donations to charity in employee's name

Local high school donations, MVP awards, by the employee

Longer breaks

Free coffee and doughnuts

your promptness in getting that report done. It helped me a lot." The less obvious ones are the countless brief conversations and two-to-three-word exchanges. These interactions often function as reinforcers.

Our phone calls, notes, and memos can also be reinforcers. We may only intend them to communicate information but they may also act as reinforcers or punishers. These small, frequent, social consequences exert lots of control over our behavior. Some employees do not receive much communication from their managers. Just a personal phone call or note about their accomplishments is often very reinforcing.

Another major category of social reinforcement is recognition for desired performance. Publicizing the accomplishments of individuals, teams, shifts, and departments is practically always reinforcing. Photographs and short descriptions of the accomplishment in in-house newsletters provide an excellent means of delivering reinforcement.

The time spent congratulating employees for their accomplishments is time well spent and pays handsome dividends in positive changes in performance.

Don't use things like "good morning," "goodbye," and "hello" as reinforcers. These greetings and salutations are merely indicative of common courtesy. If they are used as reinforcers it would mean you would say "good morning" to some and not to others. This is not recommended, even at the risk of reinforcing the wrong behavior.

Tangible reinforcers

A **tangible reinforcer** is any object or activity that is presented contingent on (based on, or after) a behavior that results in an increase in the frequency of that behavior. Tangibles are the kinds of reinforcers that first occur to people when they are introduced to the concept of reinforcement. They may range from a cup of coffee to a new car or more. In Mary Kay Cosmetics, high performers earn the use of a pink Cadillac. In some organizations taking the team out for lunch is an effective reinforcer.

Tangibles are popular with sales management and have been used successfully for many years. Through increased sales performance, sales people can earn tangibles ranging from small kitchen appliances to trips for two to exotic vacation destinations.

Managers in non-sales organizations, however, have relatively little experience using tangibles. A growing number of businesses are learning that properly planned and executed tangible reinforcers can result in significant improvement in performance and morale.

Tangibles provide opportunities to deliver social reinforcement. Every time someone earns a tangible, it provides an opportunity to relive the accomplishment and deliver praise. A common problem in using tangibles is that they are sometimes given without comment, sent in the mail with no explanation, or just mysteriously appear on a person's desk. No tangible reinforcer should be given without accompanying social reinforcement.

Any tangible reinforcer that is visible at work or at home can serve as an antecedent for future reinforcement. If the tangible reinforcer is something you use at home, it can be the source of a lot of self-reinforcement. Every time you use it you may be reminded of the circumstances under which you earned it.

Plaques, trophies, certificates and other tangibles can serve the same purpose at work. Displayed in the work place, they serve as constant reminders of reinforcement received and the performance that earned it. In addition, these reinforcers have the added advantage of prompting R+ from others: "What did you do to get that?" Also, they provide an antecedent for others, who find that particular item reinforcing, to want to earn it for themselves.

Unfortunately, certificates and plaques are not reinforcing in many companies. They have a history of being given for insignificant accomplishments or given to everyone regardless of accomplishment. But when properly done they can be effective reinforcers.

Clothing, patches, badges, and items with the company logo are some of the more commonly used tangibles. T-shirts and hats have been particularly successful with many work groups. When the group designs the titles for the T-shirt or the logo for the hat, these items become more reinforcing. This is true for both sexes as well as professional and non-professional employees.

Remember, to be considered reinforcers, tangibles must be given only *after* desired performance and must be something the person wants. The best tangibles give the recipient a story to tell. If the tangible stands for an accomplishment, when asked, "Where did you get that?" it gives the person an opportunity to recount the circumstances under which it was earned. The person might respond by saying, "Let me tell you about it." He then begins to tell how his team set a new quality, production, or sales record. He gets to tell the details of how hard and carefully the team worked. He has an acceptable opportunity to "brag."

Sometimes when asked about a tangible, people will talk more about how it was given than about the accomplishment. Perhaps it was a surprise ceremony with the plant manager personally delivering the surprise. Or, it may have been at a special luncheon or meeting.

The more enjoyment people have in receiving the tangible reinforcer, or the harder they had to work for it, the more reinforcing it will be. Whether a television set or a coffee mug, much of the future reinforcing value of the tangible will be not in the monetary value, but in what the person can say about it.

Although tangibles are not always used in performance-improvement projects, they should always be considered. A mix of tangible and social reinforcement is the best way to improve performance. Even though there is no clear data on just what the mix should be, it should heavily favor the social reinforcers, probably by a ratio of 20 to one, or more.

Potential reinforcers in the work environment. Because many managers are unfamiliar with PM concepts, they lose numerous opportunities to use naturally occurring events as reinforcers. Things such as time off, breaks, training, increased job responsibilities, and work scheduling are often given without regard to their potential reinforcing value.

Many things that are given on a seniority basis could be used as reinforcers. The reason seniority has become the basis for assigning many organizational benefits is that it is easier to assign them that way. Managers think this method will cause fewer complaints of "unfair." In reality the good performers never think it is fair for those who do not carry their load to get the same wages and benefits and other reinforcers as those who do.

Reinforcers should always be delivered based on performance. Managers should be alert to the possibility that many things given without regard to performance can be used contingently to improve performance. Reinforcers existing in the work environment include job assignment, changes in job responsibility, additional help, first choice of new equipment or tools, desired training, and others such as those listed in Figure 5.2.

Considerations in using tangibles. A primary consideration in using tangibles is whether a particular tangible is meaningful to, or valued by, the recipients. Do not assume that because something has a company logo on it that it will be a reinforcer. While some may be desirable, others may not be. Too many managers have made the mistake of ordering several dozen of every item available in the company store in order to have a ready supply of reinforcers. Most of the time, this practice will not be reinforcing.

Reinforcers must fit the occasion. Ordering caps or T-shirts with a slogan meaningful to the group or with a unit or team logo is usually reinforcing. When it is evident to the performers that some time and thought have gone into personalizing the tangible for the group or person, it will almost always be reinforcing.

Cost is another consideration. While something does not need to cost a lot to be reinforcing, even small items can be costly for a large group of performers. The expense of the tangible reinforcers should always be justified by the economic value of the increased performance.

A problem often anticipated by those considering the use of tangibles is that "people will expect them all the time." This rarely happens when tangibles are given contingently. By now it should be obvious that tangibles should not be given unless we know precisely what we are reinforcing. In many cases when managers and supervisors take a casual approach to the reinforcement process, an upsurge of unwanted behaviors often results. The problem of people coming to expect tangibles is a function of delivery, timing, and frequency, not the tangibles themselves.

Money and other generalized reinforcers. Money, tokens, and point systems are useful because they allow the performer to access a wide range of reinforcers. This increases the probability that people will actually get a reinforcer, since they have a choice of what they will exchange the money, tokens, or points for.

Points and tokens have the added value of allowing more frequent reinforcement than would be possible if the reinforcer were some expensive tangible item like a set of golf clubs. Every time the performers earn a point or token that can be saved toward some item out of a catalog or from their reinforcer surveys, they are reinforced.

Another advantage of generalized reinforcers is that they reduce the possibility that the performers will satiate on a particular reinforcer.

The most obvious reinforcer in this class is money. Although money is a positive reinforcer to practically everyone, it has several drawbacks when used in the work

place: 1) we usually cannot give it contingent on improved performance; 2) when we can give it contingent on performance, the amounts we can give are usually so small it is not reinforcing; and 3) usually money is used to pay for things people must have, rather than things they would like to have.

The first consideration is a serious one for business and industry. In most organizations it is very difficult for supervisors to use money to reinforce significantly increased productivity, quality, or cost savings. Many of the ways money is used is not effective from a PM perspective. Outstanding performers may receive only a small percentage more than the average performer. In addition, in most organizations the top performance rating is limited to only a small percentage of employees.

Typically the way the vast majority of people are paid does not allow any differentiation in pay according to level of performance. Increases are given across the board.

What this system reinforces is simply being on the payroll. Although many managers believe they are paying for performance, the contingency is only doing enough to keep from getting fired. Brethower (1972) describes the situation this way:

> We have often heard managers say with great feeling and in apparent anguish— "People should do a good job." The statement reflects a high moral tone but also reflects a willingness to ignore the facts: The people referred to are doing a poor job and they are being paid. Therefore, whether you like it or not, they are being paid for poor work.

The statement also reflects a rather thorough ignorance of the principles governing human performance and human motivation. If their wage (or salary) is the only incentive, then we should expect the very minimum level of performance, just high enough to avoid being fired. Performing below that minimum has a very clear consequence: they get fired. Performing above that level has no consequence at all, so there's no incentive for increased effort.

Obviously, very large sums of money are reinforcing to most people but are not really practical in most business situations. The issue is not whether money is something for which people will work—that's why most people come to work in the first place. The issue is that money often loses its importance in the day-to-day motivation of the average person because of the small amounts that are available and its infrequent use as a reinforcer. In most cases, small amounts of money clearly are not reinforcing in the work place. For example, if you set a production or quality record and have $5 per person to spend on reinforcers, commemorating the record with something like a T-shirt, cap, coffee mug, or other appropriate tangible will probably be much more reinforcing than $5 in cash. This assumes that these specific items have not become common through overuse, or distributed non-contingently before.

The airlines' "Frequent Flyer" programs were instituted to reinforce passengers for flying with a particular company. By flying 20,000 or more miles, passengers can earn free trips. These programs have been so successful that even the smallest airlines have them. For most frequent flyers, earning a free trip to Florida, California, or Hawaii is much more reinforcing than getting $5 or $10 off the price of each ticket.

Incentive-premium companies have established large businesses because of the fact that merchandise is more reinforcing to most people than comparable cash bonuses. There are at least two reasons for this. One reason is that once the money is spent, there is no reminder for people that they have earned a reinforcer for desired performance. By contrast, merchandise earned for performance remains as a clear antecedent for future reinforceable performance.

The second reason money is less preferable than merchandise is that money is often used to avoid or get rid of a negative rather than to obtain a positive reinforcer. The cash may

come along just in time to pay a past-due bill or an unexpected repair bill. We often have little to show for the money a month later.

NEGATIVE REINFORCERS

Another type of reinforcer is quite different from those we've discussed to this point. It is probably the most commonly used one in business and industry today—the negative reinforcer. The process of using negative reinforcers is called negative reinforcement. With negative reinforcement people do things in order to escape or avoid something they don't want. Negative reinforcement is still reinforcement. That is, negative reinforcement will increase or maintain a performance. People *will* perform to avoid something negative.

Negative reinforcement is often confused with punishment. Remember, punishment

Managers often misjudge the consequences they deliver

"What do you mean you're not getting any recognition? Two gold stars in one week is certainly recognition!"

(W. Miller. Machine Design, Dec. 1980. Used with permission of author.)

decreases performance and negative reinforcement *increases* performance.

It is helpful to remember that all work behavior is the result of reinforcement—either positive or negative. And it's important to know which kind of reinforcement is generating the behavior in the work environment. Positive and negative reinforcement produces very different kinds of performances.

With positive reinforcement, people do things because they "want to." With negative reinforcement, they do things because they "have to." When asked, "Why do you work?" most people say, "I have to!"

The *best* that negative reinforcement will produce is just enough work to escape or avoid punishment. People never do what they are capable of when their motivation is to escape or avoid some unpleasant event or interaction. Many parents often find themselves saying to their children about their schoolwork, "You only do enough to get by. You're not doing nearly what you are capable of doing." If you have ever been part of a similar conversation, you should now know that most schoolwork is under negative reinforcement control. Most children study because they are afraid of what will happen if they don't. It is only children who have been positively reinforced for learning who ever come close to maximizing their potential.

Also, in a negatively reinforcing environment, managers are in a "gotcha" situation. This means the majority of their time is spent trying to find the incorrect behavior and then punishing it. People who are not engaging in the correct behavior will hide from or avoid the manager. This is most obvious when a group of people who are talking stops and disperses when the boss comes in the room.

But when compliance is all we need, negative reinforcers can be effective. Safety rules require all employees in certain situations wear safety equipment. It is not an option, and anyone caught not wearing it is summarily fired. We may not be overly concerned that employees "like" wearing the equipment. The thing we are most interested in is that

they wear it. Where some minimal level of performance is acceptable, use of a negative reinforcer may be all that is needed to attain it. But remember, minimal performance is all you can expect.

Negative reinforcers are associated with much of our everyday behavior. We go to the dentist to escape or avoid the pain and expense associated with bad teeth. We take our cars to the shop to avoid costly repair bills and the inconvenience and expense of a breakdown. Most people pay their taxes at the last minute to avoid having to pay penalties later.

Because negative reinforcement results in people doing things as late as possible, businesses usually advertise the advantages of early responding. Dentists point out the benefits of regular check-ups. Car dealers encourage regular maintenance through special prices. The IRS encourages taxpayers to prepare their tax reports early in order to avoid the last-minute rush or possible penalties. In spite of this, most people continue to do these things at the last minute, or when they "have to." Only those who fail to act on time are punished by the pain of a toothache, the repair bills, and the tax penalties.

While constructive in some circumstances, negative reinforcers are generally less desirable than positive ones. When a manager can choose between negative or positive reinforcers, the latter should almost always be selected because of the problems associated with negative reinforcers. The best someone can do with a negative reinforcer is to avoid it. For example, one employee may receive recognition for her high-quality production while another avoids being chewed out when his quality is at or above standard. For the first employee, the better her quality productivity, the more recognition she can receive. For the second employee, once an acceptable quality level is reached, he merely avoids being chewed out. No more negative reinforcement is possible. He can't be chewed out less because he isn't being chewed out at all. In other words, negative reinforcement can only be used to increase performance to a level where one avoids the negative. You never optimize performance with negative reinforcers; only positive reinforcers can do that.

Paying taxes is a good example of the difference between the effects of a positive vs. negative reinforcer. If you are getting a refund (a positive reinforcer to most) you complete your tax return early. If you have to pay additional taxes, you wait until the last minute.

Negative reinforcers are ineffective if fear is not present to some degree. The degree may be slight, such as fear of being embarrassed in a meeting, or great, such as fear of loss of income and status. This poses a problem for the company that relies too heavily on negative reinforcers to get work done. People don't want a job they are afraid of. They will escape such work when they can by quitting. When they can't, usually because of economic circumstances, they will go to great lengths to avoid the fear, including lying, cheating, and stealing. It is not uncommon that a manager or supervisor juggles the numbers in order to meet a quota or budget. In the old days, employees were known to carry waste home in order to keep it from showing up in the waste report! Absenteeism, turnover, and poor morale are other problems associated with excessive reliance on negative reinforcers.

If negative reinforcers are used to get a performance started, positive reinforcement should be used to keep it going.

CONCLUDING REMARKS

This chapter has presented the groundwork for understanding and using reinforcement, the keystone of Performance Management. A business will not thrive on inadequate profit; neither will employees thrive on inadequate positive reinforcement—their psychological profit. Wages and other financial benefit packages are necessary for economic survival, but actual employee performance is maintained by daily reinforcement. Without it, performance falls to minimal levels. In many cases, even losing a job is preferred to working in a non-reinforcing, punishing environment.

No organization can hope to capture employees' discretionary effort without systematic delivery of positive reinforcement. Discretionary effort is performance that people can do if they want to, but receive no negative consequences if they don't. Discretionary effort amounts to doing those things they see that need to be done to increase the effectiveness of the organization. A competitive marketplace demands positive reinforcement because that is the only way people work at their best.

This chapter has presented only one of the skills needed to use R+: finding effective reinforcers. However, once you have determined what they are, you must deliver them in the proper way. Even the most potentially effective reinforcers will fail if they are delivered incorrectly. The next chapter tells you how to deliver reinforcement effectively.

NOTES

6

Delivering Reinforcement

Managers may identify a long list of reinforcers, but unless they deliver them correctly, the reinforcers may not have the desired effect. The following story illustrates how detrimental the improper delivery of reinforcement can be. We'll let the wronged party tell the story:

One of my responsibilities was to evaluate training materials and training aids for purchase by the company. I previewed a film which I thought was great and told my boss that I thought the company should purchase it. He said, "Well, set it up in the conference room this afternoon at 5:00 and I'll look at it. Oh, and I'll bring Bill [one of my peers] with me and get his opinion."

Bill, the boss, and I sat down to look at the film. I noticed the boss getting fidgety. He kept looking at the reel to see how much time was left. Once he asked me, "How long is this film?" After about one-third of the film, he stood up, turned on the lights, switched off the projector and said loudly, "I wouldn't pay $500 for that piece of crap!" and then stormed out and slammed the door. Bill looked at me, shook his head, and left the room.

The next morning, the boss appeared at my office door. I looked up as he shoved a piece of paper toward me. When I looked at it, the first thing I noticed was his handwriting across the top, "EXCELLENT WORK," with his initials as signature. He hurried away toward the next-door conference room for a meeting. On examining the page, I saw that it was a copy of a training proposal I had written five weeks earlier for one of the plants.

My perception was that overnight he had regretted the way he had responded to "my film" and was trying to atone for his wrongly delivered, punishing consequence with a positive reinforcer.

My proposal had been a routine write-up, similar to many others I had done. It did not deserve the "reinforcer" he tried to use. He had obviously shuffled through the old stuff on his desk to find something to "reinforce" me for. The fact that he chose a five-week-old memo not only meant that it was not immediate, but to me seemed insincere. Also, "excellent work" had been hurriedly scribbled, so I felt that he probably couldn't have quoted the topic of my memo if he had been asked. Lack of specific feedback indicated to me that he was only trying to be nice. The split-second delivery meant that no time was spent in personalizing it for me.

The extreme negative and the insincere positive had a cumulative effect and diluted the effectiveness of his use of consequences to me for as long as I worked for him. Since I could not see the logic of his behavior, I began to see everything he did as a result of his mood that day, or whatever, rather than contingent on my performance.

This example violates all the rules for the effective delivery of positive reinforcement.

It illustrates how important correct delivery of reinforcement is to your success in managing performance.

GUIDELINES FOR THE EFFECTIVE DELIVERY OF REINFORCEMENT

1. Personalize your reinforcement

Your reinforcers should reflect your own style. When you use tangible or social reinforcers that you are not comfortable with, they typically do not come across as reinforcing. In addition, when telling employees you appreciate their effort or accomplishments, express your praise in terms of how you feel, not in terms of the company or management. For example, use "I appreciate" rather than "We at company XYZ" or "We, the management, appreciate." Above all, avoid institutional reinforcers such as form letters. Your reinforcers should reflect not only some knowledge of the performance, but some thought as well. For example, when you send a memo or tell people face-to-face that they did a good job, don't just say, "Thanks, great job." Describe in a few well-chosen words what they did that you like and why you like it. Most important, next time you reinforce something that a person did, say something different. If you are delivering reinforcement to several people, vary the things you say so that each person receives a unique message.

2. Reinforce immediately

The best time to reinforce is when you catch people in the act. Reinforce while they are doing what you want. The longer the delay between the performance and the reinforcer, the less impact the reinforcer will have on the performance.

Reinforcement reinforces whatever is happening at the time it occurs. In other words, you cannot deliver an immediate reinforcer for a result. At best you would reinforce the last behavior in the accomplishment of the result.

Some managers think if they reinforce immediately upon knowing about an outstanding behavior or performance that this satisfies the criterion of immediacy. However, if someone told you of a performance or if you read about it in a report or memo, it has already occurred and therefore cannot be reinforced immediately. That doesn't mean that you shouldn't reinforce, because in most cases, late is better than never. But if you do reinforce late, you should be aware of the problems associated with it in order to avoid or minimize them.

Figure 6.1 shows the diminishing impact of delayed reinforcement. If you have a limited amount of time to reinforce, then spend it reinforcing on-going behaviors (immediately). That will be a more efficient use of your time than reinforcing results or reinforcing behaviors after they have occurred.

In delayed reinforcement, you always run the risk of inadvertently reinforcing the wrong behavior, because the behavior you want to reinforce may not be occurring at that time. Since what is happening at the time of reinforcement is also reinforced, you must choose the time and circumstances for delivering delayed R+. For example, if you learn of some reinforceable behavior, you should not always rush out to find the person and deliver R+.

Suppose you approach someone for the purpose of reinforcement and she is having a bad day. As you walk up she says very sarcastically, "What do you want?" This is not the time to talk to her about what a good performer she is. It is better to wait until she is back to her usually good performance. Then she will appreciate it more and it will strengthen the desirable aspects of her work.

For this reason when you are reinforcing someone who does not report to you or who works in another area, it is best to check with his immediate supervisor before you reinforce. The vast majority of the time supervisors will welcome your help in providing additional reinforcement to their performers. On occasion, though, they may ask you to come back later because of problems

Figure 6.1

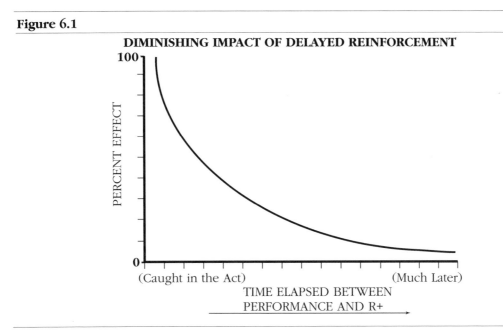

DIMINISHING IMPACT OF DELAYED REINFORCEMENT

PERCENT EFFECT

(Caught in the Act)   (Much Later)

TIME ELAPSED BETWEEN
PERFORMANCE AND R+

occurring at the time.

Delayed reinforcement also increases the risk that behaviors occurring between the desirable behavior and the delayed reinforcer may get reinforced. Sometimes these behaviors are incompatible with the desired ones. This complicates the problem of developing consistent, desirable work habits. The general rule on delivering reinforcement is: better late than never, but best immediately. When reinforcing late, the recognition must be very specific.

3. Make your reinforcement specific

Specific reinforcement generally refers to praise. Even though praise is not always a reinforcer to everyone, most people like it, so it is treated here as though it is universally reinforcing.

Being specific means telling people exactly what they did that you liked. For example, "I've noticed that you are approaching customers more immediately when they come in the department. And you always have a smile for them. I'm sure that contributed to the 12 percent increase in our sales/customer ratio. You're doing great." Don't simply talk about the result or simply say, "You're doing great."

Using data to reinforce not only helps in being specific, but also helps to guard against non-contingent reinforcement. You won't be delivering reinforcement to everyone for everything *if* you refer to data on performance.

Being specific is very important when you are in the early stages of teaching a new skill. During that time it facilitates learning to describe what a person is doing right: "Great. You're twisting it at exactly a 45-degree angle." Anytime a person is working to improve more than one behavior, or if a performance involves several behaviors, specifying the contingencies for reinforcement is necessary for efficient improvement or learning. This is especially important when delivering reinforcement to groups.

Many different behaviors go into most group accomplishments. Most of the behaviors are productive but some may not be. Therefore, if the reinforcement is not specific, you may inadvertently reinforce the bad as well as the good.

One way of being specific with a group is to ask the members of the group to tell what they did to accomplish the goal or improvement. For example, you might ask, "What kinds of things did you do, or what things did you see others do, that helped us reach our goal?" This not only helps the group be specific but has the added advantage of prompting team members to reinforce others.

There are times, however, when it is not necessary to be specific. When you reinforce immediately, or catch employees "in the act," you may not need to say anything specific. In such an instance, the situation often specifies what you are reinforcing. Simply patting people on the back as they work communicates clearly what you are reinforcing. A good antecedent for reinforcement in the work place is a poster bearing the message, "Catch Someone Doing Something Good Today." The more immediate the reinforcer, the less specific you have to be.

When good feedback systems are in place, it is not always necessary to be specific. Good feedback systems are based on the fact that the employee knows the specific behaviors that drive the graphed results. Therefore, while referring to a graph, a general statement like, "You're doing super," can still be effective.

4. Make your reinforcement sincere

The sincerity of your reinforcement is extremely important, and this applies both to what you say and how you say it. If it is not sincere it is unlikely to be reinforcing. If it appears insincere, even though it is sincere, it is also unlikely to be reinforcing.

You should never tell a person something you do not mean. If people are not doing a good job, then it is certainly not appropriate to tell them that they are. Business ethics and morality dictate against such conduct. However, ethics and morality aside, people can usually spot an insincere compliment and therefore it is more apt to be punishing than reinforcing.

Most of the problems with this aspect of reinforcement are not caused because people are insincere but because they appear insincere. A number of things are almost always associated with the perception of insincerity.

Overdoing reinforcement practically always backfires. Talking too long or using too many adjectives and adverbs practically always lead to a claim of insincerity. Overdoing it usually makes people feel uncomfortable. Words like "fantastic," "marvelous," "spectacular," and "terrific" are overused. Phrases like "best in the world," "never seen anything like it," and "unbelievable performer," are, more often than not, unbelievable. There are very few people who like to be gushed over. A general rule might be to err on the side of saying too little rather than saying too much.

Another problem results from saying the same things to everybody or saying the same thing to the same person time after time. This happened at a fast-food chain where every customer was told after a purchase, "Have a nice day." After several purchases customers got the feeling that a robot could do as well. The person who strolls around delivering reinforcement indiscriminantly and identically, regardless of what people are doing or how well they are doing, isn't reinforcing.

Remember that unearned compliments, flattery, and insincere comments are practically never reinforcing.

Humor is tricky and can be used as an effective reinforcer only if you have a very comfortable relationship with the other person. Since humor can usually be interpreted several ways, using it may cause doubts about your sincerity.

Sarcasm should never be used with an attempt to reinforce. While profanity may be reinforcing to some people, most are turned off by it. Avoid using either when trying to reinforce.

For many managers, the first conscious attempts to give their employees more reinforcement appear clumsy. They feel uncomfortable and hence appear uncomfortable to others. Employees, unfortunately, sometimes misinterpret this discomfort as insincerity and do not reinforce the manager's attempts. This makes it even harder for the manager to feel comfortable about delivering reinforcement in the future. Generally speaking, the more you

"Keep up the good work, whatever it is, whoever you are."

(*Drawing by Stevenson; © 1988, The New Yorker Magazine, Inc.*)

reinforce the more comfortable you become. Even though your sincerity may be doubted initially, if you are indeed sincere you will eventually demonstrate it through your actions, and the illusion of insincerity will disappear.

As discussed previously, an important aid to being sincere is using specific data while expressing your appreciation. People generally regard specific reinforcement as sincere.

Another good idea is to use tangible reinforcers from time to time along with your social reinforcers, a point emphasized in the previous chapter. The fact that you would spend the time, money, and effort required to select a meaningful reinforcer usually communicates sincerity.

When giving tangible reinforcers, give the social reinforcer first. This increases the likelihood that the person will hear your words and will more fully experience the impact and sincerity of your social reinforcer. When you present people with an object, all the attention tends to be absorbed in the visual stimulation of the item, or in determining how much they like the reinforcer you chose. Give the tangible almost like an afterthought—after the social sinks in.

5. Reinforce frequently

Generally speaking, the more frequently an employee is reinforced for desired performance, the stronger that performance will be. How much is enough? The answer to this question involves many factors, but to give you a perspective consider the following. In *The Technology of Teaching*, B. F. Skinner (1968) states that to teach students to be competent in basic mathematical concepts requires in excess of 50,000 contingencies. This is not to suggest that a similar number is needed to teach adults job-related skills and habits, but the amount of R+ that is needed is generally much more than most people think.

Managers sometimes say, "I reinforced him but he didn't change." Do not expect one reinforcer to change someone's life. It takes many reinforcers to develop a habit. Behaviors that are reinforced over and over again gain the status of habit and become automatic, or "our way of doing things." Therefore, when trying to develop new work habits, you must plan for many reinforcers.

A useful guide for the amount of R+ one should deliver is the **4:1 rule**. This means every time managers apply a negative consequence, they should find at least 4 opportunities somewhere in the work place to reinforce a desired performance. Of course, according to this rule, if you never delivered any negative consequences, you would never deliver any positives. But in the real world this rarely happens.

Self-report data collected on the 4:1 rule over the years indicates that managers have a ratio of 2:1 at the beginning of Performance Management training. Since the reporting of reinforcement probably served to increase the ratio, we can assume that the real ratios are less than 2:1 in the average work environment. Sadly, in many companies a quote attributed to Henry Kissinger would be applicable: "Praise around here is the absence of criticism for a brief period of time."

Remember, the 4:1 rule is only a guide to reinforcement. It is not an ideal, nor is it a requirement. The ratio can be much larger than 4:1 but should not be smaller. This ratio was suggested by research done by Madsen and Madsen (1974). In training teachers in classroom management, they discovered that teachers who had ratios of at least 4:1 had well-behaved and high-achieving students. Teachers who had less than 4:1 had classes that exhibited discipline and achievement problems. Stuart (1971) found similar ratios with parents of non-delinquent and delinquent children.

The use of this rule does not mean that if you R+ some performance of a particular person four times, you must find something to punish. Nor does it mean that when you give a negative, you must find four things to reinforce the person for. The rule is intended to help you assess your R+ level across all your interactions, not individuals. A given person may need several negatives to stop some undesirable behavior, and good performers may rarely need one.

The most important reason for using the 4:1 rule is to increase the amount of reinforcement you give. When people keep data on how often they reinforce, they begin to look for and find more things deserving of reinforcement. As people begin to keep data, they practically always discover that they do

not reinforce nearly as much as they thought they did.

Remember that the ratio is 4:1, not 4:0. The

When using the 4:1 rule remember:

1. The ratio applies to the reinforcers and punishers that a person gives to everyone, not to any single person.

2. The positives must be delivered only *after* desired performance.

---

person who gives no negatives over an extended period of time probably will be viewed by others as a pushover. This is the kind of person Leo Durocher was referring to when he said, *"Nice guys finish last."* And Benjamin Franklin (1735) said, *"Approve not of him who commends all you say."* They were describing a person who cannot set limits, who never gives negative feedback, and who pats *everyone* on the back. In the long run, this person is totally ineffective in interpersonal relationships.

If you work with any group of people long enough, there will be times when you must say "No!", set limits, ignore certain responses, or otherwise apply consequences that someone doesn't want. If you can't do that, you're as handicapped as the person who cannot pat someone on the back.

"Blame-all and praise-all are two blockheads." Benjamin Franklin, *Poor Richard's Almanack, 1733*

A **reinforcement log** (Figure 6.2) provides a convenient way to track your performance in the area of reinforcement. A log allows you to record all pertinent information about the reinforcers you give. This kind of record is particularly valuable when you set out to increase R+. It allows you to analyze not only how much you give, but also who you

HOW WE GIVE COMPLIMENTS

Dr. Mark L. Knapp (1984) and two colleagues at The University of Texas conducted an extensive analysis of compliments. They defined a compliment as, "a statement which makes a person believe that they received a positive evaluation. It may be about your appearance or performance, but it must be a positive evaluation for it to be a compliment." In one study they analyzed 768 compliments in different sections of the country involving a wide range of ages from all walks of life. Two-thirds of the respondents felt the compliments they gave and those they received were well-deserved. Over three-fourths of the compliments were positive experiences for both givers and receivers. No one expressed negative feelings about the compliments they received.   Some of the findings are presented here. *(Adapted from "Compliments: A Descriptive Taxonomy," by M. L. Knapp, R. Hopper and R. A. Bell, 1984,* Journal of Communications, *34, 12-31. Reprinted by permission.)*

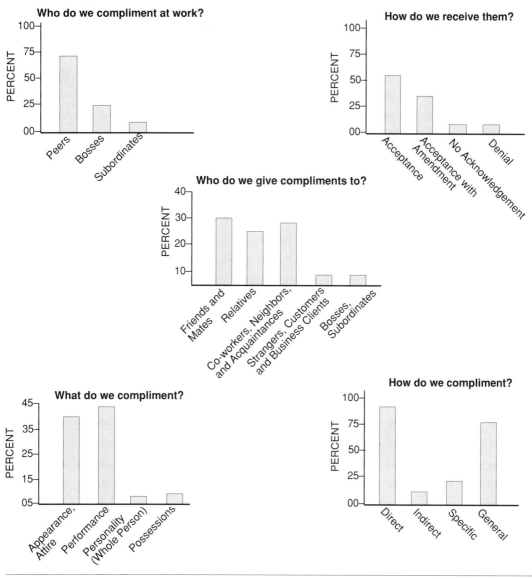

CHAPTER SIX

Figure 6.2

REINFORCEMENT LOG

NAME: *Jane S.*

Date	Performance Reinforced	Name of Person or Group	Reinforcer	Comments
3/21	*Very good job cleaning equipment*	*Courtney M.*	*Told him what a good job he did and pointed out examples of what I meant*	*He really seemed to appreciate it*
3/21	*Completed rush job without falling behind*	*A. Shift Crew*	*Coffee on me and brought boss to see how good they were working*	*Finished next day ahead of schedule*

give it to, and what you give it for. Biases in who you reinforce, restrictions in the range of reinforcers you use, and patterns in the behaviors and results you reinforce can be detected easily in this log.

6. Don't reinforce and punish at the same time

Frequently while delivering reinforcement we are tempted to express both what we did and didn't like about the performance. This causes several problems.

First, it tends to make people suspicious. If reinforcement is frequently followed by a negative, then reinforcement becomes an antecedent for punishment. The reaction to reinforcement soon becomes, "What have I done wrong now?"

Consider the probable impact of the following comments by a manager to her subordinates: "Wilson, your accuracy has improved by 14 percent this week, but I think several errors that you made could have been easily prevented." "You've done a great job, Susan. Your performance was the highest it has been, but your attitude is still causing problems in the department."

Don't confuse people by mixing reinforcement and punishment. For maximum effectiveness deliver them on separate occasions.

Some management development programs actually advise mixing reinforcement and punishment. In essence, this approach tells managers that if they must correct or discipline an employee, they should first soften the blow through reinforcement. After they praise him for something, they should tell him about the problem performance and the negative consequence for its future occurrences. Finally they should end the meeting with something positive to pick him up so that he will receive the correcting with a good attitude.

This is referred to as the **sandwich method**. A negative is sandwiched between two positives. This technique should be avoided. It creates an unpalatable sandwich which not only dilutes the impact of the negative and sets up positive reinforcement as an antecedent for punishment, it makes the reinforcement less credible at other times.

Some managers practically never say anything positive without adding something negative. Because of this practice many older employees resist being praised. This has been interpreted by their managers as an indication that they don't want praise. What they don't want is what follows it. In such cases the positive comment has become a clear antecedent for criticism.

While this procedure may soften the blow for the person doing the punishing, it does little to increase the effectiveness of the negative consequence on the performance of the person being corrected. Although such mixing is a rather widespread practice, the author knows of no research supporting its effectiveness.

Using negative consequences effectively will be discussed in Chapter Thirteen. For now, let us simply say that the constant pairing of reinforcement and punishment causes problems for both the supervisor and the employee.

In a discussion on this subject, the performance-appraisal issue usually surfaces. The typical performance appraisal usually requires that one discuss both strengths and weaknesses. This is not a problem if the performance appraisal is not the primary vehicle for reinforcement and corrective feedback. If it is, you will have problems.

If, however, you establish relationships with employees that include lots of reinforcement, the employees will actually ask for corrective feedback because they know that improvement in their performance will increase their opportunity for positive reinforcement. With this practice the formal performance appraisal becomes a time to simply summarize progress and make plans for future reinforcement which very often deals with correcting deficiencies.

7. *Don't mix goal setting and reinforcement*

Sometimes when we reinforce a performance we ask the performer for something else. For example, "Your report gave me the exact information I needed, Sandy. Thanks. But next time it would help if you get it to me earlier and type it." "Dick, you met your sub-goal this week, but you realize that you still have a long way to go."

Often these requests for additional behavior become punishers. We say things like, "You did fine. You ran one mile today; but you really should do more. I know you can do it." We are telling people they did great, but didn't do great. Don't mix goal setting and reinforcement.

A goal may be to jog six miles, but one block or one mile are achievements that can legitimately be reinforced toward that end. Set whatever goal you want, but you must reinforce improvement toward that goal. If you constantly remind people of the final, but as yet unattained, goal while you reinforce improvement, your attempt at reinforcement may turn into punishment.

The reason managers get involved in the practice of mixing reinforcement and punishment, or reinforcement and goal setting, is they think if you reinforce achieving a low goal the person will want to stay there— become self-satisfied. "Compliments encourage complacency." They believe that if they positively reinforce running one mile, the person will not want to run two. This is definitely wrong. It contradicts the entire scientifically demonstrated relationship between reinforcement and performance. The more reinforcement people receive for improving a performance, the more they want to improve that performance. When it happens that people reach a goal and do no more, it is an indication that reaching the goal was negatively reinforced, not positively reinforced.

Many managers see themselves as positive reinforcers while their employees do not. See Figure 6.3. It is not uncommon for a manager to say, "I believe in positive reinforcement. This is the way I've always managed." Yet when the employees of these managers are asked how often they are reinforced, they often respond, "Never." One of the reasons for this response is that these managers violate the "**no-but**" rule. It's not that they don't say things that are positive. They do. However, they spoil it by adding "but…". When you add the "but," you cancel the R+. Watch yourself to see if you violate the rule of "no buts" in your reinforcement attempts.

Figure 6.3

A COMPARISON OF SUPERVISORS' AND EMPLOYEES' PERCEPTION OF REINFORCEMENT

Superior Behavior	Frequency with which supervisors say "very often" (%)	Frequency with which employees say "very often" (%)
Gives privileges	62	14
Gives more responsibility	48	10
Gives a pat on the back	82	13
Gives sincere and thorough praise	80	14
Trains for better jobs	64	9
Gives more interesting work	51	9

(Adapted from New Patterns of Management *by R. L. Likert, 1961, p. 91, McGraw-Hill Book Co. Reprinted by permission.)*

If you do, try reinforcing and, if necessary, bite your arm to keep from saying "but."

REINFORCEMENT SYSTEMS

A **reinforcement system** ensures the effective delivery of reinforcement to all employees and does not rely solely on the manager to deliver it. In order to maximize performance, reinforcement must be frequent and contingent on desired performance. Left to their own devices, even the best-intentioned managers will only reinforce when they remember and have the time to do it. This generally means that R+ from the manager is at a minimum. A reinforcement system prompts the manager to reinforce and also introduces reinforcers that the manager doesn't have to deliver personally.

A reinforcement system may simply be a graph with a goal and several sub-goals on it with specified reinforcers for goal attainment. It may be as complicated as a point system where many behaviors are tracked along with

the results. The points may be redeemed for tangible reinforcers, such as merchandise chosen from a catalog.

A reinforcement system can be team-driven. For it to qualify as a reinforcement system, the members would need to know the behaviors the team must perform in order to accomplish their task or goal. They also need to know the role of feedback and reinforcement in order to properly reinforce each other's efforts in accomplishing their task or goal. Unfortunately, most teams are trained only in antecedent activities, primarily pinpointing, and have little understanding of the need for, or the effect of, systematic feedback and reinforcement. The most effective reinforcement system is an organization in which every person is able to participate in the reinforcement of every other person.

The function of a reinforcement system is to increase the amount of reinforcement within the entire work group. Every organization has systems already in place that are supposed to serve that purpose. But as we will see, practically all of them are based on results, and many of them are only loosely contingent on performance.

Compensation systems, profit sharing, suggestion systems, performance-appraisal systems, quality-improvement programs, employee involvement, and quality circles all rely on future rather than immediate consequences. The reinforcement in most compensation plans is not clearly tied to performance. Surprisingly, the typical profit-sharing plan is rarely directly contingent on the performance of most who participate in it. Performance appraisals will be discussed later, but the attempt to reinforce behaviors in the typical appraisal system can best be summarized by the saying, "too little, too late!" Suggestion systems are probably the most contingent of all the above. However, with an average participation rate in the United States of only eight percent, they do little to reinforce the majority of performers.

The most important consideration in designing a reinforcement system is to make sure that one person's reinforcement does not limit another's. If one person's success reduces the likelihood that someone else will succeed, the plan will not maximize performance. To the contrary, the system should be designed so that one person's success *increases* the likelihood that others will also be successful.

What this means is that most systems that reinforce intraorganizational competition at any level are counterproductive. This surprises most managers. Yet, data demonstrates that even in business, cooperation outperforms competition. Unfortunately, when you examine many organizational attempts at recognition systems, you discover the vast majority of them are competitive.

Internal vs. external competition

Competition may be counterproductive within an organization, but it drives the capitalist system. Competition on the open market is healthy for companies, their customers, and the economy. In fact, an organization's success depends on its ability to provide a better product or service at a better cost than its competitor. This type of competition can direct all the employees within a company toward a common goal, and therefore is a productive use of competition.

However, competition within a company is, under most circumstances, destructive. In an environment where there is a limited amount of reinforcement to divide among performers, it is amazing what people will do to get that reinforcement. Many will lie, cheat, or steal to win or avoid losing a competition between shifts, departments, or plants. When people compete for reinforcement, teamwork is minimal and cooperation is superficial.

It's sometimes difficult for managers to realize that they encourage intraorganizational competition, because the policies or procedures were not set up to be competitive. For example, ranking individuals and groups by performance data may serve a useful purpose for a manager to make decisions about personnel moves or job assignments. But when these rankings are displayed publicly, they typically produce unhealthy competition between individuals or groups.

Any time the performance of one group is held up publicly by management as being the best, problems occur. This is because reinforcement from management is very powerful. Social reinforcement from management is often associated with significant reinforcers such as money, promotions, good job assignments, perks, and status. In many organizations the only way one gets this kind of reinforcement is to beat his fellow employees. Unfortunately, this can sometimes be accomplished by such things as withholding information, not cooperating, and backstabbing.

Words like "first," "best," "highest," "top," or "most improved" should be avoided when reinforcing, unless you are comparing the person or group to its own previous performance.

Employee of the month

"Employee-of-the-Month" programs are an especially popular form of employee competition. Variations on this theme include "Salesperson of the Year," "Team of the Month," "Plant of the Month," and so on.

These programs usually provide social and tangible reinforcers to the best performer in the work unit, which may be a person, shift, department, or plant. In these programs only the performance of one person or group gets reinforced while many others get punished— this despite small differences in performance.

Another problem with "Employee-of-the-Month" programs is that if they are based purely on performance, the same person may win month after month. When that happens, management often makes the mistake of "doing the same thing harder" by increasing the number of winners to five or ten. This doesn't make the program better; it makes it worse. It may be easy to accept that you are not the best performer, but when you are not even in the top ten.... Increasing the number of winners only increases the probability that the program will be punishing to many more people.

In their usual form these programs guarantee that many adequate or even very good performances will not be reinforced. After the novelty wears off, many of those who are not winning become apathetic or even hostile. These are hardly the feelings that generate teamwork and cooperation.

The evidence that these programs do not work can be seen in many restaurants and hotels by looking for the plaque with the names of the "Employee of the Month." Such plaques are often months, sometimes a year or more, out of date. The other evidence is that nobody wins more than once. This tells you that the contest is a "pass-around." Each month a different employee is selected to make sure that everyone gets a turn. Managers rationalize this as a means of ensuring "fairness" by recognizing everyone. This means that there is no contingency between performance and the award. This is why in an informal survey I conducted of over 70 employees in various businesses across the United States, not one employee could state any performance contingency for earning the award. No wonder these programs produce little performance change but a lot of discontent.

The normal curve

Another form of competition that is almost universally disliked is the typical performance appraisal system. Under this system, rankings are given according to some "forced distribution." Figure 6.4 illustrates a typical distribution.

If a manager has ten people, under a forced distribution it is possible that no one would get a score of five, but in no case would more than one receive a five. Two or three would get a four. Four would get a three. Two or three would get a two and one person might get a one.

This system limits performance in at least two ways. First, it limits the number of outstanding performers. Second, the difference between the performer who just got into the five category and the one who just missed it may be very small. However, the difference in consequences both socially and tangibly is often quite large.

Just as in the "Employee-of-the-Month" program discussed previously, the same people tend to get the fives every time. The people getting the fours are punished or extinguished from trying to top their peers and eventually reduce their effort. In the beginning there is a lot of competition between the performers, but in the end either resignation or resentment sets in. These feelings and reactions are often hard for senior management to empathize with because they have been on the winning side of the competition.

Another negative side effect of this system is that it does not reinforce "best" effort, only "better than" your closest rival. As the lower-rated performers reduce their performance, the top performer does not need to work as hard to maintain the top spot.

The competition that the system generates is practically always unhealthy because at every level of the curve, success predicts failure. The only way one can move from one rating to another is to knock someone out of the higher group. Increasing numbers of people find this kind of environment very unpleasant. Many end up saying, "I refuse to play politics."

While it is true that every group has a distribution and that performers can be ranked, this question has to be answered: "Why would we want to?" Supporters of this approach have several rationalizations.

One is that we must have some way to administer pay increases and promotions. Promotions do not pose the problem that pay does because the average person receives very few in a career. Therefore, ranking for this purpose is more accepted. These rankings generally affect status and finances only after the promotion—an infrequent event. Appraisals, on the other hand, occur at least once a year and affect everyone either positively or negatively. The way the system is designed, most people are affected negatively, even though that is not the intent of the system.

A second excuse for appraising with a ranking method is that most upper managers have little confidence in middle managers' and supervisors' ability to appraise accurately.

Figure 6.4

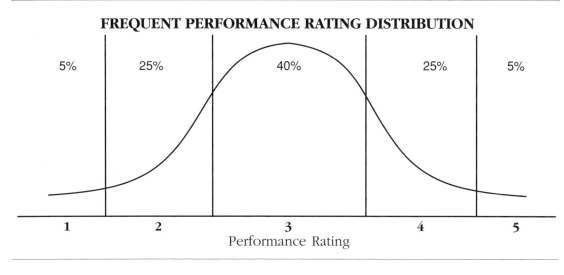

FREQUENT PERFORMANCE RATING DISTRIBUTION

5%   25%   40%   25%   5%

1   2   3   4   5
Performance Rating

That is, they tend to rate people higher than they actually perform. The "forced distribution" provides a way of making them do it right. The alternative is to train them to do it right. Then, develop an accountability system that: 1) Provides positive R+ for managers and supervisors who do it right; 2) Provides corrective feedback and additional training for those who don't.

A third reason, and probably the most compelling to many managers, is that the ranking method is easy to administer. It enables them to determine costs and to budget simply and efficiently. In addition, the distribution of ratings tells management at a glance if the system is "in control."

An alternative to forced distributions

The alternative to the negative aspects of the "forced distributions" is not, contrary to practice in some companies, to do more frequent appraisals. If the system is faulty, then doing it more often is worse, not better. An alternative consistent with the principles discussed so far is to evaluate against a standard of performance or criterion. When we spell out a performance level above which every performer gets reinforced, competition is minimized, if not eliminated.

Suppose we have a situation in which any performer whose efficiency is above 110 percent adds a value to the organization of, say, $1,000. Suppose, also, that $100 would be reinforcing to the performer. If we set a contingency under which every performer whose efficiency was above 110 percent gets a $100 bonus for the month and you are the owner, how many people would you want to get the bonus? Of course, you would want 100 percent of the employees to get the bonus because the organization would profit handsomely. We would not want to limit winners to the best performer, or even to the top 25 percent, because that would mean the organization is not doing as well as possible.

Mary Kay Cosmetics has a criterion system and almost everyone knows the prize—a pink Cadillac. Mary Kay's success is measured in terms of how many Cadillacs she awards each year—not how few. This has worked so well for her company that she has expanded the awards to a wide range of items, and every time an employee earns some tangible reinforcer she is happy because it reflects the success of her company. Her goal is to put everyone in a pink Cadillac.

This method can also be used to enhance teamwork and cooperation. If we add a bonus based on the percentage of performers who achieve above 110 percent, then it is in everyone's interest to help others get above that criterion level. This description of compensation, of course, is overly simplistic and is not meant to be a model for a compensation system. For the details of implementing a contingent compensation plan based on these ideas, see Morse (1988).

Performance appraisal that reduces competition

The mechanics of a performance-appraisal system that reduces competition are quite straightforward. All that is required is to meet with each performer at the beginning of the appraisal period and specify the rating or dollars the performer will get when specified tasks are completed or performance levels exceeded. The problem with such an approach is that the performance levels or tasks are not easy to specify in many cases. In addition, the economic value of the performance often cannot be clearly determined. While these are problems, they can be solved, resulting in improvements over the typical performance-appraisal systems that make the change well worth the effort. The question is, "Is a criterion system more consistent with the outcomes we want?" If it is, the problems you experience will at least be more palatable than those you formerly faced, and the outcomes more likely to be what the business wants and needs.

Using competition and contests effectively

Having pointed out all the problems with competition, let's look at some ways it can be used constructively. Millions of people enter contests every day. They play sports and games because of the competition. Playing without determining a winner would take all the fun out of the activity for most people. How does this square with our previous discussion?

The first thing is that in sports and other contests we enter, we do so to have fun. When they quit being fun, we quit. But at work we can't usually quit just because we're not having fun. In addition, the consequences of playing a game are not necessary to one's standard of living. Nor does losing alter one's social status in a significant way. Therefore, if we can introduce competition and contests at work that are like our play, they may offer performance improvement and reinforcement opportunities.

Below are some guidelines to setting up an effective contest.

1. Make it short

Most contests run too long. It is very difficult to sustain interest in contests that run for as long as a year. The primary reason is that a great deal of reinforcement is needed to maintain high levels of interest and involvement.

The recommended length for a contest is no longer than thirteen weeks. Weekly, monthly, and quarterly contests can be quite effective in focusing a lot of reinforcement on a specific improvement opportunity. They are relatively easy to manage, and they are over before people tire of them. With contests of these lengths you can do several in a year, if desirable, and keep people excited about all of them.

2. Do not use large tangible reinforcers

Make the reinforcers symbolic. Believe it or not, large tangibles such as TV sets and trips take the fun out of it for most people

because they think they won't win. It's much better to have many small tangibles than one or a few large ones. The best reinforcers in effective contests are for "bragging rights."

3. Compete against a standard

Although occasionally you may want to have a contest pitting one shift, department, or office against another, in most cases you will have better results when you compete against the group's previous performance, past record performances, or the performance of your external competitors.

The concept of "competitive benchmarking" offers tremendous reinforcement opportunities and is underutilized in the average business. **Competitive benchmarking** involves finding what your best competitor's performance is and setting up reinforcement on the basis of either closing or widening the gap between you and them.

4. Make it fun

Above all, make it fun. This is, of course, the whole purpose. If it is not fun it will not be reinforcing, and if it is not reinforcing it will not be effective. Many managers have trouble with a "carnival" atmosphere at work. This is because they have a history in which fun at work meant sacrificing productivity. Having fun for fun's sake is something you do at your leisure. However, if you are having fun as a result of improving quality and reducing cost, few managers would be against it. In that case they would probably say, "the more fun the better."

AVOIDING POTENTIAL PROBLEMS IN DELIVERING REINFORCEMENT

Remember that by definition, reinforcement always works. If you are confident you have a reinforcer and are still not getting the performance you desire, first consider whether the person is capable of doing the performance. Assuming she is, there is probably a problem with the way in which you are delivering the reinforcer. The most common problems of execution are listed below.

Not using a variety of reinforcers

Satiation occurs when you use the same or similar reinforcers too often. You may enjoy a particular kind of ice cream, but if you have it several times a day for many weeks, you may grow tired of it—at least for a while.

When people find a reinforcer that works, they get reinforced for using it. Naturally they are more likely to use it again. It is not unusual to hear employees say things like, "We're being coffeed and doughnutted to death!" This is often because a supervisor had some initial success with coffee and doughnuts as a reinforcer and now that is all she thinks about when planning reinforcement. The employees of one company nicknamed Performance Management "Pizza Management" because that was practically the only reinforcer used.

Although it goes against our natural instincts, the best time to change a reinforcer is while it is still working. When you change under those circumstances, you have good evidence that you will be able to use it effectively again. If you "wear it out," people will probably not be excited about using it again in the future.

Asking for too much, too soon

When we have a performance that we want to improve, naturally we want quick change. One of the more common mistakes is that we set initial goals too high.

In the early stages of improving performance, we should not wait for results before we reinforce. In the beginning we reinforce the behaviors that lead to the desired result. This is called shaping. **Shaping** is the reinforcement of successive approximations, or steps, toward some final goal.

For example, inexperienced telephone sales representatives will make very few sales during their first attempts. In order to shape their performance, you might reinforce

simply reading the presentation to the customer over the phone the first day. You could reinforce giving a memorized presentation on the second day. On the third day, you might reinforce responding appropriately to the customer's questions. In this way the firm is more likely to achieve its long-term goal of increased sales than it would if only the result of making a sale is reinforced.

Confusing rewards and reinforcers

An important distinction exists between rewards and reinforcers. You reinforce behaviors and reward results. Another term that better communicates our intent in business is celebrate. Celebrate good results.

The concept of reward has many connotations that cause problems for the performance manager. In our society, rewards are typically thought of as consequences for above and beyond or heroic performances. This implies that rewards seldom occur. If rewards and reinforcers are perceived as the same, the average person probably thinks that reinforcement should not be given often.

Another problem with the concept of rewards is that they are typically chosen by the donor without regard to whether it is reinforcing to the receiver. However, reinforcers must be tailored to the receiver.

The concept of celebration works much better than rewards for our purposes. It connotes having a good time by remembering how we accomplished our goal. We congratulate each other on what we did to make the achievement possible. We need more celebrations at work.

Confusing reinforcement and bribery

Many people think positive reinforcement is bribery. There are three things that typically concern them. One is that bribery has not worked for them. Second, they feel they shouldn't reinforce something that a person should do anyway. Third, bribery, if it worked, raises ethical and moral concerns.

Probably the most common problem many people have with reinforcement is that they reinforce before the desired behavior occurs. Of course this will most likely reinforce something you don't want, since what you want is not yet occurring. An article in the *Wall Street Journal* described a newspaper publishing organization in which morale in the newsroom was very poor. Management decided to give free coffee in order to improve the morale, only to find that at the end of the first week, the employees were complaining about the quality of the coffee!

Parents frequently make this mistake: "You can watch TV if you promise me that you will do your homework when that program is over." This is a bribe. They are reinforcing procrastination and "making promises"—not "doing homework."

Do not confuse an antecedent with a bribe. To tell a child, "After you do your homework, you can watch TV" is not bribery. The statement is an antecedent describing what is expected and what the reinforcer will be.

The second concern is often reflected by managers who say, "I shouldn't have to reinforce, that is what they are paid for." Parents say, "I shouldn't have to reinforce, because there are some things my kids should do just because they are a part of this family." But those statements reflect a misunderstanding of how habits are formed. If people are not doing something, it is because it's not being reinforced. If we want them to do it, we must find some way to provide reinforcement when they do. No one is born a hard worker or a chore completer.

Remember from the last chapter that you can get employees to do what "they are paid for" or you can get children to clean up their rooms because they "ought to," but that is all you will get—no initiative, no volunteering, nothing above the minimum required to keep you off their backs.

The third concern is that, in our society, bribery implies the use of reinforcement to achieve the selfish, and perhaps corrupt,

ends of the donor. Performance Management doesn't condone the use of reinforcement for any illegal, unethical, immoral, or otherwise unsavory behavior.

Confusing reinforcement with manipulation

Sometimes people claim reinforcement is manipulative. If they feel this way, they will resist it and it won't work.

Feeling manipulated most often stems from a manager's failure to deliver promised reinforcers after the desired performance. For example, a sales manager may promise one of his salespeople that if he continues to exceed his quota he'll get a shot at a management position. At the same time, the manager may believe the salesperson is not management material and will never advance. A reinforcer has been promised that will not be delivered. Eventually, the salesperson may feel manipulated, and indeed he has been.

To the wronged person, it matters little whether the reinforcer was not delivered because it was never intended to be, whether the other person forgot, or whether he didn't have the authority to make it happen. Never offer a reinforcer that you do not personally have the authority or inclination to deliver.

Reinforcement, as with all PM techniques, works best when everyone involved is aware of what you are doing. There is little to gain from not being open and above board. When people know you are trying to find ways to reinforce their progress, they can, and often do, tell you what reinforcers they like and don't like. In many conversations with middle managers who have been reinforced and with employees who received reinforcement from their supervisors, the answer to the question, "Do you feel manipulated?" has been answered with a resounding, "No!" Instead, people who know they are receiving reinforcement say, "I like it." Reinforcement feels good. If you doubt this, think back to the last time someone gave you some sincere praise or recognition. Did you feel manipulated, or did you feel good?

Delivering reinforcement non-contingently

Reinforcement always reinforces some behavior. When reinforcement is said to be non-contingent, it means that either what is reinforced is unknown or is unplanned. When you give reinforcers simply because someone is "such a nice person," or "it would be a shame not to include him," you are reinforcing non-contingently and cannot expect to get the results a proper reinforcement program can deliver.

Using reinforcement non-contingently usually results from a mistaken belief that "fairness" demands that what we do for one we must do for all, or because managers are afraid of negative consequences from those who do not receive the reinforcement.

Being a non-contingent reinforcer for either of these reasons will practically always generate unwanted or undesired behavior.

Delivering reinforcement insincerely

The problem of insincerity has been discussed earlier. It is mentioned again because it is one of the reasons that some people fail to get desirable results with their attempts at reinforcement. Sincerity is essentially a question of honesty. Saying things you don't believe in order to increase performance will damage your credibility and your reputation. Once you get a reputation for being insincere it is very difficult to change.

Delivering tangible reinforcement without social reinforcement

Tangible reinforcement is, for many people, a quick and easy way to give R+. They can point to a tangible item and say, "Yes, I've reinforced. I bought them a pizza," or "I gave her a T-shirt." But if the only reinforcers people receive are tangible, they may misinterpret the intention by assuming that the "token" reinforcer itself demonstrates the dollar value you place on their performance.

It is easy to see how this could cause problems. Remember, give the social reinforcers FIRST, and give them more OFTEN than the tangible reinforcers.

Not reinforcing the behavior of reinforcing

One of the basic problems with reinforcement is that many recipients find it difficult to accept. They have been taught to be humble and self-effacing and are uncomfortable with any form of praise. On being reinforced people will often say things like, "It was nothing," "I was lucky," "Anybody could have done it," or "It's just my job." Worse yet, when reinforced they may say nothing, causing an awkward silence. The end result of this discomfort about reinforcement is that the person doing the reinforcing gets punished. A colleague related the following example:

A young colleague just informed me she had submitted several articles for publication. When I congratulated her she responded, "What do you think I've been doing all this time?" If I didn't know her better, that would have been the last time I complimented her about anything.

Reinforcing is not a common behavior in most work places. If early attempts are not reinforced, the behavior will quickly stop. As with any skill, the early stages of learning to use reinforcers are fraught with mistakes. People may say the wrong things. Or what they do say is not said in the right way. Even so, if people aren't reinforced for their attempts at reinforcing, they will probably never become skilled at it.

Reinforcing the use of reinforcement is often complicated by the fact that the person giving you reinforcement is your boss. And our society has all kinds of derogatory terms for those who reinforce performance above them in business organizations. "Apple polishing," "buttering up," and "politicking" are just a few of the kinder terms. This

The SSIP Model

The previous chapter detailed the four characteristics of effective reinforcers. Reinforcers should be:

1. Readily available
2. Controllable
3. Able to be used frequently without satiation
4. Cost effective

This chapter outlined criteria for the effective delivery of reinforcers. Delivery should be:

1. Personalized
2. Immediate
3. Specific
4. Sincere
5. Frequent
6. Varied
7. Separated from punishment
8. Separated from goal setting
9. Systematic

Much of what has been said in this chapter can be reduced to four qualities that should describe the reinforcement you give:

1. **S**incere
2. **S**pecific
3. **I**mmediate
4. **P**ersonal

This is called the SSIP model of effective reinforcement. Learn and apply the model and you will increase your personal effectiveness in dealing with people at work.

situation must change. In the high-performance organizations of the future, reinforcement will be everybody's business. Reinforcing "up the organization" will be just as comfortable as reinforcing "down the organization."

All the criteria for the effective delivery of reinforcement applies to reinforcing the act of reinforcing. All employees should be taught the importance of reinforcing, how to reinforce, and their role in reinforcing. PM is not some secret weapon to be available only to managers. Rather, it grows and flourishes when everyone understands and practices it.

7

Schedules of Reinforcement

Once you know about reinforcement, its effect on behavior, and how to deliver it effectively, you must know how often to reinforce. Obviously behaviors do not need to be reinforced every time they occur. We do many things that are only reinforced occasionally. Once behaviors occur at a high and steady rate, they can usually be maintained by intermittent reinforcement. To understand why this happens and how much to reinforce, you must understand schedules of reinforcement.

A schedule of reinforcement describes when behaviors will be reinforced. When a behavior is reinforced every time it occurs, it is on a **continuous schedule of reinforcement** (**CRF**). When reinforcement occurs only occasionally, it is on an **intermittent schedule of reinforcement** (**INT**).

As you change the criterion for reinforcement from reinforcing every step to reinforcing only occasionally, you are changing the schedule of reinforcement. Changing the schedule produces changes in the rate and the pattern of the performance. Some schedules produce high rates of responding and some produce low rates. Some produce consistent patterns of responding, while others produce inconsistent ones. In addition, some schedules produce rapid extinction of a behavior and others produce very slow extinction.

CONTINUOUS AND INTERMITTENT SCHEDULES

While reinforcing a behavior every time it occurs seems impractical, in some situations it is necessary if learning or improvement is to occur most efficiently. In most cases, however, reinforcing every behavior is neither desirable nor necessary.

True continuous schedules of reinforcement are relatively rare. What behavior gets reinforced every time? Are our requests granted every time we make one? Do people always laugh at our jokes? Do we enjoy every meal we eat, every movie we see, every party we attend? Does our boss show appreciation every time we accomplish something?

Nevertheless, many of our everyday activities approximate continuous schedules. For example, when we turn the spigot, water usually flows. When we turn on the radio, we usually hear a voice or music. When the telephone rings and we pick up the receiver, someone is usually on the line. When we turn the key in the ignition, the car usually starts.

The opposite of a continuous schedule of reinforcement is one in which performance is never reinforced. Of course, without reinforcement, behavior will eventually stop. As you may recall, this describes extinction. See Chapter Three. Although we don't usually think of it as such, extinction is also a schedule. It is the opposite of continuous reinforcement (CRF).

In between the extreme of receiving reinforcement every time (continuous reinforcement) and never receiving reinforcement (extinction) are the schedules labeled "intermittent."

Intermittent schedules are those in which

behavior or performance is reinforced less than always and more than never. The relationship of continuous and intermittent reinforcement and extinction is depicted in Figure 7.1.

You will discover that intermittent schedules are the most efficient way to maintain desired levels of performance. They offer advantages to both the reinforcer and the recipient. In some situations, however, continuous reinforcement is the best schedule.

The value of continuous reinforcement

If examples of continuous schedules of reinforcement are rare in everyday life, they are even rarer at work. Nevertheless, sometimes people need as much reinforcement as you can provide. When new employees are learning job skills or when you are trying to help poor performers improve, reinforce as often as you can. Every step in the right direction and every small accomplishment should be reinforced. Continuous reinforcement is the best way to develop new behaviors or to improve performance at very low levels.

If you use continuous reinforcement in the situations noted above, progress will be maximized. Once you have steady improvement in performance, you will be able to switch to intermittent schedules to maintain the improvement. Until that point is reached, the more reinforcement you deliver, the faster progress will be.

The value of intermittent reinforcement

When you first see the effect of continuous reinforcement on performance, it appears so effective that you wonder why anyone would want to do anything else. Common sense tells us that if people receive reinforcement every time they do something, they will

Figure 7.1

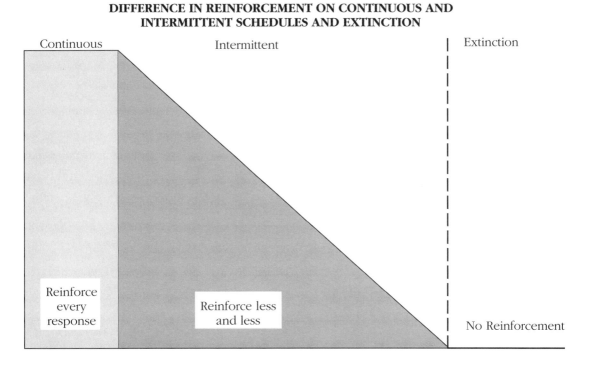

DIFFERENCE IN REINFORCEMENT ON CONTINUOUS AND
INTERMITTENT SCHEDULES AND EXTINCTION

Continuous   Intermittent   Extinction

Reinforce
every
response

Reinforce less
and less

No Reinforcement

INTERMITTENT REINFORCEMENT IN EVERYDAY LIFE

Don't get mail every time   Don't win every time

Every car doesn't stop   This doesn't happen every day

maximize their efforts. If you knew that every time you performed a certain way you'd get something you want, wouldn't you work your hardest? If you said "Yes," common sense would have led you astray.

The answer to this question, believe it or not, is "No." Once the basic performance has been well established, intermittent reinforcement generates higher levels of performance than continuous reinforcement. This finding has been confirmed by numerous research studies conducted over a period of more than 50 years (see Ferster and Skinner, 1957; Lundin, 1969; Sulzer-Azaroff and Mayer, 1977; Ayllon and Kolko, 1982; and Catania, 1984).

There are at least four advantages to intermittent reinforcement. Following is a discussion on each.

1. Intermittent reinforcement can maintain performance

If you have a reinforcer and deliver it effectively, performance will usually change rapidly. Your goals will be reached and often exceeded in less time than you ever imagined. But maintaining this performance gain in the ensuing months and years requires intermittent reinforcement. The following example illustrates this point.

What could make a fisherman spend hours sitting nearly motionless, holding onto a pole with a piece of string dangling in the water? For simplicity let's regard the behavior as "fishing" and the reinforcer as "catching a fish." Examine the following sequence of events.

On the first few fishing trips, a young fisherman is successful; he catches fish each trip. After successful trips, he goes on a trip where he catches no fish. Will he go again? Probably. Suppose on his next trip he is successful again, but on the next two trips he is unsuccessful. Will he go again? Probably.

With this kind of reinforcement history, he will most likely continue fishing for a long time even though he will have occasional trips when "the fish weren't biting." His experience has taught him that if he doesn't catch fish on one trip, he might the next time out. His performance probably will be maintained despite failure because fishing is on an intermittent schedule of reinforcement.

Some hunters hunt all season long without killing a deer. Football fans go to games in spite of long losing streaks. Many golfers have vowed to quit the game during a bad round, only to change their minds after hitting their best drive ever on the last hole.

Millions of people buy tickets to the state lotteries every week but rarely win. Many writers persist in writing in the face of numerous rejections. Thomas Edison was reputed to have said that he discovered 10,000 ways *not* to make a light bulb before he found the right way. Examples of this kind of motivation are endless. You might say that a history of intermittent reinforcement gives people hope.

People do, however, give up on projects and lose interest in hobbies and activities. If reinforcement does not reach some minimum level, extinction will occur. However, intermittent schedules produce behavior that is relatively resistant to extinction. The factors affecting the rate of extinction are too involved to cover here, but for the serious student there is an extensive body of research to review. (Lundin, 1969; Cooper et al, 1987; and Ferster and Skinner, 1957; *Journal of Applied Behavior Analysis*; *Journal of Experimental Analysis of Behavior.*)

In order to help people develop a habit that is resistant to extinction, the behavior must get a lot of reinforcement early in the learning stage. If that is done, the habits will be maintained with relatively little R+.

The advantage that intermittent R+ provides for organizations is that it permits employees to maintain high levels of performance under limited supervision. Salespeople working away from the office for extended periods of time, long-distance truck drivers, service technicians, security guards, night shift employees, auditors, entrepreneurs, and consultants are a few of the jobs that must be established on intermittent reinforcement for best performance. An additional advantage of intermittent schedules is that they allow a manager to be away from the office for a long time and not have decreases in performance due to lack of reinforcement. The advantage that intermittent R+ has for individuals is that you can't just pat someone on the head and forget about him. Some reinforcement is required on a continual basis. In other words, don't take high performance for granted. Managers frequently ask, "How

long do I have to reinforce behaviors?" The answer is: as long as you want that behavior to continue.

2. Intermittent reinforcement avoids the problem of satiation

Some reinforcers can lose their effectiveness if they are used too often. We all experience this condition when we tire of a particular food or dessert because we have had it too frequently within a short period of time. It happens with clothes, with activities, and can occur with practically all reinforcers. Satiation is especially likely when the selection of tangibles is limited. Therefore, using them only occasionally will sustain their reinforcing properties for a longer period of time. Reinforcing on an intermittent schedule and using a variety of social and tangible reinforcers maximizes effectiveness.

3. Intermittent reinforcement frees managers to reinforce many different behaviors and performances

Managers are responsible for numerous performers and their many behaviors. Reinforcing them all on a continuous schedule is impossible. There simply isn't enough time. Intermittent reinforcement makes reinforcing many individual performers possible. It's not unusual in organizations using PM for managers and supervisors to have five or more performance improvement plans underway at the same time. This is possible because as the demand for reinforcement decreases on one project, another can be started.

4. Intermittent reinforcement explains why some people seem to perform without reinforcement

You may occasionally encounter a situation where one or more people perform at a high level apparently in the absence of positive reinforcement. To the skeptic, this apparent exception "proves" that reinforcement is useful only for some problems and for some people.

Consider the star performers who are consistently prompt, efficient, and productive.

In watching them perform over extended periods of time, you may not witness any positive reinforcement. In response to surveys, they may not remember any R+. But a long time ago, most likely when they were children, they probably were given attention for their achievements and for learning new tasks by their parents. Or, perhaps as new employees, they were fortunate enough to receive a good bit of reinforcement. As they learned the job, their supervisor or trainer may have given considerable reinforcement as they made progress.

After a while, as a natural course of events, the supervisor began to reinforce them less and less often as they became more and more proficient in the job. By that time, even if new supervisors took over, an occasional comment about their work would be all it took to keep performance at a high level.

Now, years later, they seem to work independent of reinforcement. In reality, they are able to sustain high performance on a very meager schedule of reinforcement because of a rich reinforcement history.

People who respond with high levels of behavior even with little reinforcement in the present can do so because of their reinforcement history. These people are typically referred to as self-motivated, inner-driven, or self-starters. And you will discover, even these people need reinforcement on some schedule.

TYPES OF INTERMITTENT SCHEDULES

Simple schedules of reinforcement generally can be divided into two categories. You can reinforce based on the number of responses a person makes, or you can reinforce the first response after some time has passed. Schedules based on the number of responses, or the amount of work accomplished, are called **ratio schedules**. A schedule on which a period of time must pass before reinforcement is available is called an **interval schedule**. Although Catania (1984) lists 13 basic

schedules and 10 compound schedules, only four will be discussed here in detail: two ratio and two interval. For our purposes, a thorough understanding of these four will provide you with most of the information you need to diagnose productivity problems and plan corrective action for them.

The advantage of knowing these schedules is that each produces distinctive performance patterns. If you know the type of performance you want, one schedule is usually more appropriate than another. A knowledge of schedules helps you to plan and diagnose performance problems better. When you are having a performance problem, a knowledge of schedules will help you determine whether the problem is due to the schedule or to some other factor.

Ratio and interval schedules can be subdivided according to whether the conditions under which reinforcement occur are fixed or whether they are variable. This gives us the four basic schedules illustrated in Figure 7.2.

Interval schedules

1. Fixed interval

A **fixed interval (FI) schedule** is one in which a certain amount of time must pass before a given behavior or performance will be reinforced. There are two criteria for reinforcement on a fixed interval schedule. First, some period of time must go by before reinforcement is delivered; and second, at the end of this period, the desired performance must occur.

Suppose you work in an area that is inspected for housekeeping on the last day of every month. The reinforcement may be positive in that you will be praised if it is good, or it may be negative in that the most you can hope for is to avoid a "chewing out." The consequences will be delivered for having a clean area on that day. It doesn't matter whether you kept your area clean or messy during all the preceding days of the month. Reinforcement is available only on the last day. If you straightened up your work area every other day it wouldn't matter.

Figure 7.2

FOUR BASIC SCHEDULES
OF REINFORCEMENT

	Fixed	Variable
Interval R+ delivered when response is made after some time has passed	**FI**	**VI**
Ratio R+ delivered after number of responses are made	**FR**	**VR**

Reinforcement will not be delivered any sooner than on inspection day.

Because it is a monthly inspection, the performance (housekeeping) will never be reinforced (inspected) during the interval no matter how often you do it—only at the end of the interval. But remember, on interval schedules, reinforcement is not automatically given at the end of the interval. The performance must first occur. In this case the place must be clean.

Also remember that on a fixed interval schedule, responding immediately after reinforcement is never reinforced. This usually produces a distinctive performance pattern. Performance under FI schedules is often unstable. In the early part of the interval, little performance may occur, while toward the end of the interval, performance increases, often dramatically.

In the example above, it is likely that little attention is paid to housekeeping until the last couple of days in the month. At that point everybody starts scurrying around to get the place cleaned up before inspection.

If we were to graph the number of hours spent in housekeeping during the month, the graph will usually look something like Figure 7.3.

This pattern, referred to as scalloping, is generated because the response rate usually drops to zero following reinforcement. This happens because behavior occurring immediately after reinforcement is never reinforced on an FI schedule.

Figure 7.4 shows a classic example of this effect in the U.S. Congress. Most bills are passed just before the end of the session. This is such a well-known fact that legislators often consider it in deciding when to introduce their bill. That is, if the bill hits the floor of Congress toward the end of the session, it may not undergo the same scrutiny as those bills introduced earlier.

Figure 7.5 shows scalloping in research on human vigilance. Notice that as the fixed intervals get longer, the scalloping is more pronounced. That shows the rate of responding is slowing. This is a salient feature of FI schedules: the longer the interval, the lower the performance.

Figure 7.3

INDUSTRIAL HOUSEKEEPING
PERFORMANCE ON AN FI SCHEDULE

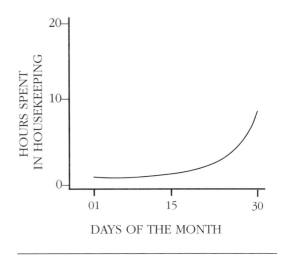

Figure 7.6 is a list of examples of fixed interval schedules in everyday life.

Given an equal number of reinforcers, FI schedules generate the lowest level of performance of the four schedules being discussed. Since most organizations are interested in producing better products and services at lower costs, FI shouldn't be the schedule of choice in most business situations.

2. Variable interval

A **variable interval (VI) schedule** is one in which the time between reinforcement varies. For example, the first time reinforcement is available may be after one hour, the next time may be 3 1/2 hours later, then again 22 minutes later, and finally, after only eight more minutes. On the average, reinforcement is available every 75 minutes, but the times it is actually available vary greatly.

Figure 7.4

CUMULATIVE NUMBER OF BILLS PASSED BY CONGRESS FROM OCTOBER 1964 TO 1968

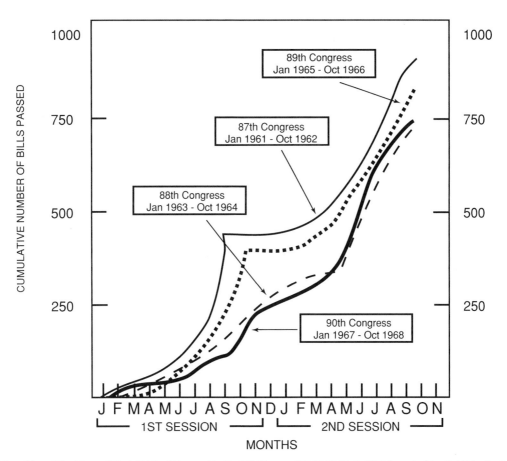

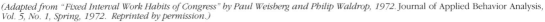

(Adapted from "Fixed Interval Work Habits of Congress" by Paul Weisberg and Philip Waldrop, 1972. Journal of Applied Behavior Analysis, Vol. 5, No. 1, Spring, 1972. Reprinted by permission.)

Figure 7.5

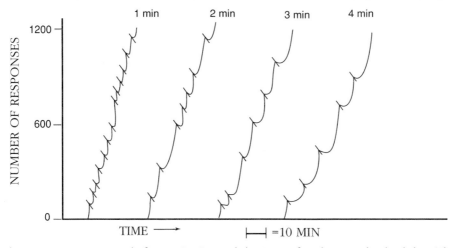

FIXED INTERVAL SCALLOPING IN "SIGNAL DETECTION" (VIGILANCE)

Cumulative Response records for 1-, 2-, 3-, and 4-minute fixed-interval schedules. The task was to detect deflections of a pointer on a dial and to reset them.

(From "Human Vigilance" by J.G. Holland, 1958, Science, *July 11, V. 128, pp. 61-67. Reprinted by permission.)*

Figure 7.6

EXAMPLES OF FIXED INTERVAL SCHEDULES

Behavior	Reinforcer
Studying for final exams	Passing the course
Cleaning up work area	Passing monthly inspection
Preparing monthly reports	Reports turned in on time
Conducting annual performance appraisals	Completing the task
Setting annual business objectives	Approved by the boss
Completing tax returns	Avoiding late penalty
Shopping for birthday gift	Response of receiver

In other words, the performer never knows exactly when reinforcement will occur.

As with FI, the performance must be occurring when reinforcement becomes available in order to get it. Since the performer can't predict whether any given response will be reinforced, VI produces a different performance pattern than FI.

On VI, in contrast to FI, reinforcement can follow reinforcement. The performance can be reinforced at any time, even if it was reinforced only minutes or seconds before. If the performer repeats the desired behavior, he may or may not be reinforced, but he does not have to wait a set period of time as with FI. A variable interval schedule produces a low to moderate, but very steady response rate.

The kind of response rate VI generates may be seen in something like listening to the radio for your favorite songs to be played. You constantly monitor what is being played because you never know when you might hear an old favorite. Since on any VI schedule the longer you wait the higher the probability of reinforcement, these schedules tend to produce patience. The result is clearly seen in those who fish off the end of a pier at the seashore. They never get in a hurry and are content to stay there for long periods of time, waiting for the fish to bite.

A nurse who checks the bulletin board to see the new work schedule also demonstrates an example of a VI schedule. Suppose the nursing supervisor posts it at various times during the week, depending on her work load. The behavior being reinforced in this case is "checking the bulletin board." The reinforcer is "seeing her work schedule." No matter how frequently the nurse checks the board, the schedule won't be posted until the supervisor has completed it. In other words, the behavior of "checking the bulletin board" does not cause the work schedule to be posted. Throughout the week the nurse will check the board from time to time because experience tells her that sooner or later it will be posted.

Even though VI produces a relatively low rate of behavior, since it produces steady or regular responding, it is the most appropriate schedule for many jobs. For example, consider the case of a security guard patrolling an area. Her performance consists of physically checking various points along the route to make sure that doors are locked, windows are latched, and lights are turned on or off as appropriate. We want her to ride or walk slowly through all the area under surveillance. One of the primary values in her performance is to let any would-be intruders know that the area is regularly, carefully, and thoroughly patrolled. We don't want her to hurry through the checkpoints.

We certainly don't want her to take a break after each patrol, slowly start patrolling again, and nearing the end of the patrol, rush through it. That is, of course, what an FI schedule would produce. If she were required to make one check every hour, that is exactly the kind of performance you would predict. But on the proper VI schedule she would slowly and methodically go through her checkpoints and on returning to the guardhouse, do any paperwork and resume her rounds.

VI schedules are appropriate for any job where patience and vigilance are more important than speed. In an age where more and more jobs require people to monitor TV or computer screens to detect certain errors or events, a knowledge of how to properly apply VI schedules is important.

Figure 7.7 shows some examples of behaviors that are usually on VI schedules.

Figure 7.7

EXAMPLES OF VARIABLE INTERVAL SCHEDULES

Behavior	Reinforcer
Policeman patrolling	Spotting a crime taking place
Usher waiting for patron	Patron arriving
Waiting for an elevator	Elevator arrives
Monitoring a machine	Getting to make an adjustment
Inspecting on assembly line	Finding defect
Monitoring a radar screen	Detecting an unidentified object

Ratio schedules

The major difference between ratio and interval schedules is that under ratio schedules reinforcement is available when a given number or frequency of behaviors occurs; whereas, under interval schedules, some amount of time must pass before reinforcement is available. With ratio schedules, the faster someone performs, the more reinforcers they obtain because they are not constrained by time. Therefore, it is not hard to figure out why ratio schedules produce higher rates of responding: the harder you work, the more often you get reinforced. For example, a typist paid by the page is likely to type more pages than a typist paid by the hour.

Figure 7.8

RELATIVE RESPONSE RATES FOR THE FOUR TYPES OF INTERMITTENT SCHEDULES OF REINFORCEMENT

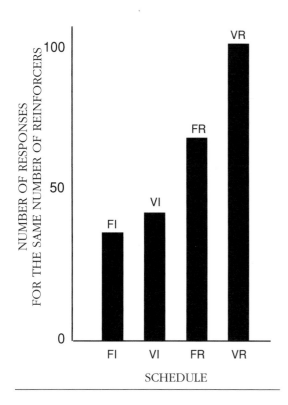

Figure 7.8 illustrates the relative difference between the various schedules in terms of level of performance. The figure assumes that the amount of reinforcement is the same for each schedule. The differences in performance levels are due solely to how the reinforcement was given, not to how much was given. Remember, in the ratio schedules, reinforcement is delivered after a certain level of performance, while in the interval schedules, reinforcement is delivered when someone responds after some amount of time has passed.

1. Fixed ratio

Fixed ratio (FR) refers to a set number of responses that must be made before reinforcement is received. Two common examples in the work setting are piecework and commissions. On piecework, employees are paid a given amount for each item or set of items they produce. Salespeople on commission are paid a certain amount for each sale they make (CRF). In the average work place, formal applications of fixed ratio schedules are hard to find because they are more difficult to track and generally require more monitoring than interval schedules. Nevertheless, employees on FR pay systems consistently outperform those on FI (fixed interval) pay systems by as much as 30 percent. Ayllon and Kolko (1982) in a survey of studies on this subject state:

> "A host of experimental work from both analogue and actual work tasks consistently points to the relative superiority of a payment system based on a specific piece-rate requirement. In particular, studies demonstrated significant improvements in productivity and task satisfaction when a CRF (fixed ratio) reinforcement schedule has been implemented following the use of a salary-based FI schedule."

FR schedules are often written as FR2, FR6, FR87, and so on. The number after the designation denotes how much performance is required in order to receive reinforcement. For example, a child who must complete six pages of homework before going out to play would be on an FR6 schedule.

Most applications of the Premack Principle (see Chapter Five) are FR: "When I do X, then I will do Y." "When I complete these tedious tasks, I'll spend an hour on a fun task." This is a very effective time-management technique. When your mother told you to do your work before your play, she was trying to teach you the value of fixed-ratio schedules. FR schedules are associated with "task orientation" and efficiency. This schedule is ideal for business. An increasing number of companies are moving to "pay for performance" in recognition of the superiority of FR over traditional interval-based pay schedules.

A characteristic usually associated with FR schedules is a pause in performance following reinforcement. This pause is called a **post-reinforcement pause (PRP)**. A post-reinforcement pause is found in both FR and FI schedules because in these intermittent schedules, reinforcement never follows reinforcement. In other words, a behavior immediately following reinforcement will never be reinforced on FI and FR. On FI some time must pass and on FR, with the exception of CRF, more than one response must occur before reinforcement is due.

The difference in the post-reinforcement pause on an FR schedule is that when the pause is over the person goes all out. Fixed ratio responding is sometimes referred to as all-or-nothing. Of course, on fixed interval the person may only need to make one response at the end of the pause to get reinforced.

The length of the pause on FR is a function of the size of the ratio. On a given performance, there would be a longer pause for FR100 than there would be for FR10. This phenomenon can be seen when people working on a project day and night for several weeks take a couple of days off when it is completed. Writers, directors, and others who work on long-term projects may take off weeks, months, or even years before starting another. One way of characterizing the PRP is as a celebration of the accomplishment. Organizations that take time to celebrate accomplishments are usually high-performing organizations.

If managers don't know about this characteristic of FR, they may get an unrealistic picture of the performers. If they happen to inspect during a PRP, they might conclude that their employees are lazy or off-task, when in reality they may be just the opposite. Many managers think that taking time to celebrate is a waste because it takes time that could otherwise be spent working. However, what they discover is that when victories or accomplishments are celebrated, people work

harder to get the celebration and work harder following the celebration than they would have done without it.

Although FI schedules also produce a pause following reinforcement, that pause differs in character from the FR pause. On FI, the performer is waiting for the next occasion for reinforcement. On FR, the performer is celebrating an accomplishment.

2. Variable ratio

On a **variable ratio (VR) schedule**, the reinforcer comes as a surprise. The person does not know exactly when the reinforcer will be delivered. However, in contrast to VI, performers learn under VR that the more they do, the more reinforcement they will get. In a variable ratio schedule, the amount of work you do to get reinforced *varies*. VR reinforcement can be planned to occur around some average, but the performer never knows exactly which response will result in R+.

A clear example of VR is playing a slot machine in a casino. The machines are set to pay off around some average. In other words, the number of times you have to pull the handle before you win is varied. (Of course the amount you win is also varied.) There is not much waiting between one pull and the next because winning on a given pull does not mean that you will not win on the next one. The sooner you pull the handle the sooner you will know if you are a winner. In contrast to FR, there is usually no pause following reinforcement. Therefore, VR schedules generally produce the highest response rate of the four.

Although there are practically no common examples of planned VR schedules at work, we typically find them where high performers are found. Because the schedule is variable, the reinforcement is often hard for the uninitiated to see when observing the performer for a limited time. But research has demonstrated that very high levels of performance can be maintained with very small ratios of reinforcement. Sometimes hundreds, even thousands, of behaviors or performances may occur before reinforcement.

For example the artist may paint many pictures before being satisfied enough to exhibit one. The athlete may repeat a performance hundreds of times before getting it perfected. The commissioned salesman may call on many customers before one buys. The researcher may test hundreds of variables before discovering one that works. According to research conducted by Scott & Fetzer Co., World Book Encyclopedia salespeople average making five presentations for every sale. Kirby Vacuum Cleaner salespeople make, on average, one sale for every three in-home demonstrations.

Not only do VR schedules produce high rates, they also produce steady rates. In contrast with FR, where there is a pause following R+, VR has no pause. The term high and steady rate (HSR) is associated with VR schedules. People who are always active are probably operating on a VR schedule. Those who work all the time are most likely people whose performance is reinforced on VR schedules.

Anyone you know who is obsessed with a vocation or avocation is most likely operating on a VR schedule. We call these people hobbyists, zealots, enthusiasts, type As, or workaholics. No matter what the behavior or performance, they all have one thing in common: they pursue it with a vengeance, or at a high and steady rate.

VR schedules offer a significant advantage because they can generate and maintain high rates of performance even when reinforcement cannot be delivered frequently. Under VR schedules people will work long and hard without reinforcement because their experience has taught them that sooner or later it will pay off.

This allows managers to manage—effectively—people they don't see every day. For this to be possible, the performers must already be working at a high and steady rate. Many performers fail because they are put into situations where reinforcement is infrequent before they have reached the HSR state. Sales organizations are particularly guilty of this practice. Before they become proficient, trainees are often put in the field where reinforcement levels are extremely low. It isn't uncommon for the failure rate of new salespeople to exceed the success rate. The problem can usually be solved by providing more reinforcement during training and when they first go into the field.

Finally, VR schedules are often associated with enthusiasm and excitement. You have only to watch an athletic contest to understand this side effect. The fact that we rarely have excitement at work that rivals what we see in sports is in large part due to the lack of VR schedules in the work place.

CONCLUDING REMARKS

This chapter has introduced you to the subject of schedules of reinforcement. It is a very complex subject, but an understanding of it is essential to maximizing performance. Since all behavior at work is on some schedule, you can't hope to understand the problems and opportunities presented to you every day unless you have some understanding of this subject.

The next chapter describes how schedules can be applied to problems at work.

NOTES

8
Applying Schedules of Reinforcement in the Work Place

THE APPROPRIATE USE OF SCHEDULES

When first introduced to schedules of reinforcement, many managers are attracted to variable ratio schedules because of the high performance they produce. They often want to apply VR to every performance, regardless of the kind of work involved. This, of course, would be a mistake. Remember that every schedule produces distinct performance patterns. That means that schedules are appropriate or inappropriate depending on the type of performance you want.

For example, if you want something delivered only at a certain time, a fixed interval schedule is the most appropriate one. If we want vigilance, a variable interval is most appropriate. If a job requires patience, we would not want VR to be the dominant schedule. If you understand the nature of the performance required in the job and the performance characteristics of the various schedules, you will be able to solve significant performance problems.

Many organizations make the mistake of putting salespeople on salary (FI), when ratio performance is what they need. Some organizations have abandoned "piece-rate" pay for hourly pay, not understanding that performance practically always declines. What these organizations fail to understand is that performance problems occurred not because the original schedules of reinforcement were wrong, but rather the contingencies for that reinforcement were flawed.

For example, many organizations have found that under piece rate, production increased but quality suffered. Rather than changing the contingency for pay to quality production, they switched to hourly pay, and of course, production suffered. Sadly enough, in most cases, quality did not improve significantly under this arrangement either.

SHOULD FI BE THE MOST COMMON SCHEDULE?

Though ratio schedules produce the highest rate of performance, fixed interval schedules are much more common in work settings. The reason for this seems to be that they are easier to administer. We can pay everybody at the same time, give raises at the same time, and give performance appraisals once or twice a year. We can manage projects by timeliness or deadlines, report on results at the end of the month, or set annual goals and objectives.

FI allows us to set a deadline and forget the performer until the end of the interval. When the performer or event comes up on our tickler file we can check on progress, or lack thereof.

As you might suspect, organizations pay dearly for this convenience. Remember, FI not only produces a low performance, but also unstable rates of performance. That means the rate of performance varies greatly from the beginning to the end of the interval—the scallop. Since on an FI schedule, reinforcement never follows reinforcement immediately, response rates often fall dramatically following R+.

We have all witnessed this following a reinforcing weekend. People drag in to work on Monday. They talk to other employees, straighten up their desks, read the newspaper, get a cup of coffee, and so on. As the morning wears on, they gradually get down to business. About an hour or so before lunch, they suddenly realize that half the day is gone and then they bear down, getting more work done in that hour than in the previous three. The same thing happens after lunch and continues until the rush to finish certain tasks before it is time to go home.

This is, of course, not the performance we want, but it is typical of FI. Performance on FI can be improved a bit by shortening the interval of reinforcement. We can have daily inspections, rather than weekly. We can have weekly meetings rather than monthly, and we can set shorter deadlines for projects. The teachers who give weekly quizzes could give daily tests and would probably get an increase in hours studied. Of course, there will still be some scalloping, in that no matter how short the interval, performance will increase toward the end. The problem with this solution is that it generates more work. Someone has to plan more meetings, conduct more inspections, monitor more deadlines, and construct and grade more test papers. If the response cost (the amount of effort expended) for the small improvement that you get doesn't justify it, choose either a VI (irregular inspections, impromptu meetings, pop quizzes) or a ratio schedule (when you finish you can take a break, go home early, start on a more enjoyable or challenging task), depending on the kind of performance you need.

USE A VARIETY OF SCHEDULES

In everyday life we are subject to a wide variety of schedules. All our behavior is on one schedule or another. On first learning about schedules of reinforcement, many

people realize that a lot of business performance is on the wrong schedule. Even so, most employees are unable to correct the problems because they often involve corporate-wide systems such as compensation and performance appraisal. However, if the schedules these systems are on are not the ones that produce the kind of performance you need, you can still do something to improve performance, even if you can't change the schedule.

By overlaying the desirable schedule on the existing one, you will be able to overcome some of its undesirable characteristics. For example, if salespeople are on salary, you can give additional reinforcement for sales earlier in the sales accounting period. Or you could increase reinforcement for sales above a certain level.

If you are a teacher, you could give a pop quiz occasionally. This would increase the amount of studying and distribute it more evenly over the quarter. You could also give bonus points or other reinforcement for completing extra assignments. In manufacturing, with hourly or salaried employees, you can overlay FR schedules on FI by celebrating accomplishments. Don't always wait till the end of the week, month, or year.

It isn't necessary that you use the same reinforcer for the overlaying schedule as the original one. For example, if you are using a salary for sales, you could use merchandise, some other form of tangible, or even social reinforcement to reinforce higher levels of performance.

By using a creative mix of schedules, you will be surprised how much you can improve performance over that predicted from the basic schedule. Maximizing that opportunity, however, requires a thorough understanding of the four basic schedules: fixed interval, variable interval, fixed ratio, and variable ratio.

SCHEDULES OF REINFORCEMENT AND EXTINCTION

Just as performance differs while each

schedule is in effect, so it does during extinction. As you remember from Chapter Six, when you stop reinforcement completely, you are practicing extinction.

What happens to performance under extinction depends on the history of reinforcement on the prior schedule. As noted earlier, there are four things that often happen when a performance is undergoing extinction:

1. Initially, the performance will increase. This is known, technically, as an extinction burst.
2. Negative emotional behaviors, such as verbal abuse, tantrum-like behavior, and even aggression occur.
3. The rate at which the desirable or undesirable performance decreases will vary widely depending on the schedule, but be prepared for a gradual decrease.
4. Once the performance has stopped, it frequently recurs later, even though it has not been reinforced after extinction began.

The first three characteristics describe quite well what happens during extinction on a continuous schedule (FR1). We have all heard people make an assessment of someone with a behavioral problem such as, "He will have to get worse before he can get better." They are referring to an extinction burst. An extinction burst occurs when, early in extinction, there is a dramatic increase in the behavior of concern in an attempt to get the usual reinforcement. Unfortunately, if the attempt is successful (gets reinforced), the rate of the behavior will be higher than before the extinction effort.

For example, in trying to extinguish behaviors like temper tantrums, many parents have noted that they actually got worse. This often occurs because when the child screamed longer than usual or turned bluer than usual, the parents gave in and thereby reinforced the child for a larger variable ratio. In other words, if he screamed longer than usual, he would be reinforced. This will, of course, make extinction more difficult in the future.

A person who has been getting attention for complaining about co-workers may complain more frequently if his manager suddenly ignores his complaints. The manager who doesn't understand that extinction bursts are a predictable aspect of extinction may think that the ignoring isn't working, when it is.

Emotional behaviors are more likely to accompany extinction on fixed schedules. The extent of the emotional reaction is due to the schedule and number of reinforcers received on it. Everybody has witnessed at least a mild form of this phenomenon. When a person puts money in a vending machine several times only to have it returned each time, he may try to shake the machine, or even hit or kick it before giving up. That person is exhibiting emotional behavior characteristic of extinction under fixed ratio schedules. Parents who say things to their children like, "You can cry all you want but you're not going to go," are dealing with the same problem.

When people are accustomed to receiving reinforcement on some predictable pattern and suddenly it stops, you can expect an emotional response from them. These responses may range from complaints of "That's not fair," to tantrum-like behavior. Variable schedules typically produce less emotional behavior during extinction.

In regard to Item 3, behavior previously reinforced under FR1 extinguishes faster than the other schedules. Next comes FI. Variable schedules take much longer. Factors affecting the rate of extinction of a behavior under a particular schedule include the size of the ratio, or length of the interval, and the number of reinforcers received on the schedule. In any event you may not see an immediate change in the behavior and should be prepared for a gradual, rather than sudden, decline.

A predictable characteristic of extinction that frustrates most people is the phenomenon of resurgence. **Resurgence** is the re-emergence of previously extinguished behavior. After a period of time when the behavior has not occurred, it often reappears for no apparent reason.

This occurrence is what has led many people to conclude that "You can't really change people." Their evidence for this is that people may change in the short run but they seem to always go back to their old ways of doing things. What they are witnessing is a common occurrence in extinction—resurgence, or as it is more traditionally called, spontaneous recovery. Sulzer-Azaroff (l988) prefers the term resurgence to spontaneous recovery because she says the latter term implies a certain lawlessness, while resurgence is a lawful phenomenon.

As Epstein (1985) has discovered, when a new behavior undergoes extinction, the old behavior comes back. In other words, if the new behavior does not get sufficient reinforcement, the old behavior will return. What happens to the old behavior when it returns is critical, since any reinforcement will put the behavior on a much thinner variable schedule and make it more difficult to extinguish in the future.

Knowledge of the four factors will help you recognize when extinction is occurring. Extinction bursts, emotional outbursts, resurgence, and a reduction in performance are all fairly easy to spot. On investigation, if it appears that extinction is the problem, your knowledge of reinforcement will allow you to remedy the situation easily and quickly in most cases.

In addition, if you want to extinguish some undesirable behavior, knowing the signs will allow you to anticipate them. If they are anticipated, you should be able to extinguish the behavior in the most efficient manner.

THINNING: HOW TO CHANGE SCHEDULES

When you change a schedule of reinforcement from continuous to intermittent, you are "thinning." Similarly, when you change FR2 to FR3 or FR11, or anything higher, you are thinning. Any change within any kind of schedule that results in less reinforcement is called **thinning**. Thinning allows you to maintain or increase performance with less reinforcing.

The advantages of thinning are two-fold. First, it allows you to have more time to reinforce other behaviors more frequently. In other words, the organizational purpose of thinning is not so that managers will have to spend less time reinforcing, but to provide them with extra time to reinforce other performances. In fact, if thinning is used as a vehicle to do less overall reinforcing, the result will usually be a decline in performance.

Another advantage to thinning is that it prevents satiation. Satiation is reduced when schedules are thinned. Therefore, the reinforcer remains effective longer.

The purpose of thinning is not to try to squeeze as much work out of people for as little reinforcement as possible. That is exploitative and manipulative. It has been stressed throughout this book that PM and reinforcement will not maintain their effectiveness if they are practiced in a secretive, manipulative manner. If people think you are trying to get them to work harder for less, whatever you do will in all probability not be reinforcing. Clearly then, thinning must always be done very carefully. It is done best with the understanding and support of the performers.

Thinning should not be confused with changing the value of the reinforcer. Let's say a manager has a party every Friday after work when the group has met or exceeded the goal for the week. Suppose she decides after several weeks to change to every other week, every month, or every now and then. In this case she would be thinning. On the other hand, if she went from having a party with steak to having hamburgers and later to having only hors d'oeuvres, she would not be thinning. She would be changing the reinforcer.

A schedule can only be thinned so much. If you thin too quickly or reduce reinforcement too much, the level of performance will erode. Therefore, there are several guidelines to follow when thinning a schedule:

1. Do it gradually.
2. Continually monitor graphed performance.
3. Watch for any signs of frustration (ratio strain).

Gradual thinning of the schedule is important. For instance, do not go from reinforcing behavior several times a day to reinforcing it once a month. Figure 8.1 provides a graph of the process of thinning for "sandpaper slitting machine efficiency." Note the improvement in performance as reinforcement is gradually thinned.

When you decrease reinforcement, it is very important to watch your data closely. When performance reaches a desirable level, managers often get lax in monitoring the data. The best evidence that you are thinning too rapidly or too much is a decrease in performance. By continuous monitoring you will be able to see small decreases, which will signal you to change your thinning procedure before performance is markedly affected.

Remember that a natural pause usually follows reinforcement on an FR schedule. It is usually short. However, if the schedule of reinforcement is too thin, the pauses get longer and more frequent. This will eventually produce a rather erratic performance. When high performers begin to lag in their performance, if there is not some physical reason for it, it is often because the amount of reinforcement they are getting is too little for the amount of performance that is required. Technically, this is called ratio strain.

Ratio strain occurs when the amount of reinforcement received is less than the amount required to maintain the performance. It usually occurs when the ratio is very large (much behavior/little R+) or there is an abrupt increase in the size of the ratio.

When good performers start complaining about how hard their job is, or that it isn't as satisfying as it used to be, or that they are getting burned out, it is highly likely that they are suffering from ratio strain. People often say these things before they actually decrease their level of performance. Therefore, these comments should be taken seriously. They predict that performance will decline if you don't increase reinforcement.

One of the reasons some companies think incentive pay doesn't work is that, over time, they engineered-out the reinforcement. They

Figure 8.1

AN INDIVIDUAL'S PERFORMANCE ON A SANDPAPER SLITTING MACHINE

J. O'Connell

continually asked for more work for the same, or little increase in, pay. Many an employee has been heard to say in those situations, "It's not worth killing myself for that little increase." The companies wrongly conclude that the incentive didn't work when from the performer's perspective there was no incentive.

Another type of behavior that will indicate that you may be thinning too much is emotional behavior. If you see changes in the level of emotional outbursts or aggressive behavior, especially with senior employees, you may have ratio strain.

The secret to avoiding these problems is to monitor performance data and reinforce while performance is high. A good rule to follow is to reinforce sometimes when you feel you don't have to. The best mistake to make is to reinforce too much. The worst mistake is to reinforce too little.

TANGIBLES AND THINNING

A final consideration in thinning concerns fixed schedules and tangible reinforcers. Thinning is not easy when you are using tangibles such as merchandise. Many people have experienced this problem when using monetary incentives. Any change is resisted, unless the change makes earning easier. This does not mean you should not occasionally use such programs, only that they should be carefully planned.

If you are planning a program using tangibles, always state clearly at the beginning that the program will end on a specific date. "Program" in this context means a point system in which people can accumulate points to exchange for merchandise or other tangibles. You may want to run it for three months or six months, but state the ending date.

Generally, you will probably want to leave open the possibility of renewing. In other words, you may say, "The program will end on June 30, at which time we will evaluate the results and if it is working well and every-

body is enjoying it, we will make a decision about continuing it."

KEEP REINFORCEMENT CONTINGENT ON PERFORMANCE

When using intermittent schedules, managers often do not make their reinforcement contingent on performance. Reinforcers should always be contingent upon desired performance. This principle is violated especially when variable schedules are used.

As you recall, on variable schedules reinforcement is a surprise to the performer. The everyday definition of surprise is different from its definition within a schedule of variable reinforcement. Usually, a surprise is something that is totally unexpected. This is not true of reinforcement on variable schedules. People often expect reinforcement even if it is on a variable schedule. This is illustrated by sayings like, "If you work hard enough, you will eventually be successful." They know they will be reinforced, but only if they are performing at or above some desired level. What they don't know is exactly when the reinforcement will come.

When managers confuse the everyday definition of surprise with the surprise of a variable schedule, they spring reinforcement on others for no apparent reason. The reinforcement does not follow any particular level of performance. Sometimes it may actually follow poor performance. The result of this misuse of reinforcement is the gradual deterioration of performance and morale. You must plan when and what you are going to reinforce.

The contingency requirement is often violated when people use fixed interval schedules. As noted earlier, on interval schedules there must be a response before reinforcement is delivered. If positive reinforcement occurs without any responding on the part of the performer, it is called a **fixed time (FT)** or **variable time (VT)** schedule. Catania (1984) differentiated these two non-contingent schedules from the contingent schedules, FI and VI. On fixed- and variable-time schedules, reinforcement is response independent. That means that reinforcement comes no matter what the performance or behavior. Birthday presents, Christmas presents, and other holiday presents are usually given independent of the behavior of those receiving the presents. In business most benefits such as holidays, pay raises, and health insurance are practically always FT or VT. The problem is that these schedules typically produce, at best, superstitious learning. Superstitious learning refers to behavior that is learned through accidental or chance reinforcement. Obviously, these schedules should be avoided.

When using FI or VI, you must be careful not to let them deteriorate into FT or VT. "Employee-of-the-Month" programs, as mentioned earlier, are classic examples of this non-contingent, pass-around type of schedule. With FT and VT schedules people are simply reinforced for being on the payroll. In a productive enterprise, the mere passage of time is rarely an appropriate reason for positive reinforcement.

CONCLUDING REMARKS

As you have learned from this chapter, the proper understanding and application of schedules of reinforcement will create the most productive and satisfying place in which to work. The subject is very complex and this chapter has exposed you to only the most basic aspects. Hopefully, many readers will want to learn more about the subject by referring to the listed references.

9

Dealing with Unwanted Behavior

When people do things that are unsafe, unhealthy, or unfair, they cannot be ignored or allowed to continue. When people do things that are annoying, disruptive, or counterproductive, they can be ignored but that may not solve the problem. These are cases in which the consequences of punishment or extinction are indicated.

Remember that punishment and extinction decrease behavior (Figure 9.1). Punishment occurs when a behavior is followed by a consequence the performer doesn't want. Extinction occurs when a consequence the performer wants is removed or withheld. Punish-

ment and extinction only stop or decrease behavior. Stopping an undesirable behavior does not mean that a desirable one will replace it. That is why many people who stop smoking gain weight. Reducing one bad habit (smoking) increases another (overeating). Frequently, punishing one unsafe act results in the person doing another unsafe act; or stopping one quality shortcut results in another.

While effective in decreasing or eliminating behaviors, punishment and extinction provide no new behaviors to replace the old, troublesome ones. To avoid the problem of replac-

Figure 9.1

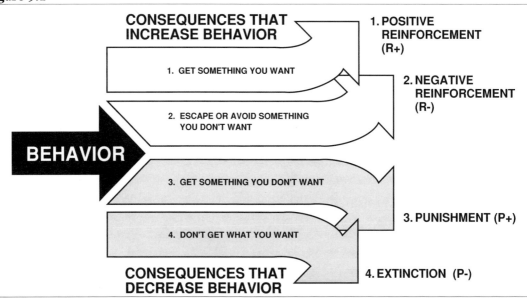

CONSEQUENCES THAT INCREASE BEHAVIOR

1. GET SOMETHING YOU WANT

2. ESCAPE OR AVOID SOMETHING YOU DON'T WANT

BEHAVIOR

3. GET SOMETHING YOU DON'T WANT

4. DON'T GET WHAT YOU WANT

CONSEQUENCES THAT DECREASE BEHAVIOR

1. POSITIVE REINFORCEMENT (R+)

2. NEGATIVE REINFORCEMENT (R-)

3. PUNISHMENT (P+)

4. EXTINCTION (P-)

ing one bad habit or behavior with another, you can use either correcting or differential reinforcement techniques.

Correcting consists of punishing the undesirable behavior and reinforcing the desirable performance. **Differential reinforcement of alternative behavior** (**DRA**) involves extinction of an undesired behavior and reinforcement of a desired behavior.

CORRECTING

The only reason to use punishment in a business or other setting is to increase the person's future reinforcement. Therefore, if you use punishment on an undesired behavior, you must be prepared to reinforce a constructive alternative. An illustration of the effect of reinforcing a constructive alternative behavior appears in Figure 9.2.

In common usage, the word punishment often refers to some physical act, such as spanking a child or restricting movement such as "grounding" a teenager or putting a criminal in prison. None of these are appro-

priate in the Performance Management context.

Punishment in this context simply means any active consequence that reduces behavior. It could be a frown, disagreeing with someone's idea, a verbal reprimand, criticizing a presentation, or any of a million other things that happen to people that they don't like. Sometimes punishment is done deliberately; other times accidentally. In either case, if it results in a behavior or performance decrease, it is technically called punishment.

Don't confuse punishment with a threat. Simply telling people they will be reprimanded is usually not punishment. It is simply an antecedent. Threats do tell what the punishment will be, but threatening to punish seems to happen much more often than actual punishment. Some people threaten punishment all the time and never follow through. In such cases, the threat has practically no effect on the behavior in question.

The only way a threat can be considered a punisher is if it follows some undesirable behavior and decreases or stops that

Figure 9.2

EXAMPLE OF RELATIVE EFFECTS OF PUNISHMENT AND DIFFERENTIAL REINFORCEMENT ON RESPONDING

The graph shows the relative effectiveness of punishment when no alternative response is reinforced. Line A is a behavior occurring at a high and steady rate. Line B shows that when the behavior is punished, and no alternative response is reinforced, there is a reduction in the rate of occurrence. However, when the behavior is punished and an alternative response is reinforced the rate of the original behavior dropped to zero. (*Adapted from W.K. Honig, 1966, Operant Behavior; Areas of Research and Application, New York, Appleton-Century Crofts, Inc., p. 404. Reprinted with permission.*)

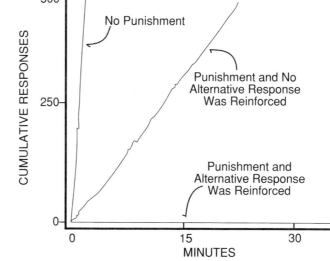

behavior. Suppose you catch someone in an unsafe act, and you say, "If I catch you doing that again, you will be fired." If she never does it again, then the threat acted (technically) as a punisher for the unsafe act.

When to correct performance

Performance must always be corrected in the following circumstances:

1. When a performance is unhealthy, physically dangerous, or life-threatening to the performer or to others;
2. When someone is doing things that are destructive to the organization, such as being dishonest or unfair;
3. When you catch someone in the act of some undesired performance.

While these are not the only circumstances that indicate punishment, failure to use punishment when these do occur in a business situation can result in negative consequences for management and the organization. For example, if a supervisor sees someone doing something unsafe and says nothing and the person is injured later, the employee may bring legal action against the supervisor and the company for not taking the proper action to secure a safe work place.

It is fairly obvious to most people that you cannot ignore dangerous acts. If you see someone walk on a moving conveyor belt to avoid walking around it and you know that several ankles have been broken in the past by such behavior, you cannot ignore that behavior but must correct it every time it happens.

If you see someone lifting something in a manner that is likely to result in a back injury, you must correct the situation as it could pose a serious health risk to the person. If people are overexerting themselves, even to the ultimate benefit of the company, you must do something to stop it.

Judgments about unfair behaviors are generally more subjective than those about observable actions, but some are fairly clear. In this context, behavior that is unfair includes not only that directed toward other employees, but also toward customers and the company. Unfair would include any act of dishonesty such as lying, cheating, and stealing. Of course, most people don't have a problem understanding the necessity of applying punishment in these cases. But there are other cases where people are unfair that are equally demanding of swift negative consequences.

Any act of discrimination should be dealt with immediately. Sexual harassment has received much attention in the work place lately, and rightly so. Such behavior can have serious consequences, not only to the person being harassed, but to the organization as well. When you have knowledge of such behavior you must take immediate steps to prevent its future occurrence.

You also need to correct an employee any time you witness them engaging in undesirable or inappropriate behavior. For example, suppose you overhear an employee talking rudely to a customer or you bump into someone leaving work early without permission (and in both cases the person is aware you saw this behavior).

You might think that if you do nothing the performance won't be repeated so you shouldn't make a big deal of it. But in all of these cases, doing nothing is doing something. Your silence may be interpreted as your consent and consequently may act as an inadvertent reinforcer for the behavior you don't want.

Guidelines for correcting

"Correct" correcting is not easy. To decrease unwanted performance you must pay careful attention to several guidelines. While following the guidelines, you will discover that you really are correcting performance, not simply punishing it. You are helping people do the right thing as well as reducing the chance that they will perform in an undesirable way.

Point 1: Always specify the performance being corrected

The first step in correcting performance is to pinpoint the problem behavior or performance and the correct or desired performance. It is not enough just to point out what someone is doing wrong. You must also specify clearly what behavior is needed. For example, it is better to tell the ward secretary on a hospital floor that the physicians' orders are not being posted on the patients' charts within the ten-minute standard than to tell him that he is wasting time. Pinpointing the performance that needs to be changed and letting the performer know what you want reduces the emotionality of your interactions. The performer is less likely to get defensive when he is asked to change a specific performance than when reprimanded in vague and general terms.

Point 2: Use data

Use data when you correct. Ideally, information of this sort should have been available as feedback all along; however, this is often not the case. For example, the ward secretary should have received regular feedback on his accountabilities. In the absence of this information, the head nurse must accumulate specific data before correcting him. She must be able to say something along these lines: "For the last three days you posted orders on time only 56 percent of the time."

The important thing to remember in collecting data for correcting is to collect data on the performance you want as well as for the performance you don't want. Build a case for improvement, not for dismissal. If you use data in this way, you also achieve the significant advantage of focusing attention and correction on the performance, not the person. When your correction is specific, individuals realize that you are referring to what they did, not who they are—an important distinction. People are much more likely to change their performance if they believe

that your criticism is not personal.

Another important use of data is to confirm that what we think is a punishing consequence is, in fact, punishing. As noted in Chapter Three, what we think is punishing may in fact be reinforcing! Suspension may be the equivalent of a free day off for some people, or reprimanding someone publicly may make him feel good that he really "got your goat" by making you lose control. Only careful monitoring of data on the performance you are intending to punish will let you know for certain whether you are, in fact, using punishing consequences. If the person keeps repeating the infraction, you may very well be using the wrong consequence.

Point 3: Provide reinforcement for what you do want

Of all the guidelines for correcting, this is the most important one. If you only punish what you don't want and don't reinforce what you do want, improvement in performance is unlikely. People perform in undesired ways because they are reinforced for doing so. If your punishment works and they stop the undesired behavior, they will behave to obtain reinforcement in other ways. Ideally, you should be ready to substitute new sources of reinforcement for desired behavior.

To provide reinforcement for the behavior you want, you must first pinpoint the behavior you want. Often what you want is a performance that is incompatible with the unwanted performance.

An incompatible behavior is one that cannot occur at the same time as the behavior targeted for change. Examine the list in Figure 9.3. You can't be working at your work station and taking breaks at the same time. Therefore, if you increase being at the work station, you will automatically reduce excessive breaks.

The key, however, is to identify what you want, even if it is not fully incompatible with the undesired performance. Be prepared to provide reinforcement for desired performance before you punish the unwanted

Figure 9.3

EXAMPLES OF INCOMPATIBLE BEHAVIORS

Unwanted behavior that needs to be stopped	Desired incompatible behavior
Takes too many breaks	Working at work station
Arrives late too often	Arrives on time
Unsafe acts	Working safely
Always negative about changes	Makes positive statements about changes

performance.

Point 4: Correct immediately

Consequences are most effective when they are delivered during or immediately after the behavior. Just as you should try to reinforce immediately, you should also administer punishing consequences during, or immediately after, undesired performance.

In their day-to-day actions, many managers violate this guideline. When they attempt to correct someone's behavior with a delayed consequence and the performance doesn't change, their solution usually is not to make the consequence more immediate, but more severe.

Correcting is most effective when the person is caught in the act. As was pointed out earlier, when you bump into someone doing something wrong, you should correct immediately. Of course, this doesn't happen often, and once people are caught and punished, it will be much harder to catch them again. In contrast, once you "catch" people doing something right and reinforce them for it, they will try to be caught next time. People want to receive reinforcement.

Unfortunately, grievance procedures,

company and government regulations, and increasing employee litigation all make it difficult to respond immediately to instances of undesired performance. Still, the longer the delay between the occurrence and the consequence, the less effective the correction will be.

Point 5: Don't correct when angry

Never attempt to correct while you are angry. It's better to delay punishment and deliver it calmly than to deliver it immediately while you are upset. There are at least three reasons for this:

First, when you are angry, you are likely to say things you don't mean or can't follow through on. In anger, we tend to use "hollow threats," instead of simply stating the real consequences of the unwanted performance. In correcting you should never threaten.

Second, correcting in anger may reinforce the very performance you want stopped. The person may find it very reinforcing to see you get upset. When you get angry at people, they usually get angry in return. Obviously no one wins in such a situation.

Third, your anger may prompt the person being corrected to offer excuses or denials.

For example, suppose you say, "How many times do I have to tell you that we don't have enough engineers? When are you personnel people going to get off your rear ends and get some in here?" The response may be, "Don't you know anything about what's going on in the outside world? There is only one engineer for every five jobs. And, furthermore, your attitude certainly doesn't help our recruiting efforts."

The calm manager is more likely to be able to say something like, "What do you think we can do to increase the number of engineers available for the Kosmas project?" The personnel director may still respond, "There are not that many to go around." But the manager whose judgment is not affected by anger can make an appropriate response like, "You're right, Joanna. But what can we do to at least get our share?"

Point 6: Be consistent

When you state the consequences of a particular behavior, you must be willing to follow through. It is important to deliver the consequence for every instance of the problem performance. If you punish a performance once, you should punish it when it happens again. Inconsistent follow-through will weaken your correcting efforts.

Point 7: Maintain a ratio of 4:1

Correcting is aided by maintaining a high ratio of reinforcement to punishment. Make the work environment reinforcing. Maintain a ratio of at least 4 to 1. Reinforce all behaviors that deserve it. This practice makes any instance of punishment that much more prominent by contrast. In this kind of environment, people notice the punishment more because it is in stark contrast with all the reinforcement they receive for their accomplishments.

Maintaining a minimum ratio of 4:1 also predisposes people to accept correction. Knowing from experience that the boss has your best interests at heart, you view correc-

tion as an attempt to help you grow, rather than as a put-down. The more reinforcement people receive, the more secure they become about their abilities. The more secure they are about their abilities, the more open they are to correction.

If punishment is effective, you will seldom need to use it. If punishment is used too frequently, people may become insensitive to it. The only recourse then is to increase the severity of the punishment, and it's always best to prevent the situation from reaching that point.

Point 8: Do not use the sandwich method

The sandwich method, described in Chapter Six, is a punisher put between two reinforcers. As pointed out, this is an ineffective way to correct performance. Sandwiching detracts from the reinforcement value of the positive comments and diminishes the corrective value of the punishing consequences.

Correcting involves the use of both positive reinforcement and punishment, but they are used at separate times on different behaviors. If you punish an undesirable response on one occasion, you should reinforce the desirable or correct behavior on another occasion. You don't reinforce what you want and punish what you don't want in the same breath. These activities should follow the behaviors they are intended to affect.

Point 9: Never correct publicly

If providing positive reinforcement for the desired behavior is the most important guideline in correcting, this one is the second most important. Don't tell people they are doing wrong in front of other people. Make sure that when you correct someone, other people can't hear you. Ideally, others should not even see the interchange. When possible, ask the person to join you in a private area where the problem can be discussed.

Correcting in public embarrasses the person being corrected. While public embarrassment might seem to be a small punisher, it is not. Few things at work are more punishing than to be criticized in front of your peers. In fact, more often than not, public criticism will set up revenge as a positive reinforcer. Everybody is aware of the wasted and counterproductive time spent by people trying to "get even" following public punishment. Public punishment creates another equally serious problem. Since everybody fears being humiliated, if a manager humiliates others, peers will side with the person being punished, even if they feel that punishment is needed. This is often indicated when you hear people say things like, "That was no reason for her to do a thing like that!" or "If he ever does that to me, I'll quit."

The feeling that fellow employees are being punished unjustly or in an unnecessarily cruel way can lead to grievances and walkouts in union environments and to establishing unions in non-union work places. Some managers believe that an advantage of public punishment is that it sets an example for others. Aside from the moral issues involved in such a strategy, the negatives generated by

Figure 9.4

GUIDELINES FOR CORRECTING

1. Always pinpoint the behavior being corrected.
2. Use data to:
   a. build a case for improvement, not for dismissal;
   b. focus correction on behavior, not the performer;
   c. confirm that the consequence is a punisher.
3. Provide reinforcement for the desired behavior.
4. Correct immediately, when possible.
5. Don't correct when angry.
6. Be consistent.
7. Maintain a ratio of 4:1.
8. Do not use the sandwich method.
9. Never correct publicly.

such action more than cancel any benefit derived from it.

The guidelines for correcting are summarized in Figure 9.4.

THE NEGATIVE SIDE EFFECTS OF PUNISHMENT

The side effects of positive reinforcement are positive, but the side effects of punishment are negative and numerous. Clearly, punishment is a costly procedure. This is why the emphasis must be on preventing performance problems rather than correcting them. A discussion of some of the side effects of punishment follows.

Punishment creates escape and avoidance behavior

If people are being punished, they will try to escape it. When they have been punished, they will try to avoid it in the future. As you know, the escape and avoidance behaviors are maintained and strengthened through negative reinforcement.

Escape and avoidance behaviors take many forms. People may become defensive, blame others, blame equipment, or blame materials. They may lie and cheat, or hide when they see the agent of punishment coming; they may be absent or they may quit. They may be cautious to the point that they reduce production. They may delay turning in reports and doing paperwork, fearing criticism or other punishment. They may counterattack by criticizing the person doing the punishing. When you see these behaviors occurring, you should question the source of the punishment, its appropriateness, and its effectiveness.

Punishment may decrease desired as well as undesired performance

As with positive reinforcement, punishment may generalize from the behavior being punished to other behaviors. In other words, by punishing undesired behavior, you unintentionally may punish some desired behaviors as well. For example, a part of an engineer's job was to visit all the plants in her division and report on quality procedures. The engineer was very thorough, and on her own initiative prepared detailed reports. When she reported to the boss, he liked the report; but, unfortunately, he always criticized something about each one. After a while she never seemed to have time to do the write up for the boss. The boss liked the reports and his criticism was only intended to "help her improve her note taking," but she generalized the criticism to the act of reporting as well.

We have all been in meetings where the boss criticizes several people's input at the beginning of the meeting, only to have the meeting continue with no voluntary contributions. She may have only meant to criticize *what* they were saying, but it generalized to *all* verbal behavior as well.

Those who have been in the army learn quickly to "never volunteer!" Those who do always seem to get more or harder work. When punishment is used frequently, initiative, creativity, and extra effort are substantially reduced, if not absent. We have all heard people make statements like, "I only do what I'm told." While many might interpret this as lazy or a bad attitude, it simply may be the person has experienced more punishment than reinforcement from attempts to do more than was required.

One of the cardinal rules of brainstorming is: Do not evaluate. Leaders of this activity have learned that if you criticize some aspect of an idea, you will get fewer of them. If you reinforce all the ideas, you will get more of them.

Courtney Mills relates an amusing incident:

When I was consulting with a newspaper, the advertising department had one room with about 50 people who took want ads over the telephone. There was a microphone on the supervisor's desk up front that was to be used for passing messages only. The department manager came in one day and saw one employee not working. He picked up the microphone and said, "You people get off your tails and get back to work." One person went back to work and 49 people stopped.

The 49 people who were working began looking around to see who was being chastised, interrupting their work. How much more effective would it have been to deal specifically with the person individually and privately?

Punishment never increases performance

Probably the most compelling reason that punishment should not be used alone is that punishment does not increase performance. Punishment doesn't teach any new skills or increase any performance. At best, it is a stop-gap measure. Punishment does not solve a performance problem; it only gets you in a position to take positive action.

Punishment increases aggression

When people are punished, they may react aggressively. They may attack verbally or sometimes physically. The aggression may be overt or it may be covert—overt in that they may do something like tear up a report, make verbal threats, or actually hit someone; covert in that they may sabotage or even steal to "get even." Sulzer-Azaroff and Mayer (1977) report a laboratory study in which subjects receiving mild electric shock showed a 900 percent increase in aggressive behaviors. Should punishment-induced aggression occur, be sure it does not get reinforced.

Punishment is difficult to utilize effectively

Azrin and Holz (1966) have identified 14 guidelines to follow to use punishment effectively. When correcting performance, you need to follow not only the guidelines for punishment, but also those for selecting and delivering reinforcers outlined in Chapters Five and Six. In other words, proper correcting involves many considerations and activities. Because there are so many steps, there are many opportunities to make a mistake.

A mistake when administering punishment is much more serious than one made while administering reinforcement. If you attempt and fail to reinforce someone for a desired performance, the worst that can happen is that the performance doesn't change. If you deliver a punishing consequence improperly, one or more of the negative side effects discussed earlier may occur. However, even when you punish effectively, you may get unwanted side effects.

People often make the mistake of using something they think is punishing when it is not. It is not advisable to test a punisher. With positive reinforcement, you can easily try something with few, if any, negative side effects. If you said to a person or a group, "I wanted to try this [reinforcer] to see how you like it," the response to your efforts would probably be positive. However, if you said, "I wanted to try this to see how punishing it is," it doesn't take a genius to know that the best response you would get is that people would think you were stupid.

A classic example of this happened with a plant housekeeping program. The "punisher" for the department with the worst housekeeping got the "Eight-Ball Award." The "Eight-Ball Award" was a large cardboard mock-up of a billiard ball. The award was displayed in the department for a month. In addition, the employees had to pose for a picture with their heads sticking out from "behind the eight ball." The picture was published in the plant newspaper. On some slow news months, it even made the front page.

Before you read further, guess the effect this "punishing consequence" had on housekeeping. (Hint: The people in the picture were always smiling.)

Poor housekeeping probably received more reinforcement than all the productive work in the plant. You might imagine that the plant management focused considerably more attention on what was not accomplished or what was wrong than what was right. Although people did not necessarily try to get the award, they certainly didn't seem to mind.

When management was asked about the program, they replied, "They really hate to get that." How could they be so wrong? For one thing they believed that what would be embarrassing for managers would be so for everybody. Secondly, they had no data. They went on what they believed would happen, rather than measuring what actually happened. All they knew was that somebody got the award every month, so the program must be working. Although this might be an extreme example, we've seen many variations on this theme in offices and plants throughout the country.

Another variable that makes punishment difficult to use is the fact that intense punishment is more effective than mild punishment. Many people have trouble administering any form of punishment, but delivering intense punishment is distasteful to almost everybody. Generally speaking, we tend to start with the mildest punishment we can think of and gradually move to more and more severe punishment. However, when mild punishment is gradually increased in intensity, it tends to lose its effectiveness because people will adapt to it.

Sulzer-Azaroff and Mayer (1977) state, "Individuals appear to adapt easily to very mild aversive stimuli that are presented repeatedly and to those that are gradually increased in intensity (as many teenagers adapt to loud music), whereas the effects of strong aversive stimuli appear to be more enduring."

This finding has been reported by many others as well. It brings into question the progressive discipline programs in which offenses such as absenteeism are subjected to increasingly more severe consequences, finally resulting in termination. Would more people be helped if only one consequence existed? Only the data can tell us. If these problems are not enough to convince you of the difficulties involved in using punishment effectively, consider the following. The success of punishment also depends on the amount of reinforcement the person is receiving for the punished activity. For example, an avid duck hunter may miss work on the first day of hunting season, knowing that there will be negative consequences at work. Mild punishment by a supervisor will probably be offset by the reinforcement of his hunting buddies and by shooting the ducks.

For an interesting variation on how one might handle the problem of chronic absenteeism with a bit of novel negative reinforcement, refer to the sidebar below.

WHY IS PUNISHMENT SO POPULAR?

With all the problems associated with punishment, you would think that it would rarely be used. Yet daily examples can be given from almost every work environment. Why do we so often resort to punishment to solve a problem? The answer lies, of course, in the consequences to the person using punishment.

When you use punishment, if it is going to work, it will work right away. That is, the behavior will stop, at least temporarily. If the behavior stops, that is what you wanted. The

---

Novel Use Of Negative Reinforcement

We often use antecedents for which there are no certain consequences, either by failure to communicate these consequences, or failing to actually follow through on the consequence once it has been stated.

Take the example of a southwestern manufacturing plant which had serious problems with absenteeism. Company policy stated that excessive absenteeism would result in review, and if continued, termination. These were the consequences stated in the policy manual.

The catch—the plant was new, which meant training people and keeping them there once they were trained in order to get production rolling as fast as possible. Employee turnover had to be kept to a minimum. As a result, management was willing to compromise "within reason" on absenteeism to avoid turnover.

However, once production was up, the absenteeism rate remained so high it was a problem.

One manager took hold of the situation with an employee who frequently enjoyed his "bachelor status" and missed a lot of work due to late nights. The manager sat down with the employee and plotted his termination date! By using the standards set by the policy manual, the manager figured that if his absenteeism continued at the present rate he would be fired for excessive absenteeism (on the date printed on the graph for the performer to see). Weekly the employee sat down with his manager to see how the date was changed by his attendance during the past week. Increased attendance moved the date further out in the future and poorer attendance moved the date closer to the present. By actually seeing the date he would be let go, the employee had a clearer picture of the consequence. His attendance improved immediately. Negative reinforcement increased his attendance. It should be noted the manager also used small tangibles such as coffee and doughnuts to reinforce good attendance and often made positive comments on the employee's improved attendance.

J. DANIELS

use of punishment gets reinforced. In other words, you receive a PIC for using punishment. This is the "punishment trap." Having received a PIC (positive, immediate, certain) for punishing, the probability that you will use it in the same or similar circumstances has been increased. By contrast, when you reinforce, you rarely see immediate results.

When you reprimand those who are doing something wrong, they will usually stop immediately. If you reinforce someone who has done something right, you will usually have to wait for some period of time to see if the reinforcement worked. This is why many people mistakenly think punishment is more effective than reinforcement in solving problems.

Punishment is reinforcing to the one punishing, not only because it works but because you don't have to do it as often as reinforcement. With punishment, you can just sit back in your office and wait for problems to be brought to you. This is called "management by exception"—when people do something wrong, go out and let them have it; any other time, ignore them. People don't foul up as often as they perform adequately. So a good deal of your time can be devoted to other things, like solving the problems generated by the negative side effects of using punishment. This is called "crisis management." The crisis manager never runs out of work.

Many managers realize the shortcomings of punishment but don't know how they would solve their problems if they decreased their use of it. They will likely continue to use punishment but will do it more and enjoy it less. A manager who retired from a maintenance superintendent's job at an auto plant said in a speech to new supervisors, "In my 35 years in this plant I can remember the names of about 50 people who were really no-good. They continually caused problems. I can remember about 10 who were really outstanding. But the thing that bothers me is that I can't remember the names of the hundreds of people who helped me be successful during my career here. I hope you

don't retire with that burden on your conscience as I have." He was implying that he wished he had expressed his appreciation to the people who had helped him.

When people experience success with positive reinforcement, they will often make dramatic changes in long-standing patterns of relating to people on the job. One supervisor, after learning PM, withdrew her retirement papers. A retired safety manager, who returned to participate in auditing "safe behavior" in a PM safety program, remarked that he was popular for the first time in his career because his presence now signaled positive reinforcement rather than punishment.

DIFFERENTIAL REINFORCEMENT OF ALTERNATIVE BEHAVIORS

Differential reinforcement of alternative behaviors (DRA) involves withholding reinforcement for the undesired performance (extinction) and positively reinforcing the desired one. Extinction generally takes longer to decrease a behavior than punishment does, sometimes much longer. However, the negative side effects are considerably less with extinction than with punishment. The amount of time required for extinction is a primary consideration in choosing to use differential reinforcement over punishment. All things being equal, we would always choose DRA. It is easier on the performer, less time consuming, and has fewer negative side effects. It is, however, not always the appropriate choice.

When to use DRA

For certain behavioral problems, withholding your attention when the unwanted behavior occurs and reinforcing an appropriate one can be a very effective way to change performance. This will work if your attention is the reinforcer that is maintaining the unwanted performance. The key is that your attention is a consequence over which you have full control. You can give it or you can withhold it. If you don't have control of the reinforcer, or can't influence it, DRA will not work. There are numerous behaviors at work that are maintained by consequences that you don't control.

Peer reinforcement is one of these consequences. When people regularly horse around and their fellow employees enjoy their antics, withholding your attention will do little to stop this behavior. You may stop smiling or not look at what is going on, but if the other employees laugh and talk about it, the behavior will likely continue. Correcting will be more effective than DRA in such cases. You should use differential reinforcement only when you have control over the major reinforcers for the unwanted behavior.

DRA is also not the method to use for dealing with behavior that is unsafe, unhealthy, or unfair. When these behaviors occur, they must be stopped as soon as possible. Correcting is recommended in these cases because it produces quicker results than DRA.

DRA works best on behaviors that can be tolerated during the extinction process. Nuisance behaviors and negative verbal and social behavior are particularly appropriate targets for DRA. Nuisance behaviors are usually those that prevent other people from performing optimally or that irritate others, such as idle chit-chat in their work area, excessive personal phone calls, and bad manners.

Typical verbal behaviors on which DRA is appropriate are excessive jokes and wisecracks, excessive arguing, complaining and excuse-making, and excessive defensiveness. Everyone argues and complains occasionally or gets defensive; therefore, none of the verbal behaviors listed above are problems themselves. The problems are determined by when or how often these things occur. There are some situations in which arguing is inappropriate; and although practically everybody likes a joke, you can tell too many. In cases where you don't

want to totally eliminate the behavior but want to reduce its frequency, a variation of differential reinforcement is helpful. It is called **differential reinforcement of low rates (DRL)**.

With DRL, reinforcement is delivered if the frequency of the behavior does not go above a particular level. For example, if a person usually disrupts a meeting by telling too many jokes or making wisecracks, his jokes should be ignored unless they occurred at a low level, say one or two. In other words, it is not the joke telling that is the problem, but the fact that no comment is made that he doesn't offer some humorous comment. Therefore, as the leader you might reinforce his more appropriate behavior in the meeting (tell him you appreciate how he conducted himself during the meeting) if the total number of jokes and wisecracks totaled two or less.

Differential reinforcement of alternative behavior is the method of choice for reducing troublesome behaviors. With the few exceptions mentioned, always try DRA before resorting to correcting. Figure 9.5 will help you make a decision about which method to use.

Guidelines for using differential reinforcement of alternative behavior (DRA)

When using differential reinforcement, the following guidelines will help you be more successful in solving your problem.

Point 1: Be prepared for extinction to work very slowly

Extinction is a gradual process. Depending on the reinforcement history of the behavior in question, it could take weeks or months to completely extinguish it. In many cases it will be considerably shorter. As a matter of fact, the more frequently you reinforce alternatives, the more rapidly extinction will occur. In any event, if you choose to use DRA, you must consider your ability to withhold reinforcement from the

Figure 9.5

WHEN TO USE DIFFERENTIAL REINFORCEMENT OF ALTERNATIVE BEHAVIOR: WHEN TO USE CORRECTING

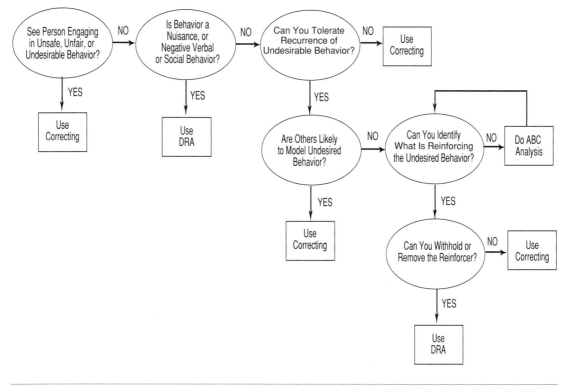

unwanted behavior for a long time.

Point 2: Be prepared for initial increases in unwanted performance—extinction burst

Shortly after extinction begins, there is a predictable increase in the frequency of the unwanted behavior called an extinction burst (see Chapter Seven). The increase can be sudden and dramatic, and if you don't expect it you are likely to think that extinction is not working. In fact, the occurrence of an extinction burst is evidence that you have successfully identified the reinforcer.

The jokester may tell more jokes or the chronic complainer may complain more after DRA has started. However, if the "burst" is not reinforced, the behavior will soon begin to decrease in frequency until it reaches some previous baseline level, which in many cases, is zero.

Point 3: Be prepared for a later recurrence of unwanted performance—resurgence

This is probably the trickiest characteristic of extinction.

Just about the time you think you have solved the problem, the unwanted behavior appears again even though you did not reinforce it. This is a fairly predictable response to extinction.

Even though it was not reinforced, the reappearance of a behavior that has undergone extinction is called resurgence (see Chapter Seven).

Fortunately, if the resurgence is not reinforced, it will be fairly short-lived. The key to long-term success is, of course, to make sure that the new behaviors are getting sufficient reinforcement.

Point 4: Be prepared for emotional behavior

During extinction, and especially during the extinction bursts, you should be prepared for emotional reactions from the individual whose reinforcement is being withdrawn. Occasionally, people become upset and even hostile when their performance is put on extinction. They may talk loudly and aggressively, slam doors, and kick or throw things.

Fear not, however. If you continue to reinforce what you want and ignore these emotional outbursts, they will stop as well as the specific undesired behavior you originally wanted to stop.

Point 5: Once you stop reinforcing the problem behavior, don't start again

When you decide to withhold reinforcement for the unwanted behavior, your determination should remain firm. In other words, once you begin extinction, you should never reinforce that behavior again. This is the most important guideline for extinction.

If you ignore behavior on some occasions and reinforce it on others, you are in effect putting the behavior on an intermittent schedule of reinforcement. You will recall that intermittent schedules extinguish more slowly than continuous reinforcement, and larger ratios extinguish more slowly than smaller ones. Therefore, by starting extinction and later giving in, you inadvertently increase the ratio, delaying the solution of the problem.

For example, Herb is the most argumentative person you have ever known. Ask him to do something and he'll give you three reasons why it's a bad idea and two reasons why he couldn't do it anyhow. Herb's disagreeableness is reinforced by the attention his manager gives him for it. Whenever Herb begins complaining, his manager sits down with him and has a talk. The talk involves trying to understand Herb's position and getting him to see the necessity of doing the task in question. While this was the appropriate thing to do the first time Herb complained, or even the first few times, it has now reached the point that the manager spends more time with Herb than all the other employees combined. At this point the

Figure 9.6

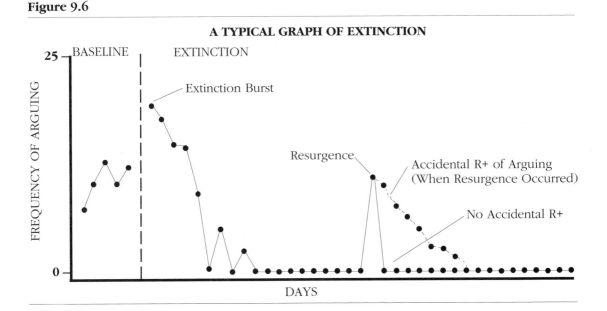

A TYPICAL GRAPH OF EXTINCTION

manager should simply state what she wants and politely excuse herself when Herb starts arguing. In other words, the manager should begin extinguishing Herb's argumentative behavior by withholding her attention, the suspected reinforcer.

If the manager did this we would expect to see results like those represented in Figure 9.6. Notice that on the first day, the rate increased—an extinction burst. However, following this was a gradual decrease, until arguing stopped altogether.

Let's say that after the behavior stopped for some period of time, one day out of nowhere Herb becomes argumentative again. If the manager fails to realize that this is resurgence, she may become fed up with the problem, call him into the office, and "read him the riot act." Unfortunately, this attention may be reinforcing and the behavior may quickly return to pre-intervention levels. Following this, extinction will be even more difficult.

This guideline is like many rules: easy to state but hard to follow. Ignoring the behavior of someone who is doing something wrong is difficult for most people, yet it is essential if differential reinforcement is to work. Remember: the first requirement of differential reinforcement is that you withhold the reinforcer totally. If you can't, don't start.

Point 6: Before DRA begins, explain to the individual why you want to extinguish the particular undesired performance

The importance of giving clear antecedents in all work situations has been stressed throughout this book. It is particularly important when using DRA. Although you may think that people are aware of the problem behavior, always pinpoint the problem with them. You will be surprised to find that many problems obvious to everyone else are unknown to the performer.

In addition to pinpointing the problem, when using DRA you must also pinpoint the desired performance. Just by doing this you will have gone a long way toward solving the

problem. Don't be afraid to spell out exactly what you are doing. Remember, the point of this intervention is to help the performer be successful. If you are not doing anything illegal, unethical, or immoral, there is no reason for not sharing it with the performer.

Point 7: Ignore behavior, not people

You must be careful to ignore the specific behaviors that are problems, not all behaviors. If you ignore people, you not only stop reinforcing a particular behavior, you stop reinforcing everything they do. This is not the correct use of extinction. If people do something wrong and you ignore them, you will produce employees who are lazy and unmotivated. Performance will soon deteriorate to levels just sufficient enough to maintain employment.

Point 8: Reinforce frequently

If DRA is successful, the person will receive more reinforcement in the future than in the past. The more good performance is reinforced, the less time the person will have to engage in undesired behavior. The more time you spend reinforcing the good, productive, quality behaviors that are going on around you, the less time you will have to inadvertently reinforce the wrong things.

Figure 9.7 lists the eight guidelines for using differential reinforcement effectively.

DISCIPLINE AND PERFORMANCE MANAGEMENT

To most people the term discipline implies something negative. When you discipline someone, you apply punishment. When you think of disciplining someone at work, you think of taking serious negative action to correct a problem.

Discipline is usually the last step before termination. Many companies have some form of "progressive" discipline. This means that once a serious problem has been identified, there are several steps before termination. Each step involves what is planned to be a

Figure 9.7

GUIDELINES FOR DIFFERENTIAL REINFORCEMENT
OF ALTERNATIVE BEHAVIORS (DRA)

1. Once you've stopped reinforcing unwanted performance, don't start again.
2. Be prepared for extinction to work very slowly.
3. Be prepared for an initial increase in unwanted behavior (extinction burst).
4. Be prepared for emotional behavior.
5. Be prepared for later recurrence of unwanted behavior (resurgence).
6. Reinforce desired behavior frequently.
7. Ignore the unwanted behavior, not the person.
8. Before extinction begins, explain to the individual why you want to extinguish the particular undesired behavior.

more punishing consequence.

The problem with most of these programs is they do not include reinforcement for improvement, other than "getting to keep your job," which is negative reinforcement. If you use the methods described in this chapter, you will seldom have to take such drastic steps as progressive discipline and termination.

NOTES

10

Pinpointing

CHARACTERISTICS OF PINPOINTS

To be most effective in changing perform-ance, you must be able to describe perform-ance in detail. For example, consider the term "lazy." An employee who is called lazy may come to work late, take long breaks, have a high scrap rate, and not volunteer to help others on the team. All of these things describe the specific aspects of what we call lazy.

Pinpointing is the process of being specific about what people do. The specifics may be either the behaviors of the performer or the results produced by the behaviors. Therefore, pinpoints consist of behaviors and results.

Behavior consists of someone's actions. It's what you actually see if you observe some-one working. The individual may be typing, talking to a customer on the telephone, making a presentation to upper management about a proposed project, drilling holes, or teaching a class. These are all behaviors. Results are the outcomes or products of behavior.

A result is what is left when the behavior is completed. For the behaviors cited above, possible results would be: a typed letter, a satisfied customer, approval for the new project, a board with holes in it, and trainees who can use the new equipment correctly.

Results are pinpointed in order to make sure that we don't occupy ourselves with re-inforcing behaviors that produce no value to the organization. Deming (1986) and his

associates have focused much attention on the fact that if a system is "in control," then it is inappropriate to either punish or reward the performer for changes in the results because they are being produced by normal variation in the system and not by changes in the behavior of the employees. If we have not pinpointed the behaviors we want from the beginning, we will be unable to deter-mine if changes in the results are performer-produced or system-produced.

Another reason to pinpoint results is that without them we get caught up in managing many behaviors that have no useful purpose. Activities that produce no measurable out-come must be called into question if they consume personnel and material resources.

Pinpoints are measurable, observable, and reliable

A pinpoint must have several characteris-tics. For example, anyone can observe and measure the amount of scrap a person produces, the number of miles driven per gallon, the number of milestones met on time, or the amount of time someone spends on the phone. These are clearly measurable and observable results.

Furthermore, measurement of these results needs to be reliable. Evidence of reliability can be obtained by two or more independent observers. The extent to which their measures agree is an estimate of the reliability of the pinpoint.

To check the reliability of a pinpoint, ask

one or more of your peers to measure it independently at the same time you do and then compare your results. If you agree completely, you are quite likely to have a pinpoint. If you do not, then you may want to refine it further. As you will see, pinpoints do not have to be perfect to be useful in solving performance problems or for improving performance. The more reliable they are, however, the more effective your intervention will be.

For example, describe the behaviors that cause you to characterize someone as friendly, courteous, or neat. Then give this list to some peers and ask them to observe the same person at the same time. As you observe, however, don't tell each other what you think. Simply check the items you see that indicate the person is friendly, courteous, or neat. Compare your answers. If you go through this process several times with different people and different observers, you will discover how reliable or unreliable your pinpoints are.

The pinpoints of scrap, miles per gallon, and errors are typical pinpoints frequently measured in business. These pinpoints are results. Writing computer code, stacking boxes, and typing are behaviors. Although behaviors are not usually measured in business settings, they constitute an important category of pinpoints, because behaviors lead to results. We will examine both behaviors and results in detail.

Pinpoints are not interpretations

Pinpoints are not beliefs, attitudes, or anything else internal, subjective, or abstract. Terms such as "motivation," "personality," "morale," "communication," and "rapport" require pinpointing because each of them represents a collection of behaviors and/or results. Over a period of time you observe many different performances from which you conclude that a person is motivated, has a pleasant personality, communicates well, establishes rapport easily, or has high morale.

For example, when people say that a person has a positive attitude, they may be referring to the fact that the person is rarely late or absent, seldom complains, keeps the work area exceptionally clean, takes short breaks, and maintains high quality and productivity. In another example, when someone says that a person works well with others, is congenial, or communicates well, the behaviors they may be referring to are: smiling a lot, saying "yes" and agreeing often, answering questions quickly, using familiar words and expressions, initiating conversations, volunteering to help frequently, and so on.

Once you realize that a "bad attitude" is composed of many behaviors, it is easy to see why people accused of such have a difficult time changing. They may change one or even several behaviors and still not change the one that bothers you.

PEANUTS ®   **By Charles M. Schulz**

(©1958, United Feature Syndicate, Inc.)

Managers frequently use vague terms to describe an employee's performance. They may say that an employee has a poor or negative attitude. When asked what they mean, they say things like: "He has no pride in his work," "He just doesn't care," or "He's just plain lazy."

A person may be labeled "uncooperative" if she frowns when her manager asks her to do something. Labeling in this way does not help correct the problem. But by giving the person feedback on "frowning," the problem is more easily solved than it would be if you only told her she is uncooperative.

All these descriptions summarize a collection of non-specific behaviors. When solving performance problems, people should think in terms of measurable, observable behaviors rather than vague non-pinpointed descriptions of performance. Figure 10.1 summarizes the relationship between behaviors and results.

Sometimes through pinpointing you discover that what you thought was a problem is not a problem, or is not a significant one. For example, a woman complained to her therapist that her husband did not love her. In the process of helping her pinpoint what her husband did that led her to that conclusion, the therapist discovered that her main complaint was that he did not *voluntarily* say, "I love you." The magnitude of this problem was quite different from the one originally stated.

People may suggest that attitudes can be measured by surveys and polls, implying that attitudes can be observed. This approach presents several problems to managers. To measure attitudes reliably, psychologists and test experts need to be consulted—a costly and time-consuming activity. Without a systematic and reliable approach, informal surveys, straw votes, or opinion polls conducted by the manager may produce both invalid and unreliable results.

The most serious problem with measuring attitudes is that people's responses to questionnaires or interviews may not predict their behavior. For example, the most sophisticated techniques were used to analyze voters'

Figure 10.1

RELATIONSHIPS BETWEEN BEHAVIORS AND RESULTS

Summary terms for a collection of behaviors/results	Behaviors	Possible results (the behaviors may or may not lead to these results)
Unmotivated, bad attitude	Being late Being absent Refusing to help others Complaining Arguing with manager	Low productivity Low quality Late shipments/reports
Aggressive, hostile, poor disposition and personality, uncooperative	Frowning, doesn't smile Interrupting Saying no Complaining Ignoring people when they are talking to him Arguing with manager	Customer complaints Cancelled orders

attitudes toward Reagan and Carter before the 1980 presidential election. The polls concluded that voters were almost evenly divided in their attitudes toward the two candidates. Voting was the behavior these attitudes were supposed to predict. However, people's behavior did not express their carefully measured attitudes. Fifty-one percent voted for Reagan and 41 percent for Carter. People's expressed attitudes are often different from their actual behavior. For this reason, manage behaviors, not attitudes.

An employee attitude survey indicates, at best, whether a problem exists. A survey that tells you morale is low only provides the most general indicators of what the problem is. Moreover, the survey tells you nothing about how to solve the problem. Morale is certainly important, but it must be pinpointed if you are charged with improving or maintaining high morale.

Pinpointing is one of the necessary steps to changing behavior, but it is not sufficient alone. Performance Management gives us all the essential steps to changing performance. We have described two of them in previous chapters: 1) providing effective antecedents, and 2) providing consequences that are positive and immediate.

Pinpoints must be under the performer's control

Besides being measurable, observable, and reliable, your pinpoints must be under the performer's control. Persons responsible for pinpointed results must have the major influence on changing the results. That is, their behavior, more than anyone else's, determines the result.

For example, in many organizations human resources departments are held responsible for employee attendance. Yet immediate bosses have at their disposal many more opportunities to reinforce the employee than do people in the personnel department. As such they are more accountable than personnel for attendance. Thus it is inappropriate to hold a front-line supervisor accountable for griev-

ances that result from an industrial relations policy over which the supervisor has no control. Similarly, it would not be appropriate to hold front-line supervisors accountable for quality problems which are due to defective raw materials. When evaluating which pinpoint to focus on, you must ask: Does the performer have the major influence over the behavior or result?

PINPOINT BOTH BEHAVIORS AND RESULTS

Every job has specific behaviors and specific results associated with it. If you can't recognize the difference between them, you might end up managing only results or only behaviors. Either strategy often creates problems in the long run. When you pinpoint behaviors only, you may not always get the desired result. When you pinpoint results only, you may inadvertently reinforce the wrong behaviors.

Some behaviors lead to the desired result and others do not. For example, we often emphasize attendance and short breaks for clerical personnel. Coming to work and taking breaks are behaviors. The poorest performer in the organization could be someone who takes no breaks and has perfect attendance. Without results these behaviors have little value in and of themselves.

Yet, results are often overemphasized. Sales managers typically hold their salespeople accountable for meeting sales quotas. Meeting the quota is a result. The behaviors going into making a sale may be ignored while reinforcing or punishing is based only on the results. Failure to meet a quota is a serious problem in the typical sales organization, and the consequence is usually to punish the performer in some way. But instead of punishing those who are not meeting quotas, managers should tell them what behaviors they should perform to make sales, such as getting lists of prospects, calling them, making appointments, preparing presentations, etc. Then, if they do these things and still don't make sales, they could still get feedback and reinforcement on the improvement in their sales behaviors. Eventually, if they perform all the behaviors at satisfactory levels and the sales are not forthcoming, then the manager should re-examine the pinpointed behaviors.

Pinpointing verbal behavior

People's verbal behavior, that is, what they say to each other, is a very important behavior. Most people want to hear good news. We especially like to hear people say things like "I agree with you," "You're exactly right," and "Great idea." Many people may unknowingly reinforce verbal compliance but punish disagreement. Of course, this causes people to remain silent when they disagree and speak up only when they agree. This creates what has been called "yes men." While no one consciously wants to do this, it is a problem in many organizations. Managers who relate to their employees this way produce subordinates who recycle the manager's ideas, good or bad, and make no contributions of their own. This occurs because the managers are unaware of what they are reinforcing and punishing, often because they have not pinpointed the verbal behavior they want.

Avoid confusing behavior and misbehavior

Behavior has a very narrow meaning for most people. They use it as a term to label problem behavior. Most people associate the term "behavior" with misbehavior. Children who are acting as they should are said to be "behaving" and children who are not acting as they should are said to be "misbehaving." These connotations have carried over to the work place in that we talk of someone who has a behavior problem.

Use of the term behavior in this book refers to all of what people do—good, bad, and neutral.

Distinguish between behaviors and non-behaviors

The best way to learn to distinguish between what is a behavior and what is not is to study many examples. Figure 10.2 lists some typical non-behavioral descriptions used in the work setting, along with some possible behavioral referents.

We should not be surprised that people don't understand what actions they need to take to improve their performance when such non-specific terms are used. What exactly are you supposed to do if you are said to "lack enthusiasm?" On the other hand, if you are told that you need to: 1) volunteer to help others when you complete your assignments, 2) make more suggestions to improve the product or service, or 3) talk more positively about your work, you will know much more about what to do than if you are simply told, "You need to show more enthusiasm."

Pinpoints should be active

Pinpoints can be active or inactive. For example, you might pinpoint a problem as either "attendance" or "absenteeism." Attendance requires an action (behavior). Absenteeism is inactive in that the person does not have to do anything in order *not* to come to work. The difficulty with an inactive pinpoint was explained by Casey Stengel, former manager of the New York Yankees baseball team, when he said, "If the fans don't come out to the park, you can't stop 'em."

It is best to specify active pinpoints because they communicate what we want. Inactive pinpoints like "absenteeism," "zero defects," or "have no accidents" typically tell people what we don't want. People perform best when they know exactly what they should do. Even if people stop doing the wrong behavior, that does not guarantee they will do the correct behavior. For example, many a supervisor has tried to reduce tardiness by punishing people for being late, only to discover that absenteeism increased. If you tell people to stop making personal phone calls, they may stop the calls but talk to fellow employees instead. On the other hand, if you tell them to complete the previous day's invoicing by noon, they will know much more clearly what to do.

A test for whether we have an active pinpoint is the "**Dead Man's Test**" (Lindsley, 1965) which means, "If a dead man can do it (the pinpoint) perfectly, it won't solve your problem." Dead men don't make errors, have accidents, leave their work stations, or upset others. You could have an organization where all these things don't happen, and still have serious problems. We can, in fact, make less errors, have less accidents, not leave our work station, and not upset others by simply *doing nothing*. We hire people for *active behavior*. We want them to produce error-free work, work safely, work productively, and work cooperatively with others. The ability to pinpoint *active* behaviors and performances is often the difference between the success or failure of a Performance Management intervention.

Sometimes, though, we can get by with focusing on inactive pinpoints because the behavior we want is incompatible with the inactive pinpoint. For example, in a plant where the performer does not have control over the quantity of material to be processed

or assembled, as on an assembly line or in a continuous process, you can get away with "reducing waste" as a pinpoint because "reducing waste" automatically increases yield—an active pinpoint.

The active pinpoints that we are interested in involve positive behavior. This provides another reason for using active pinpoints—reinforcing is easier. It is easier to reinforce someone for what you want than for what you don't want. It is easier to say, "Thanks for being here," than "Thanks for not staying home." It is more likely to be reinforcing when you comment on what someone did—"I really appreciate the large number of orders you wrote today"—than commenting on what they didn't do—"I appreciate your not taking so many breaks today."

Pinpointing results

A result is what is left after a behavior is completed. The performers do not have to be present for the results of their behaviors to be observed. For example, testing computer programs for errors is a behavior (actually several). The number of programs tested is a result. You can count the number of programs tested when the performer has gone home. At the end of the day you can look at

Figure 10.2

BEHAVIORS AND NON-BEHAVIORS

Non-Behaviors	**Possible Behaviors**
1. Energetic	1. Completes assignments early; volunteers to help others
2. Responsible	2. Always completes assigned tasks on time
3. Immature	3. Plays practical jokes on friends at work
4. Neat	4. Puts all tools and materials in their proper place
5. Uncooperative	5. Argues with manager; refuses requests to help team members
6. Trustworthy	6. Reports own errors
7. Safety-conscious	7. Performs job, following all safety procedures

a production report and see the number of units produced (a result).

You can distinguish results from behaviors by the fact that, while behaviors are active, results are static and inactive. You can't observe people doing a result; you can only see them perform behaviors. You can't watch someone doing a completed report. The report has already been done; it is completed—a result. You can only examine it (a behavior). However, you can watch individuals writing, typing, editing, and copying a report. These are all behaviors.

Results—like behaviors—must be measurable, observable, and reliable. And results—like behaviors—should be stated in positive terms. For example, run time is better than downtime as a pinpoint. It's more effective to reinforce someone's rate of production ("Your quality production is up over last week. I am really pleased with your progress") than for what she didn't produce ("Your off-quality is down this week, thanks for the effort").

Words and phrases are cues for behaviors and results

In statements that contain both behaviors and results, you will find certain words and phrases that tell you which is which. The most common cues are terms such as:

the number of .... (result follows)
in order to .... (result follows)
so that .... (result follows)
to achieve .... (result follows)
by .... (behavior follows)
through .... (behavior follows)

Examine the following: The number of claims processed without an error (result) can be increased by referring all problem cases to your supervisor (behavior). All problem cases should be referred to your supervisor in order to test the effectiveness of our training procedures (result).

"Ing" words are a clue that a behavior is being described. Thus "filing," "typing," and "writing" are behaviors. Results would be "documents filed," "letters typed," and "reports written." Another way of separating the two is that behaviors are usually in the present tense, while results are described in the past tense. You cannot do a result in the present since a result is something that has been completed or finished. By the same token, behaviors that have been completed are results, at least for purposes of reinforcement.

We usually refer to completed behaviors as a performance. A performance may involve doing the same behavior many times, as in an assembly-line job, or it could involve doing many behaviors, as in playing 18 holes of golf. When we speak of "performance," we mean the sum of the behavior and its results. When we speak of "performance management," we mean knowing not only what was accomplished (the result), but how it was accomplished (the behaviors). This is the only way we will know whether to "celebrate" the result. That is, in order to celebrate we need to know that the result was, in fact, due to changes in the behaviors and not just due to system effects.

Figure 10.3 provides a summary of different ways to differentiate behaviors from results. As described in the beginning of this chapter, the purpose for specifying behaviors and results is to pinpoint the specific performances we want to increase or maintain.

THE VALUE OF PINPOINTING

If you aren't precise in describing the performances you want, you are likely to have problems in applying consequences for the right thing at the right time. Pinpointing is also essential for delivering feedback. People need useful information on how they are doing. That's what feedback is. But only if you have pinpointed their performance can you give people information they can use.

A third value of pinpointing is its communications potential. A pinpointed goal or problem described in terms of specific per-

Figure 10.3

POINTS FOR DISTINGUISHING BEHAVIORS FROM RESULTS

Behavior	**Results**
1. What people are doing	1. What people have produced
2. What you see people do when they are working	2. What you see after people stop working
3. Must see people working	3. Not necessary to see people working
4. Tends to be expressed in present tense, verbs ending in "ing"	4. Tends to be expressed in the past tense by noun-adjective pairings: "documents filed"
5. Cue words: by, through, to	5. Cue words and phrases: in order to, so that, to achieve, to be able to
6. Commonly used terms: input, process, activity, means	6. Commonly used terms: output, product, outcome, achievement, ends
7. Examples: inspecting, designing, conducting meetings, reinforcing, giving feedback	7. Examples: production, yield, run time, milestones met, suggestions made

formance rather than vague generalities allows others to understand and to act on your pinpoint.

A crucial component in PM, the collection of data on performance, requires pinpoints. You can't adequately measure whether you've achieved a goal unless you've pinpointed it first. What would you measure if your goal were not pinpointed, for example, "increased cooperation among shift supervi-

sors?" Only by pinpointing "cooperation" could you eventually know if a training program directed toward correcting such a problem was successfully solving that problem.

As an aid to pinpointing, Figure 10.4 provides a checklist containing the criteria that a pinpoint should meet. Use this checklist to make sure that what you plan to reinforce is pinpointed.

Figure 10.4

CHECKLIST FOR EVALUATING A PINPOINT

Directions: Answer "yes" or "no" to each question. If you have an adequate pinpoint, all the answers to questions 3 through 7 should be "yes." Modify the pinpoint for any "no." If you can't correct the pinpoint, drop it and get a new one.

Pinpoint _____   Name _____

	YES	NO
1. Is it a result? *	____	____
2. Is it a behavior? *	____	____
3. Is it measurable?	____	____
4. Is it observable?	____	____
5. Can two independent counts agree?	____	____
6. Is it under the performer's control?	____	____
7. Is it an active performance?	____	____

*If it is not a behavior or result, it is probably not a pinpoint.

NOTES

11

Measurement

Once you have pinpointed the behavior or performance you would like to change, you are ready to begin measuring. If you have a reliable pinpoint, measurement is easy. The most basic measurement is counting. Pinpoints allow you to count, because the specificity of a pinpoint enables you to determine if the behavior or performance occurs or exists. As you will see, pinpointing allows you to measure many abstract performances or states such as morale, attitude, and creativity. Once you have established the precise behaviors you will accept as evidence of these qualities, counting them is easy.

WHY MEASURE?

Just as we manage organizational performance by data, we should manage human performance by data. If we pinpoint what we want from people, the next logical step is to measure the performances.

In many organizations, problems sometimes arise when we start measuring what people do. People may say things like, "You can't measure what I do," "You don't trust me," or "It's not fair." These comments indicate that the performers have a history in which measurement has been an antecedent for punishment. This is understandable because a lot of what we measure is negative. We measure things like errors, defects, accidents, and waste. Quite naturally people are not delighted when someone suggests

counting the number of errors they make.

One major reason for measuring in a PM system is to increase the appropriate delivery of reinforcement. Measurement allows you to see smaller changes in performance than you would be able to see through casual observation. Seeing these small improvements allows you to reinforce more often. This will guarantee faster change than if you wait until some final result has been attained. Certainly, measurement exposes poor performance, but knowing about poor performance helps us know when improvement occurs so we can positively reinforce.

Progress requires measurement

Measurement is the key to progress. In many areas of past human endeavor, progress was slow until effective measurement techniques were devised. The telescope and microscope generated great advances in astronomy and biology because they allowed better and more precise measurement than was possible with the naked eye. The computer accelerated progress in science, technology, and business for the same reason. Similarly, human performance benefits from advances in measurement because it permits us to detect subtle changes in behavior.

If you don't measure, you don't know if you're going forward, backward, or nowhere. Under those conditions, improvement results from chance, rather than from rational planning and evaluation.

Feedback and reinforcement require measurement

Feedback—useful information on performance—is an essential part of PM. Therefore, the effective application of PM requires measurement. Feedback depends on data—data obtained by measuring relevant performance. How are people to know how they are doing if their performance is not measured?

Optimal performance requires both feedback and reinforcement. Measurement increases the effectiveness of reinforcement because data helps you separate real from apparent change. Without measurement you may think there is an improvement when there is not—or vice versa. Without data you may reinforce the wrong behavior, or reinforce at the wrong time. In other words, data helps you plan when to reinforce. By watching the data, even small improvements can be detected and reinforced when appropriate.

Measurement also helps you identify positive reinforcers by giving you a way to measure the effect of various reinforcers on performance. You may think you have an effective reinforcer, but if the behavior doesn't increase, then it is not a reinforcer. By using measurement you can discover this earlier than you would without it.

Data also will inform you when the value of the reinforcer you have been using is beginning to lose its effect through satiation. If the performance begins to decline over time, data will show that the value of the reinforcer has changed. With data you can correct the problem before a serious deterioration in performance occurs.

Measuring increases one's credibility

A popular saying among some quality professionals is: "In God we trust, all others bring data." When people disagree, the one with the data is most likely to prevail.

People perceive individuals who offer data to support their points as objective and persuasive. Since solutions are often suggested by analyzing data, those with data are more likely to have solutions than those who don't. Those who offer more solutions are more likely to command respect and have more influence in decision making.

Measuring reduces emotionalism, increases constructive problem solving

Using objective, unbiased data on performance reduces emotionalism. People get upset when they don't understand why someone says they are not doing well. Measurement helps us communicate the specifics of performance. If people understand why you've made a particular decision about performance, they're more likely to discuss the decision calmly and accept it than if they think the action is arbitrary.

Managing effectively requires performance data. If you don't have data to support your assessments, you may appear opinionated, subjective, and irrational. When data is continually collected and openly displayed, performance trends become more apparent. This allows the performer to take action to correct problems sooner than would be possible if they did not have measurement.

The introduction of Statistical Process Control methods (SPC) by Shewhart (1939) promoted by Deming (1986) and others has made it possible for companies to make significant improvements in quality. With these measures managers are able to separate variance in the process from variance in the performer. Therefore, when these measures are available, if performance is down as a result of variation in the process that is out of the performer's control, performers are less likely to be blamed for the decrease. Another significant benefit of Statistical Process Control is that the data also will tell performers when to take action to keep their process in control.

Data also increases the probability that you will make the right decisions about promotions, suspensions, performance appraisals, and of course, positive reinforcement. People who have the appropriate data, have a clearer basis for devising effective solutions to problems. For example, displaying data at crew, shift, sales, or other meetings puts the focus on performance, not on excuses.

As a necessary condition for developing and maintaining optimal performance, measurement is one of the key attributes of PM. Yet, if it is so useful, why don't people do it more often?

BARRIERS TO MEASUREMENT

There are a number of reasons that people don't measure. However, most of them can be grouped under the following four headings.

1. Thinking some jobs can't be measured

People often insist that some things can't be measured. This has probably been said in the past about a large number of basic measures in biology, physics, chemistry and other sciences. But if you take the position that everything can be measured, you will discover many more measures than if you take the contrary. Performance measures have been developed in the widest possible range of jobs, from "job shop" operations to research and development organizations.

2. Thinking measurement is hard to work with

While it appears that some performances are harder to measure than others, on closer analysis it is not the measurement that is difficult, but the pinpointing. As you move on the measurement continuum from judgment to counting, you are moving from a vague description of performance to a pinpointed one. Once you determine what you want people to do, the measurement of it is fairly straightforward. It's true that we can measure behaviors more easily than traits. When we want to measure such things as cooperativeness and teamwork, we make little progress in doing so until we

ask questions like, "What do we want the performers to do?" Once that has been determined, measurement is easy.

3. Thinking of measurement as an antecedent for punishment

The most common reason performance is not measured is that in business, measurement frequently is associated with punishment. Performance measurement has often been used to catch those performing below some standard. Those who were performing above standard were usually ignored. Measurement meant accountability and accountability has too often meant punishment. To overcome this problem, once again remember to maintain a ratio of positive reinforcers to punishers of at least 4 to 1. By doing so you will be able to pair measurement with positive consequences much more frequently than with negative ones. When measurement is usually the source of good news, people will look forward to measurement, rather than try to avoid it.

In an insurance company, it was announced that a new department was being formed to develop measures for all clerical jobs—about 1,200 employees. As the corporate job-measurement staff tried to schedule their work, the departments to be measured came up with a myriad of excuses like, "We're not ready; give us some more time," "It's our busy time of year" or, "It makes more sense to start with Dept. A before you do us."

Some months later a PM system was installed. One of the reinforcers the employees could earn for meeting their quality performance goals was time off. The only way to earn the time off was to have a measured job. As you might guess, department managers and section supervisors started lining up at the door of the corporate performance measurement director, asking when their department or section was scheduled to be studied. They actually had to increase their staff to keep up with the demands for developing job measures.

4. *Thinking there isn't enough time to measure*

The comment that has been heard by practically every consultant helping with measurement is: "We don't have time to establish an elaborate measurement system." In the first place, a measurement system doesn't have to be elaborate to be effective. In fact, the rule is: the simpler, the better. Start simple. Add and refine only as necessary.

Often, when people are working under a lot of time pressure, they resist job measurement. This is because other job responsibilities still must be accomplished in the face of the added demands brought on by measurement. Initially, the establishment of a measurement system may require extra time. In the long run it will save time by helping you generate higher performance and by significantly reducing the performance problems that consume so much of your time.

MEASUREMENT CATEGORIES

Four categories of measurement are of most interest to business: quality, quantity, timeliness and cost. Gilbert (1978) includes timeliness as an aspect of quantity. However, with the current emphasis on deliverability and Just-In-Time inventory control systems, we list it as a separate category.

Ideally, all performance should be measured in all four categories. For example, quantity without quality is of questionable value; quality at an excessively high cost cannot be sold; quantity and quality that is late may have no value.

Quality

When we begin to measure the quality of a performance, we find that there are a number of dimensions to be considered. Three are: accuracy, class, and novelty.

Although accuracy is a measure of what we want, errors are probably the more commonly measured aspect of quality. They are usually measured as deviations from specifi-

cations or standard. We typically measure the errors resulting from some deviation in performance and not the performance itself. For example, quality inspection in manufacturing means examining the product for cosmetic and functional defects. Finding a defect in the product does not always tell you what behavior needs changing to correct the error. In fact, *errors are always a measure of something other than the behavior of interest.* In other words, making errors is not what we should be concerned with, rather, doing the job correctly. In PM we usually want to convert "error measures" into "accuracy measures" because "increasing accuracy" is an active performance, whereas "decreasing errors" can be accomplished by doing nothing (inactive).

When you measure the quality of performance on something other than accuracy, you are usually measuring an aspect that Gilbert (1978) calls class. He defines **class** as "comparative superiority of a product beyond mere accuracy." Class is usually harder to measure because it is not as easily pinpointed as accuracy. However, it is often just as important, and in some cases is the only quality measure of interest.

When we are interested in the *way* that someone does something, we measure class. Form, style, manner, and technique all refer to the measurement of class. Although it is harder to develop reliable measures of the class of a performance, there are many that are used and accepted as valid indicators of quality.

Class is the best measure for the quality of many athletic performances. Gymnastics, ice skating, diving, and others have highly sophisticated systems for measuring this aspect of quality. In these sports, accuracy is the major concern in the "compulsory" part of the competition while class is what matters in the "free style" performance. Although to the uninitiated these measures appear totally subjective, they actually contain very detailed lists of pinpointed behaviors. A judge in these sports must have extensive training.

Housekeeping is an item in business situations that is usually measured on class. Customer service is another. A person may handle a customer correctly, technically, but the "way" in which he does it might irritate the customer so much that she won't return. In business situations where we are concerned with the "attitude" aspect of a person's performance, we need to develop a class measure of quality. For example: When waiting on a customer, does a salesclerk smile, make eye contact, talk in a pleasant tone of voice, and thank the customer, rather than simply take the money, throw the purchased item in a bag, and thrust it wordlessly at the customer?

The third aspect of quality measurement is novelty. Novelty is the unusual or unique aspect of a performance. Novelty is not of concern with every performance, but when it is, you need a way to measure it to make sure you get more of the kind of novelty you want. We typically don't want novelty just for the sake of novelty, but toward some outcome. That outcome will help define the measure.

The aspect of novelty is important in jobs such as engineering, maintenance, and computer programming. It is also of considerable interest to suggestion-system evaluators and administrators.

With the emphasis on improving quality that exists in business today, new ways are highly desired, and as such, novel solutions are now more important in all jobs. Examining quality from the perspective of novelty adds an opportunity for reinforcement that would be missed if we only looked at accuracy and class.

Quantity

Of all the measurement categories, quantity is the category most often used. It involves only counting. Counting is usually reported either in terms of frequency (number of occurrences or units) or rate (frequency per unit of time). Rate is usually the preferred performance measure. We want to know not just how many, but how many per minute, hour, or day.

Many organizations have gotten into trouble because they have set up compensation or other reinforcement plans to reward people only for quantity. This is rarely appropriate. As previously stated, reinforcing quantity without reference to its quality practically always causes problems.

Timeliness

This category of measurement is concerned only with *when* something gets done. Meeting deadlines is a measure of timeliness. The crucial performance for a reporter is not just to write stories of good quality, but to write them by some deadline. Similarly, marketing information is often measured not just by amount, but how up-to-date it is.

As mentioned earlier, fast customer service is a priority for companies trying to excel. In customer service, timeliness is one of the most important measures. As a matter of fact, Bill Abernathy, a productivity expert in banking, says the greatest impediment to customer satisfaction in banks is the time customers have to wait in line. The inventory control system introduced by the Japanese, called *Kanban*, or Just-In-Time, puts timeliness at a premium.

Cost

The final measurement category is cost, an area measured in most businesses. Cost accounting typically determines the cost of manufacturing a specific product or delivering a particular service. However, in PM we are primarily concerned only with how much the performance costs. As such we separate raw material costs from the performance costs. Performance cost is determined by measuring the cost of behaviors that add value to the raw material.

We can subdivide these costs in three ways: labor, material and management. Of course, cost is practically always expressed in monetary terms.

Labor includes wage, salary, bonus, commission, benefits, insurance, and taxes involved in the performance. The cost of tangible reinforcers should also be included here. Additionally, all the costs of social reinforcers, such as celebrations, should be added into the cost of the performance. Of course, you would not hold the performers accountable for this aspect of cost since they don't control it.

Material cost includes physical resources like buildings, supplies, machinery, energy and so on. Generally, the only one of these for which the performers are held accountable is supplies, and then, only when the performers have some control over their use.

Management cost reflects the expense of providing the non-material support necessary to produce the desired results. This would include all supervisory costs, secretarial and clerical support, computer support, technical training, and all team and management training provided for enhancing performance.

Although management costs are known, they are rarely separated as a performance cost that can be used to evaluate their effectiveness in aiding performance improvement. With the increased competitive pressure that most firms find themselves under, these costs are being closely scrutinized. Unfortunately, management costs are usually cut before determining value added.

Most managers have experienced that when business conditions soften, the first thing to go is training. But if more training could reduce the cost of the product, management might actually increase these resources.

When some organizations cut back on supervisors, the cost of performance may actually increase because the value added by supervision was more than its cost. Until these costs are known and analyzed as to value added, many mistakes are likely to be made in providing the highest quality product or service at the best cost.

Figure 11.1

SUMMARY OF MEASUREMENT CATEGORIES

Category	Measure
Quality	
Accuracy	Degree of conformity of a measure to a standard or true value
Class	A judgment of the comparative superiority of an accomplishment beyond accuracy
Novelty	Judgment of the degree to which an accomplishment involves a new or unusual combination or variation of objects, words or events
Quantity	
Frequency	Number of occurrences
Rate	Number of occurrences in a given period of time
Timeliness	The degree to which a product or service is completed and arrives at an agreed time and place
Cost	
Labor	Total of all performance and performance-related costs such as wages, benefits, reinforcers, etc.
Material	Total of all material costs related to an accomplishment
Management	Total of costs of supervisory practices and supporting functions

Of course, if they cannot control it you would not hold performers accountable for management cost. As you can see, cost is typically not a relevant measure for front-line performers but is very relevant at the management level. See Figure 11.1.

Which measurement categories are relevant?

Quality, quantity, timeliness, and cost are considerations in every performance. Therefore, you should measure every performance you want to increase or maintain in each of the categories described. It is rarely necessary to measure every aspect of a pinpointed performance. But you must examine the performance in terms of each category before dismissing any as irrelevant.

As stated previously, cost is often not a relevant measure for the performer. In some cases, quantity is not relevant either. On an auto assembly line the number of cars that come down the line during the shift are not under the performer's control.

To determine which measurement categories are relevant for performers, you should ask the following questions for each category:

1. If performance varies on this measure, does it matter?
2. Does actual performance typically vary on this measure?
3. If performance does vary on this measure, is the variation large enough to require action?

As you ask these questions about a particular measure, if you get a "no" to any question, the measure is not relevant for that performance. See Figure 11.2. For example, let's look at a job of putting liners in the trunks of cars. Is quantity a relevant measure for this job? The answer to the first question is "yes." One liner must be put in every car. If it is not, there is a problem.

The answer to the second question is "no." It's almost unheard of that a car would come off the end of the assembly line without a trunkliner. Therefore, we would not need to measure this performer on the number of liners she installed each day.

By going through these questions, you can limit your measures to those that are necessary for the performers to exercise maximum control over their performance. For many organizations, this may mean providing additional measures. However, if the principles discussed in this book are followed, the return to the organization will be considerably greater than the cost.

MEASUREMENT METHODS

There are two major measurement methods: counting and judging. While counting is the preferred because of greater reliability, judgment can be a valid way of measuring; it allows us to get the benefits of measurement in areas that would otherwise go unmeasured.

Counting

Counting is very straightforward. We can count the number of parts made, engineering drawings completed, lines of computer code written, or hours of overtime. Counting is the preferred method of measuring because practically everybody can do it—and with a high degree of reliability. It is easy and usually can be completed in a minimum of time.

Another advantage of counting is that when we do not need to count every instance of a behavior or result, we can sample. **Sampling** involves counting at random times or inspecting random units of production. The process of sampling is highly scientific and as such there are rules about how to select a sample and how many observations or counts constitute a representative sample. Most statistical books cover this subject in detail. Those readers who have been trained in Statistical Process Control are very familiar with sampling methods and processes.

Figure 11.2

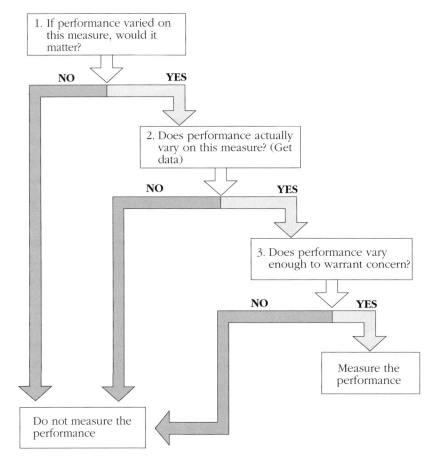

**FLOWCHART FOR DETERMINING WHICH MEASUREMENT CATEGORIES
ARE RELEVANT FOR A PERFORMANCE**

1. If performance varied on this measure, would it matter?

NO   YES

2. Does performance actually vary on this measure? (Get data)

NO   YES

3. Does performance vary enough to warrant concern?

NO   YES

Measure the performance

Do not measure the performance

Sampling errors are common in business and everyday life. We often draw conclusions about both behavior and results based on too little information. If you are not counting every occurrence of something, you must make sure you have counted enough instances to have an adequate sample.

Judgment

When the pinpoints you have selected

can't be made specific enough to permit counting, you can use the judgment technique of measuring. Judgment is the process of forming an opinion or evaluation by discerning and comparing.

Even though judgment is less reliable and more subjective than counting, it has at least two very practical uses in PM. First, judgment allows you to measure any performance. Second, in most cases when you use judgment measures, you discover new ways to count. Counting is nearly always preferred to judgment. However, when you can't count, there are four techniques that are helpful in making judgments about performance. They are:

1. Rank performance based on opinion.
2. Rate performance based on opinion.
3. Rank performance based on pre-established criteria.
4. Rate performance based on pre-established criteria.

These alternatives are presented in the four cells of Figure 11.3. They range from a general opinion about who is better in Cell 1 to a much more specific rating of performance in Cell 4.

When making judgments you need a frame of reference. As a starting point, this reference is usually your experience or point of view—in other words, your opinion (Figure 11.3, Cells 1 and 2). By ranking or putting a number to your opinion, it practically always forces you to be more specific. It causes you to think things like, "Would she rank fifth or sixth? I believe I'll rank her fifth because she is more friendly than Ted when she waits on customers," or "I think Jamie would rank above Jack on 'responsive to customers' because he asks more questions." If each time you rate or rank you get a little more

Figure 11.3

FOUR TECHNIQUES OF MEASURING BY JUDGMENT

TYPE OF COMPARISON		Opinion	Pre-established Criteria
	Ranking	**Cell 1** In my opinion, Laura ranked second in neatness among the ten first-shift mechanics	**Cell 3** Laura tends to pick up debris after her job is done more often than, about as often as, less often than the other mechanics
	Rating	**Cell 2** In my opinion, Laura's neatness was **1** **5** **10** **Poor** **Excellent**	**Cell 4 (BARS)** **10** – Picks up tools and debris, organizes area, wipes surface clean, and cleans safety goggles for the next person **8** – Picks up tools and debris, organizes area, wipes surface clean, and cleans safety goggles for the next person **6** – Picks up tools, organizes them, picks up major debris **4** – Picks up tools, organizes them by major compartment **2** – Picks up all tools

specific, you will be surprised at how quickly you increase the reliability of your judgments.

For example, suppose we have a supervisor who wants to measure a mechanic's neatness but doesn't know exactly how to do it. Let's start by asking him to rate the performer on a "neatness scale" where 0 is the messiest mechanic he has ever known, and 10 is the neatest mechanic he has ever known. Also, at the end of the job, ask the mechanic to rate himself. Have them compare the ratings. If they both agree, the supervisor has some evidence that they are measuring neatness in similar ways.

Most often they won't agree. What the mechanic sees as very good (an 8 on the scale), the supervisor may see as average (a 5). This will immediately cause questions to come up like, "Why did you give me a 5?" or "Why did you give yourself an 8?" The answers to these questions will add more definition to the scale so that with repeated measures their ratings will become remarkably similar.

Over time, this opinion-based measure can be made more objective by specifying distinct criteria for judging performance. Once this happens, judgments can be made on the basis of observation (Figure 11.3, Cell 3 and Cell 4).

Let's assume one element in "neatness" is to clean up the debris produced before leaving the job. This creates what is referred to as a "pre-established" criterion.

Look at the samples in Cells 3 and 4. Note that the determinations about neatness are based on observation, rather than simple opinion. Cells 3 and 4 are still somewhat subjective, but they are much more objective than Cells 1 and 2.

The measure in Cell 4 is called a "Behaviorally Anchored Rating Scale," or BARS for short. Each number on the scale represents a specific set of observable behaviors. This measure is the most objective technique of the four cells in Figure 11.3. BARS are what we strive for in judgment measures. Although we do not always start with a behaviorally anchored rating scale, we can usually develop one for every performance.

As noted in Figure 11.3, we can rank or rate. Ranking involves comparing the performances of individuals against each other (Cells 1 and 3). You simply decide whether the performance you are considering is better or worse than the one closest to it. You are in effect lining up the performers from best to worst.

Using ranked scores may cause problems when the results are fed back to the performers. When you rank how well people do, you distribute performance measures across the full range from best to worst. In other words, you establish only one winner, just as the typical contest does. As discussed previously, if you have only one winner, you limit reinforcement for all other performers, thereby ultimately reducing the overall performance. Consequently, ranking should be used only when ratings are impractical.

Performances are judged independently when using ratings, thus avoiding the problem encountered in ranking systems of limiting reinforcement. In a rating system, all performers could attain a perfect score at the same time.

If your ratings are based on opinion, your labels will be terms like *poor* to *excellent*, or *never* to *very often*. Your judgments involve only your impressions of the performance (Cell 2). If you start out measuring using "rate opinion" (Cell 2), and do not eventually move to "rate pre-established criteria" (Cell 4), your measure is probably not important to the performer. If it is important, the performers will want to know why they received the ratings they did and what they have to do to get a higher score. When you are able to tell them, you will have what you need to develop a "pre-established criterion" scale.

Figure 11.4 is another illustration of the four types of judgment techniques. This example includes only a few of the possible criteria that might be used to measure the value of a suggestion. However, it does demonstrate some of the ways you could measure a "good idea."

Figure 11.4

MEASUREMENT METHODS USING JUDGMENT

Performance To Be Measured: Quality (Class) of an Employee Suggestion

		Opinion	Pre-established Criteria
TYPE OF COMPARISON	**Ranking**	**Cell 1** Of the ten suggestions we received, this suggestion is the best	**Cell 3** — As compared to other suggestions offered by employees, this suggestion is: 1. <u>more likely</u> to be accepted by upper management, <u>about as likely</u> to be accepted by upper management, <u>less likely</u> to be accepted by upper management 2. <u>more likely</u> to work, <u>about as likely</u> to work, <u>less likely</u> to work
	Rating	**Cell 2** This suggestion is 1 5 10 **Poor** **Excellent**	**Cell 4 (BARS)** This suggestion is an improvement on an existing procedure ⊢ 3 This suggestion is a new procedure 2⊣ ⊢ 1 This suggestion is similar to one working in another area

---

1. Point systems

Most organizations use multiple measures of performance. These measures are most often of results. They may include quantity, quality, cost, morale, and others. When two or more different measures are used to evaluate performance, it causes questions like "What do you want—quality or quantity?" With multiple measures, priorities often become confused and communication suffers. Look at Figure 11.5. Which supervisor performed better? It is difficult to tell. Unless you know the relative value of each of the accountabilities, you cannot make an informed judgment. One way to handle this problem is to combine the measures into an index. We do this by developing a point system.

A **point system** is a way of weighting different aspects of a job performance according to their value (priority) to the organization at a given time. A point system shows strengths and weaknesses, while at the same time yielding an overall measure of job performance. Point systems are especially valuable in three types of situations.

The first is where two or more different measures of performance are being used. Suppose a supervisor is measured on the fol-

Figure 11.5

EXAMPLE OF EVALUATING PERFORMANCE USING MULTIPLE MEASURES

Supervisor

Accountability	#1	#2	#3
Production	+	–	+
Quality	–	+	+
Cost	+	+	–
Deliverability	–	–	+
Morale	+	+	+
Safety	+	+	–

+   Met or Exceeded Goal
–   Failed to Meet Goal

lowing results: productivity, quality, yield, attendance, and morale. What does it mean when productivity and quality are good, but yield, attendance and morale are poor? Is the supervisor doing a good job? It could be that she is judged as performing poorly because her boss is currently more interested in yield and morale. The reason for this is the plant manager has just chewed out managers because of increasing manufacturing costs and the plant's poor showing on a corporate morale survey. When these improve the next month, but productivity and quality dip slightly, the supervisor will probably still receive a poor rating because by that time priorities may have changed again.

To the supervisor and manager in the situation above, a point system would be very helpful. One month the boss may say, "We've got to get more production. We must reduce our backlog." The next month she says, "Our yield is terrible. We've got to get these costs under control!" The supervisor may begin to wonder if the boss will ever be satisfied, and wishes upper management would get its act together.

When managers are asked, "Which variable is most important?" the most usual answer is, "All of them!" This can happen only in a perfect world. In our everyday work, people are constantly having to make decisions about where to focus their time and energy. Point systems help people make those decisions.

Point systems are also helpful when many individual numbers are collected under a single category. For example, over the course of six weeks, an employee's performance on productivity or quality may be 100 percent, 95 percent, 88 percent, 92 percent, 97 percent, and 92 percent for an average performance of 94 percent.

The employee may conclude that he is doing a good job because, even though he has had one week in the high 80s, he still performs in the high 90s most of the time. The supervisor, however, may consider any score below 95 to be poor and may put a lot of emphasis on consistency. Consequently, he would be unimpressed with the performance. Using a point system in these situations can clarify standards and expectations.

Figure 11.6 shows how this supervisor might use a point system to communicate expectations better.

A third indicator for a point system is in a situation where goals tend to change frequently. For example, a particular sales quota may be appropriate when the economy is healthy, but much too high when economic conditions weaken. Even though the quota was realistic at the beginning of the year, now only 60 percent of that number would represent a significant accomplishment.

Most people face the situation where monthly objectives and standards are agreed to but later some unexpected project comes down from corporate with an urgent priority. Working on the urgent problem may cause performance against objectives to suffer. However, under a point system, point values could be adjusted to reflect the new priority and if performance were constant, the rating would not suffer. In these situations, a point system can maintain continuity because goals can be changed as often as necessary to

maintain high-level performance.

2. Checklists

A simple checklist of items to be accomplished represents a point system where all items have the same value. Much of the value of such lists is lost when they are not scored. By scoring them you are able to see trends and make adjustments where necessary. When you start with a simple checklist and the scores are correlated with some outcome, it will almost always evolve into a "weighted" checklist. The weighted checklist is one in which some items on the list earn more points than others. This allows you to match reinforcement to the effort or difficulty of the particular demands of the task. Figure 11.7 is an example of such a list for maids in a hotel.

USING POINT SYSTEMS EFFECTIVELY

The following are important considerations

Figure 11.6

ILLUSTRATION OF CONVERTING EFFICIENCY SCORES TO POINT SYSTEMS

WEEK	EFFICIENCY	SCORE	SCALE OF POINTS	
			EFFICIENCY	POINTS
1	92	2	99-100	10
2	97	8	97-98	8
3	92	2	95-96	6
4	88	0	90-94	2
5	95	6	Below 90	0
6	100	10		

Four consecutive weeks at/above 97 = 5 point bonus

CHAPTER ELEVEN

Figure 11.7

EXAMPLE OF A WEIGHTED CHECKLIST FOR HOTEL HOUSEKEEPING

				Page 1

Housekeeping Quality Audit

Property_____   Room Number _____ Date _____

Total Points Earned _____   Points Possible_____

			Point Value
1.	General Appearance (Guest Room)		
	101. Carpet raked and fluffed		30
	102. Beds neat and spreads tight		40
	103. Pictures straight		5
	104. Lamp shades (straight w/seams to back)		5
	105. Towel Presentation		
		01	3 wash towels	10
		02	3 hand towels	10
		03	3 bath towels	10
	106. Vanity Presentation		
		01	mirror clean	25
		02	ice bucket	5
		03	clean ashtray (w/matches)	10
		04	3 bars soap	15
		05	clean wastebasket	15
		06	3 wrapped cups	10
	107. Triplex Presentation		
		01	Bible	5
		02	fresh DIA Directory	5
		03	fresh comment slip	5
		04	clean wastebasket1	5
		05	mirror clean	20
	108. Nightstand		
		01	telephone presentation	5
		02	cords hidden	5
		03	clean telephone book	5
	109. Air Conditioner Top		
		01	reach out	5
		02	ashtray (w/matches)	10
		03	draperies neat, straight, pulled even with a/c top	10
		04	Do Not Disturb sign	5
	110. Lighting		
		01	all lights working	15
		02	all lights turned off	20

(continued)

when formulating a point system.

1. Focus on R+—not punishment

Point systems must be used to deliver positive reinforcement, not punishment. One way to increase the chance that the system will be reinforcing is to allow those whose behavior will be measured to assist in setting it up. In addition, if you do not have a specific plan of what you will reinforce and how you will reinforce it *before* you implement the system, you are asking for trouble.

2. Show small improvements

The system should be designed to reinforce improvements as well as to attain final goals. Performers should be able to earn points for desired behavior and results, even if those performances represent only small steps in the right direction.

3. Focus on merit—not demerits

Point systems must not become demerit systems. They should focus on what performers are doing right, not what they are doing wrong. For example, it is better to award points to maids for what is clean rather than to subtract points for what is dirty.

4. All measures should lead to a one number score

Your point system must combine all measures into one overall index of performance. The advantage of the point system is lost if more than one number represents performance. This number must describe the performer's total job. The purpose is for the index to represent the degree to which the performers have met the expectations of their jobs.

5. If rating, use BARS

If ratings are used, make them Behaviorally Anchored Rating Scales (BARS). BARS provide the most specific information of all the judgment techniques and typically produce the best results.

6. Use simple accounting

Base the system on easily calculable numbers. Typically, a 100- or 1,000-point total is best. It is easier to relate to scores as a fraction of 100 or 1,000 than a total point value of something like 150 or 1,200. Distribute points so they total 100 or 1,000. For example, you have a better idea of what a score of 93 of 100 means than 106 of a possible 120. Also avoid fractions. If you have fractions, multiply point values by 10 or 100. Generally speaking when earning points, people find larger numbers more reinforcing than smaller ones.

7. Build in flexibility

Change point values and weights as situations change. When factors outside the performer's control change, change the system to reflect them. This means that points could increase or decrease for a particular item. If outside factors make it easier or more difficult to achieve, then the points should be changed to reflect it.

Generally, these systems are reviewed at weekly or monthly intervals. That is the time to make any adjustments to the values. If conditions change in the middle of a week or month, do not change points for the current period; rather, wait until the end of the period to make changes in the points for the following scoring period.

PERFORMANCE MATRIX

The performance matrix is a point system that enables you to measure any job. It provides a way to combine judgment measures and counts into a single index representative of the total performance that you expect of a person or a group. The judgment measures can include all the techniques discussed above, although BARS and checklists are the ones most often used.

The performance matrix evolved from Riggs' (1986) objectives matrix (OMAX). His work on the matrix began as he tried to measure TLC (tender loving care) during hospital productivity studies in 1975.

TLC is one of those variables that people often say cannot be measured, yet if you have ever been a patient in a hospital, you have measured it. You know whether the hospital had it and have an opinion of the degree to which it was present. The BARS enables you to measure all such variables, and the performance matrix allows us to relate them to other more traditionally measured items so that we can get a total picture of how the person is performing against expectations. In effect, the performance matrix is any combination of BARS, checklists, and counts that covers all aspects of a person's or group's job. You develop one by first defining the areas of accountability and pinpointing them as best you can. This is usually a joint process between supervisor and subordinate.

Once you have this completed, select the appropriate measure for each pinpoint (behaviors and results) from the techniques presented in this chapter.

Next, determine the current level of performance on each of the pinpoints. Then set a goal for each one.

Finally, give each one a weighting. The total weightings must add to 100.

Look at the form in Figure 11.8. Notice the measurement scale is from 4 to 13. This allows you to anchor the current performance at 5, and the goal at 10. Eleven, 12, and 13 provide opportunities for overachievement. Some people prefer a scale of 1-10, with 3 being current performance and 7 being goal. Which you choose is not important. However, many have difficulty relating to 7 as goal and do not feel good about reaching goal because they did not get a 10. Generally speaking in our society, 11 "feels" more like overachievement than 8. In any

Figure 11.8

PERFORMANCE MANAGEMENT MATRIX

Name ______________________ Position ____________________ Manager ___________ Date _____

Behavior/Results	4	5	6	7	8	9	10	11	12	13	X Weight	Raw Score	Points
		Current Performance					Goal		Overachievement				
				Sub-Goals									

Score

REINFORCEMENT PLAN

POINTS	R+	COMMENTS	PLANS

Next Review Date ______________________

case, use the one that makes most sense to the performers.

The chart opposite shows monthly figures for a manufacturing department. This is not a real case, so do not find fault with either the pinpoints or the measures. This example is to show you the mechanics of developing a matrix.

Let's see how these figures would look in a performance matrix. Figure 11.9 shows a matrix for the department management team. On this matrix a score of 500 would show no overall improvement and 1,000 would represent goal attainment.

Accountability results: May
Productivity.............................588,700 lbs.
Cost..1.032 per lb.
% Grade 01..............................96.6%
Yield..81.1%
Successful R+ plans.................88%
Morale Survey Results.............92% favorable
Number of processes using control charts............37

Figure 11.9

PERFORMANCE MATRIX

Name Toe Hold Mgmt. Team   Position _____ Manager _____ Date 6/3/89

Behavior/Results	4	5	6	7	8	9	10	11	12	13	X Weight	Raw Score	Points
Productivity (in thousands of pounds)	548	550	560	570	(580)	590	600	605	615	625	20	588,700	160
Cost	111.5	111	108	(105)	103	101	1.00	99.5	99	98.75	20	1.032	140
% Grade 01	87	88	89.3	90.6	91.9	93.2	95	(96.3)	97.6	98.9	25	96.6%	275
R+ Plans Developed and Implemented		48	64		(88)		100	100% by 6/24	100% by 6/17	100% by 6/10	15	88%	120
Morale Survey Results	—	84		87		90	(92)	95	100		10	92%	100
Number Processes Using Control Charts	—	15	20	25	30	32	35	(37)	38	40	10	37	110

Current · · · · · · · · Goal

Score 905

REINFORCEMENT PLAN

POINTS	R+ CRITERIA	COMMENTS	PLANS
700		Boss will visit area to see successful PM projects	Spend time with each team (serve refreshments)
850	With no score below an 8	Have meeting over lunch away from office	
1,000	Items 1, 2, 3 must be above 10	Visit to customer	

Next Review Date _____ 7/5/89

The weights are assigned according to departmental priorities. The points are derived by multiplying the weight by the number of the column in which the circled number appears. For example, in the column on "Cost," $1.05 is circled because the monthly cost of $1.032 did not meet the criterion of $1.03. Therefore, the team received a score of 7. Seven is multiplied by 20, the weight for "Cost," giving the team 140 points.

Notice also that some blocks on the scales don't have numbers in them. Depending on what you consider reinforceable, you can have numbers in every block, or several with no numbers.

At the bottom of the form is a section for a reinforcement plan. There is not enough room for a complete plan since the team would probably want to identify behaviors that need to be reinforced to reach the goals they have set. The plan should be continued on the back.

The matrix is a very flexible instrument. Pinpoints, goals, weights and reinforcers can be changed as often as required. This makes it a highly desirable way to communicate

Measuring Creativity

While people often see the application of PM to the more routine jobs, many ask, "But can it be used in creative jobs?" An application used by Mike Vincent of Maritz Motivation, Inc., St. Louis, proved it does, in fact, work—and it works well! Mike managed artists and writers who prepared advertising copy and illustration. By using a matrix he made substantial improvements in the performer's creations as measured by customer acceptance, outside judging, and use of the ads. Not only did the performers turn out a better product when Mike used PM, but the artists and writers felt that communication with their supervisors was much improved as a result.

In order to measure the artists' performance a matrix like the one below was developed. Illustrations were judged on eight dimensions, and BARS were created for each. The matrix below is the one used by the manager to rate the illustration on the opposite page.

	15	10	5	0	
	OUTSTANDING	GOOD	MEETS MINIMUM REQUIREMENTS	UNSATISFACTORY	COMMENTS
CREATIVITY INVOLVED	12				
COMPOSITION	13				
CRAFTSMANSHIP			8		
TECHNIQUE		11			
USE OF COLOR		10			
REPRODUCIBLE	12				
ILLUSTRATES COPY	14				
TIME TO PRODUCE	13				
TOTAL	93/120 78%				

J. DANIELS

priorities and reinforce performance in hard-to-measure jobs.

THE BEHAVIOR OF MEASURING (COLLECTING THE DATA)

Measuring a performance is itself a performance. It is often time-consuming and tedious. Sometimes collecting the data is as much a problem as developing the measures. If collecting the data is too time consuming, over a period of time it will not be collected.

There are several ways to simplify the data-collection process. The first is to use data that has already been collected. It is surprising how many times data is thought to be needed on a particular variable, only to find that data has already been collected. Check it out before developing your own data-collecting procedure. Sometimes, what you need can be obtained just by breaking the data out of existing records. At other times, if what you need is not available, it can be obtained at little extra cost or effort at the same time other data is being collected.

Finally, the performers can collect data on their own performance. You cannot do this, however, if existing data is not already being used to reinforce performance. If measurement is used primarily for pointing out errors and substandard performance, self-monitoring may precipitate a crisis.

If performers are asked to self-monitor, the first reinforcer they receive should be for collecting the data. Once data-collecting procedures have been worked out, the performers can be reinforced for accurate recording and then for the performance itself. Self-monitoring is highly desirable because it gives the performers immediate feedback on how they're doing, thereby allowing them to make frequent adjustments to their performance.

SUMMARY OF MEASUREMENT METHODS—COUNTING AND JUDGING

Counting is the preferred measurement because it is the simplest, easiest, and most reliable of the two. When the performance that needs to be measured is not easily counted, you may have to use a judgment technique. Within the four techniques of judgment, the use of pre-established criteria (Cells 3 and 4) is more objective than opinion-based approaches (Cells 1 and 2).

The three steps to developing measures:

1. Selecting relevant measurement categories (quality, quantity, timeliness, cost).
2. Selecting relevant measurement category division (quality—errors, class, novelty; cost—labor, material, management).
3. Selecting measurement methods (counting or judging).

Figure 11.10 is a summary of measurement methods.

Figure 11.10

SUMMARY OF MEASUREMENT METHODS

Measurement Method	When To Use	Advantages	Disadvantages
Judgment: Rank-Opinion	Can't use counting, ratings not suitable and hard-to-measure areas, especially quality unrelated to accuracy	Makes everything measurable	Subjective Limits who can be reinforced
Judgment: Rate-Opinion	Can't use counting, hard-to-measure areas, especially quality unrelated to accuracy	Makes everything measurable	Subjective
Judgment: Rank- Pre-established Criteria	Same as 1, and if you can identify specific criteria	Makes everything measurable, and more objective than 1 or 2	Less objective than counting Limits who can be reinforced
Judgment: Rate- Pre-established Criteria	Same as 2, best method to use of 1-4	Makes everything measurable and more objective than 1, 2 or 3	Less objective than counting
Counting	For measurement areas such as behaviors, units produced, yields, accuracy, run-time THE PREFERRED METHOD.	Most objective	Some things can't be easily counted

* Refer to Figures 11.3 and 11.4 for complete examples of judgment methods.

NOTES

12

The Right Pinpoint

This chapter describes the process of identifying a job's most important result—its mission. Once specified, this result lays the groundwork for all further pinpointing. The final section of this chapter covers when to emphasize behavior and when to emphasize results. Knowing which to emphasize—and when—is critical to effectively and efficiently managing performance.

IDENTIFYING THE MISSION

You will get more of what you reinforce. This sometimes causes a problem because reinforcing the wrong thing will get you more of the wrong thing. You may reinforce something that is insignificant to the overall result desired. To avoid these problems, you must identify the job **mission**—the most important result a job should produce.

Just as every organization has its mission to perform a particular service or produce a product, each job has a mission that contributes to that organizational mission. This is true of work at all levels, from the president to the head of research and development, to the mechanic on the production line.

Once the job mission has been identified, pinpoints and measures flow naturally from it. However, the vague description of a personnel supervisor's job as "supporting the organization by providing human resources" does not naturally lead to job measures.

But if you describe the job as "keeping job positions filled," several possible measures become apparent. They are: percent of job positions filled, time required to fill open positions, percent of job openings with qualified applicants available, and percentage of new hires retained after probationary period.

Most jobs require many behaviors and produce many results. However, until you know the most important result, priorities are often confused and much time and energy is wasted producing results that are insignificant or in some cases counterproductive.

The best way to determine a job mission, to list first all the results of the job (with appropriate measures). Then try to extract from the list the single most important result of the job. This is the job mission. Once you have a mission, go back and check all other results against it. If achieving the other results doesn't help achieve the mission, it is secondary to the mission, or it belongs to some other job.

The process, then, of identifying the most important results of a job consists of these three steps:

1. List all the results for which you are accountable.
2. Extract from the list a single result which explains why the job exists.
3. Check each remaining result against the mission and determine which ones are critical to the accomplishment of the mission.

An example of a job's mission

Let's illustrate this process by looking at the job of personnel supervisor, mentioned earlier. The list below contains some possible important results for this position.

- EEOC requirements met
- Employee files current
- New applicant files available
- Recruiting interviews conducted
- Exit interviews conducted
- Jobs filled with qualified personnel
- Job openings filled within target time

With this list, it is easy to see that the one overall result the job is directed toward is "jobs filled." But how do we know this is an adequate statement of the job's mission?

Evaluating the mission— the ACORN test

Listed in Figure 12.1 are five criteria developed by Gilbert (1978) representing a simple test for you to apply to any result you think might be a job mission. They are abbreviated as ACORN (Accomplishment, Control, Overall Objective, Reconcilable, and Numbers). The following section shows how these criteria would apply to the mission, "jobs filled."

Accomplishment

The mission, jobs filled, is stated as a result, not a behavior. You never need to see the personnel supervisor perform any specific behavior; you only need to look at the effects of the behavior—a report of percent of positions filled.

To fill these jobs the person may have placed advertisements, visited schools, and attended conferences, but none of these are the job's mission. A mission must be stated as a result. You can't compromise on this point. If you have questions about whether a potential mission meets the criteria for a result, review Figure 10.3, Points for Distinguishing Behaviors from Results.

Control

If the personnel supervisor engages in the right behaviors, jobs will be filled. Consequently a person in this position must have more authority to fill jobs than anyone else.

A question to ask yourself in evaluating a job for "control" is: "If the job holder did

Figure 12.1

SUMMARY OF THE ACORN TEST FOR DETERMINING A JOB'S MISSION

Accomplishment	It is a result, not a behavior.
Control	The performer has the predominant influence over the accomplishment.
Overall Objective	The accomplishment which represents the major reason for the job's existence, not just one of several objectives for the job.
Reconcilable	The accomplishment must have minimal conflict with the requirements of other jobs.
Numbers	It must be possible to generate practical, cost-effective data to measure the accomplishment.

everything in her power and authority, as outlined in the job description, and used all the resources available to her, could she significantly impact the results?" The answer, of course, must always be "yes." If she could not significantly affect the desired outcome when other people didn't do their part, then she doesn't have enough control for it to be considered her mission. If other people have enough control to prevent the performer from being successful, then you have not identified the mission. Certainly, it would not be appropriate to hold the person accountable for those results. Yet, it's done all the time.

Many sales managers are held accountable for increasing sales. Yet, the only way a sales manager can directly increase sales is to call or visit a client and get an order.

Supervisors are often held accountable for increasing yield. The only direct way that a supervisor, middle manager, or even plant manager can increase yield is to go down to the front line and take a position working on the production line.

A nursing supervisor's mission may be described as "increasing patient care." The only way a nursing supervisor or hospital administrator can directly influence patient care is to go into a patient's room, fluff his pillow, dispense medications, change the bedpan, take his temperature, and fulfill all his requests. Yet, the responsibility for improving patient care is usually at the supervisory or administrative level.

In these examples, if the managers increased sales, increased yield, or increased patient care, they would be doing somebody else's job—their subordinates'. The managers in these situations do not have the most control over these results. The salesperson, the production operator, and the nurse do. Yet many organizations hold managers accountable for this type result.

For example, suppose a supervisor has five operators responsible for producing 100,000 yards of tape. In the typical plant, the supervisor would be held accountable for 500,000 yards. If the supervisor's boss has two

supervisors, the boss would be accountable for 1,000,000 yards. If a manager is simply responsible for the sum total of his subordinates' results, why do we need the manager? In this type system, all managers and supervisors are responsible for the same thing. Therefore, there is no individual accountability. All share the glory or the blame.

The question to ask is, "What do the supervisors accomplish that the operators can't?" Whatever those things are is what the supervisors are accountable for. The mission of a supervisor is very simply to create successful employees. The supervisor who has five operators, each responsible for 100,000 yards, is responsible for the success of five operators, not the production of 500,000 yards of tape.

Figure 12.2 shows how managers under this system can be successful even when employees fail. This illustration is from a real example. The boss received a bonus and four of the five performers had their jobs put in jeopardy.

If you have supervisors who can be successful when employees are not, then you will have constant productivity and morale problems.

If the mission as described does not satisfy the criterion of control, redefine the mission until it does. If you can't do this, then select another result to test against the mission criteria. Don't bother to check a possible mission against the rest of the ACORN criteria if the performer does not have sufficient control over the results. No matter how well you satisfy the other criteria in the ACORN test, if the control is not there the job will produce little for the organization and will frustrate whoever tries to accomplish it.

Overall objective

The basic question to ask when evaluating whether the mission statement represents the job's overall objective is: If the result is completely achieved would anything else be expected? If the answer is "yes" then the result described in your mission statement

Figure 12.2

EXAMPLE OF A TYPICAL ACCOUNTABILITY SYSTEM: THE SUPERVISOR CAN BE SUCCESSFUL WHILE MOST OF HIS EMPLOYEES ARE NOT

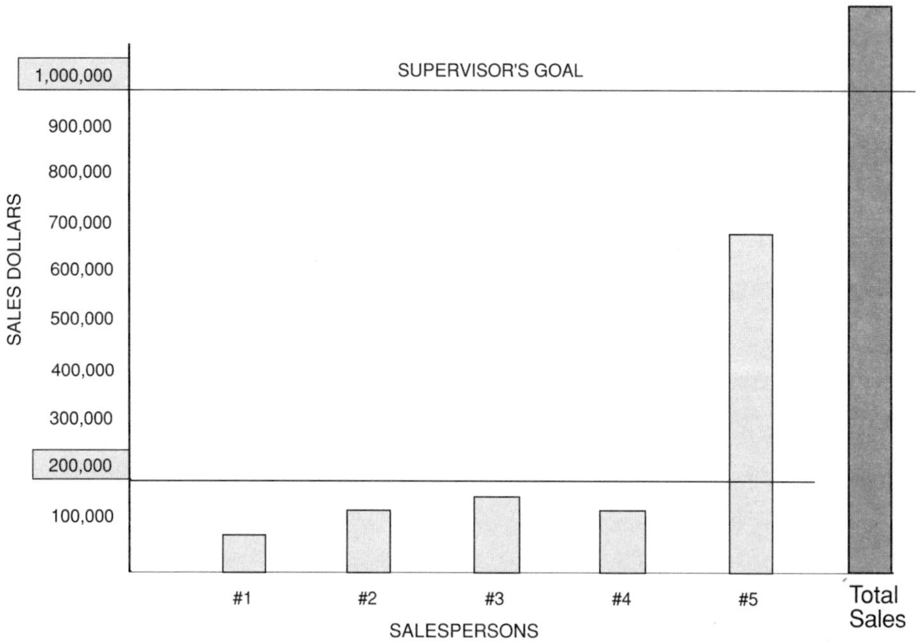

does not meet this criterion. In our example, you would not have selected the overall objective if all jobs were filled with qualified applicants, but there were other significant results the boss still expected to be done. There will always be things to be done when jobs are filled, such as maintaining up-to-date and accurate personnel files, but these things should support the mission of "filling jobs with qualified applicants." If the personnel supervisor is responsible for plant security, then "filling jobs" may not be the overall objective. (In your organization this may not be the mission of the personnel supervisor. This was selected only to illustrate how to generate a job mission.)

Reconcilable

The key question here is: "If this mission

were accomplished perfectly, would the missions of other jobs be hampered?" For example, if the mission of the training department is defined as "training," then its ultimate result would be for all employees to be continuously involved in training. No one would ever be doing anything except being involved with training. This, of course, would interfere with every other job in the organization. Therefore, this mission clearly is not reconcilable with the missions of other jobs.

In some organizations in the past, the missions of the production manager and the quality manager were not reconcilable. The production manager was responsible for meeting a production schedule to get the product out the door. The quality manager often had the mission of "preventing poor quality from leaving the plant." In many cases, the quality manager would stop production, hold up shipment, inspect more slowly, etc., all of which had a negative effect on the production manager's mission.

The classic clash of missions has occurred most often between manufacturing managers and sales managers. The mission of sales managers is frequently to sell all they can. The mission of manufacturing managers has often been to make the product as cheaply as they can. As a result, the sales managers want to make the product in an infinite number of sizes, shapes, and colors, whereas the manufacturing managers want to make it in one size, one shape, and one color.

As for the example of "jobs filled," it is hard to imagine this would interfere with other organizational missions. If all jobs are always filled, what other department or job in the organization would be hampered? The answer is: None.

The ability to reconcile job missions within an organization is critical to the overall success of the organization. Unless all jobs in the organization support each other in contributing to the organizational mission, results will be less than optimal. We can extend this analysis to performance, that is to say, "Is an increase in what I do valuable?" Many people start reinforcement programs without thinking about the impact of an increase in the results of their job, team, or department on the rest of the organization. Sometimes an improvement in one part of the organization can create problems in other parts of the organization. All work performance occurs as a part of some system. One person does things that enable others to do their thing. We are all aware of what happens when people do not do their thing correctly or on time; but we don't always think about what an improvement in one area will do to the performance of others.

Goldratt and Cox (1986) show dramatically in their book, *The Goal*, how important it is to understand the system in which performance occurs. They point out how the constraints of the system affect final outcomes. Bottlenecks, they say, ultimately define the productivity of a system.

In any system where bottlenecks exist, more is not always better, except in the bottleneck. What this means to performance managers is that if your job, team, or department produces products or services for a bottleneck, then increases in your output should not be reinforced because they will actually increase costs and add no value. If you precede the bottleneck, increases in your productivity should be reinforced only up to the capacity of the bottleneck.

Once your production reaches the capacity of the unit ahead of you, then things other than productivity should be reinforced, such

"By 'Fair' do you mean 'Good Looking' or 'Evenhanded'?"

(© 1988 Malcolm Hancock, reprinted by permission of the author from "American Health", 1988, September, p.112.)

as helping clear the bottleneck, or any number of other things that will increase the effectiveness of the system.

This means that what gets reinforced in the most effective organizations may vary from day to day, or even hour to hour. Those employees who know when to switch reinforcement from one thing to another and have the personal flexibility to do so will become increasingly valuable to their companies. Those who think "more is better" and that problems are solved by "doing the same thing harder" will become increasingly ineffective and a larger drag on their fellow employees and their organizations.

Until you have asked the question, "How will this improvement in performance affect those before us and those after us?" you have not completed reconciling.

Numbers

There are many possible measures for our personnel supervisor's mission. The primary measure is simply "percent of jobs filled with qualified applicants." Quality, quantity, timeliness, and cost of fulfilling this mission can all be measured. You could measure the degree to which applicants meet job requirements or specifications. You could measure the number filled. Other measures are how quickly open slots are filled and how much it costs to fill them and keep them filled.

Chapter Eleven described how everything can be measured. The issue, then, is not whether the mission can be measured, but whether the measure is practical. Practicality involves two factors:
• Cost of measurement: Will it be too high?
• Validity: Is the measure valid?

Most managers tend to overestimate the cost of measuring, thinking in terms of sophisticated computers, time-consuming reports, and extensive outside assistance required to develop industrially engineered standards. As you saw in Chapter Eleven, simple measurement techniques can be developed if you have a good pinpoint. By using good sampling techniques, you can get highly reliable data that is inexpensive and easy to obtain. Involving the performers in measuring their own performance, for example, is inexpensive and has the added benefit of providing immediate feedback to the performer.

The second factor, **validity**, refers to the extent to which a measure measures what is purported to be measured. Sometimes measures don't give us what we want or need. This is most often a problem with indirect measures of a mission. For example, the number of hours worked may not be a valid measure of the mission of "producing accurate engineering designs on schedule." A person could put in a lot of time but spend it inefficiently and thereby not meet a schedule.

BARS, matrices, and point systems must be tested for both validity and reliability. Reliability refers to the degree to which two or more people get the same number when measuring a performance. **Reliability** refers only to the fact that the measurement system remains consistent from one time to the next. Just because the measure has high reliability does not mean that it is valid. We can have high agreement among the measurers on a BARS or matrix, but the number still may not measure the performance we want.

However, you don't need to wait until you have a perfect measurement system to start. An imperfect system is better than none at all. Once you begin to measure you will find that certain problems arise, causing you to refine your measure. If you wait until it's perfect, you may never begin.

In defining the mission of a job, you identify all the important results of that job. The last step in defining the job mission is to compare each of the results to the suggested mission. Each result should support the accomplishment of the mission. If a result does not support that accomplishment, it may belong to another job.

Examine Figure 12.3. EEOC requirements ensure that job slots will be filled with legally qualified applicants. Up-to-date files allow personnel to take prompt and proper action

Figure 12.3

Job
Personnel Director

Mission
Job slots filled

Possible Accomplishments
- EEOC requirements met
- Employees' files kept current
- New applicant files available
- Exit interviews conducted
- Jobs filled within target time

to hire and maintain employees. Conducting interviews is essential to filling jobs. Exit interviews reveal why employees leave jobs and provide valuable information to correct problems. Jobs filled within target time is a measure of how efficiently the job is done.

The process of identifying job missions and their results is often difficult and time consuming. However, time spent on this activity will invariably pay significant dividends in the long run. The only way any organization can operate in the most efficient manner is to identify and reconcile every job mission. By doing this you can eliminate unnecessary jobs and make sure that all jobs support the overall mission of the unit or organization.

BEHAVIORS AND RESULTS: WHICH SHOULD YOU EMPHASIZE?

Every job was created to produce particular results. We have just finished discussing how one can identify what these results should be. Clearly, then, results always need to be pinpointed. And if something is worth pinpointing it is worth measuring. Therefore, one simple rule we can state concerning behaviors and results is: Pinpoint both behaviors and results, but always pinpoint and measure results first.

However, the necessity for pinpointing and measuring at least some of the behaviors required to produce results may not be clear to some people. Why worry about the means (behavior) if the end (result) is justified and being accomplished? The answer is that if you don't pinpoint relevant behaviors, one or more of the following problems may occur:

1. People may engage in illegal or morally reprehensible behavior.
2. Behaviors necessary for the maintenance of long-term results may be neglected.
3. Results data may be falsified.

The Watergate scandal that led to the resignation of President Nixon is an example of the first type of problem. In that case, individuals were told to obtain certain information about the Democratic Party. The result, "maintaining a Republican president," was the important thing. Any behaviors that would lead to that end were considered justifiable by those involved and were reinforced by their superiors. As a consequence, those involved committed crimes (behaviors) that included "conspiracy to commit breaking, entering, and misprision of a felony." The course of American history was dramatically altered as a result.

Those involved could have attended speeches by the Democratic politicians. They could have talked to supporters and reporters. They could have analyzed the information obtained to understand the strategy the Democrats were taking. These are all legal activities (behaviors) directed toward the same end as the break-in of the headquarters of the Democratic National Committee in the Watergate complex. (See Shannon, 1974). Obviously, monitoring to see that the results were obtained by legal behaviors rather than illegal ones would have avoided a major political scandal and saved the country countless dollars and untold grief.

Newspapers and television news constantly report problems of this nature. Under the pressure to win (result), college coaches engage in illegal behavior in order to recruit star high school athletes. Athletes use steroids and other illegal substances (behavior) in order to set performance records (result). Stockbrokers engage in insider-trading and other illegal activities (behaviors) in order to make money (result). The list seems endless. Systems that emphasize results to the exclusion of behaviors may encourage otherwise law-abiding individuals to perform illegal, immoral, or unethical acts.

Managers who focus exclusively on results may unwittingly create lying, cheating, and stealing. This is a frequent occurrence when there is a lot of pressure to produce results or else lose one's job or status within the organization. If employees know the boss is only interested in the results, they may falsify the data or engage in other behavior that is even more reprehensible in order to avoid the punishment for not achieving those results.

Another problem that occurs when only results are evaluated is that behaviors necessary for long-term results will be neglected. In other words, short-term gains will be reinforced at the expense of long-term results. For example, preventive maintenance may be neglected in order to maximize short-term productivity. Of course, this may cause equipment failure in the long run and subsequent production losses far in

excess of that gained from not doing the required maintenance. When there is pressure to "get it out the door," quality may suffer in favor of meeting a shipping schedule. The problems caused by shipping poor quality goods are practically always greater in the long run than those created by missing the shipping schedule. An organization is headed for trouble when you hear managers say things like, "I don't care how you do it, I want those chemicals disposed of by the end of the month," or "I don't care how you do it, but you had better make those budget cuts by the end of the month."

In essentially every case, you should pinpoint and monitor both behaviors and results. Even though you should monitor both, you will usually need to focus reinforcement on one or the other.

Behavior as the focus

When managers pinpoint and measure performance, they are more likely to focus on results than behavior. Often, in fact, they typically believe that the behavior of their subordinates is not their responsibility. This erroneous view should be corrected. Because behavior contributes directly to results, it must be of primary concern to managers.

Behavior should be the focus of reinforcement in the following five circumstances.

(By permission of Johnny Hart and NAS, Inc.)

1. When current performance is a long way from final result (goal)

When a goal is far above the current level of performance, providing reinforcement for goal attainment rarely supplies enough R+ to keep the performer going. This is particularly true of new or poor performers. When people don't know the behaviors necessary to produce the results, or can't perform them very well, those behaviors should be pinpointed and reinforced.

2. When the link between the behavior and the result it produces is not obvious

Sometimes the relationship between behaviors and a result is not clear. This is particularly true in situations in which a result can be achieved even when all the prescribed behaviors are not completed. For example, a pilot may not complete a pre-flight checklist but still have a successful flight; a salesperson may get an order without asking for it; a teacher may have a good class but not follow an outline; a programmer may develop a successful computer application without doing required tests; machines may run efficiently even when required preventive maintenance is not done; people may not have an accident even when safety procedures are not followed. In all of these situations, though, we know the absence of these behaviors eventually will adversely affect the results.

There are other times we engage in many behaviors to produce a result when, in fact, only a few of them are actually related to the accomplishment of the result. This relationship was suggested many years ago by Vilfredo Pareto, an Italian economist. Pareto's observations have been interpreted to mean that of all the possible causes of a result, only a small percentage actually are responsible for most of the effect. Known today as Pareto's Law, or the **80-20 Principle**, we interpret in this context to mean that 20 percent of employee behaviors probably produce 80 percent of the results.

In many situations employees are expected to engage in numerous behaviors that contribute little to results. For example, sales-people locate potential customers, send letters, make follow-up telephone calls, schedule appointments, take customers to lunch and dinner, do market research, prepare presentations, and on occasion even play golf with customers. Their presentations involve many behaviors. They may assist the buyer in making presentations to others in his company. They "establish rapport," assess the customer's need, describe or demonstrate the product or service, identify and address customer concerns, supply references, and ask for the order. They may dress and speak a certain way.

Of all the above, the one that is probably stressed the most in sales training is "asking for the order." For some salespeople, particularly new salespeople, asking for the order is requisite to making a sale. Unfortunately, it is also the behavior they are most likely to forget or have difficulty doing. A national grocery-products company conducted a survey of salespeople who averaged 17 years in selling and discovered that they asked for the order less than 45 percent of the time.

The reason new salespeople don't want to ask is because they are punished by a "no" more often than they are reinforced by a "yes." The reason senior salespeople get out of the habit is because they make some sales when they don't ask. The act of "asking," without feedback and occasional reinforcement, gradually undergoes extinction. If managers don't define the "critical few" behaviors necessary to produce a result and reinforce them in these situations, many superstitious behaviors can be the result.

A good example: I went into a Burger King to get a cup of coffee and review some notes before going to a meeting. When I ordered the coffee, the clerk asked, "How about a hot apple pie?" I replied, "That's a good idea." At that point her boss leaned over and said to her, "See—it works!"

No doubt he had told employees that if they tried "suggestive selling" they would sell more. He did the right thing by providing immediate, positive, social reinforcement.

What should the manager have done if I

had said "no"? He should have reinforced
her! She did exactly what he wanted her to
do. He might have said, "You did that
exactly right. Keep it up and you will sell a
lot of hot apple pies." In this way he would
have reinforced the behavior that would
create results, even though it did not in that
particular instance.

3. When the result is long delayed

Some results take a long time to produce.
Engineers often have projects that take many
months or several years to complete. The
same is true for sales of "big ticket" items like
real estate, heavy machinery, or large computer systems. Any product or service
costing large amounts of money usually
requires weeks or months to sell. In these
situations, behaviors must be reinforced
because the results do not occur frequently
enough to provide the amount of reinforcement necessary for maximum motivation.
Many long-term projects are late because of
this lack of consistent reinforcement. Managers may need to monitor the performance in
these situations and reinforce the behaviors
involved in the result, rather than wait until
the project is finished to have a celebration.

Another way to manage these performances is to break the task into smaller tasks to
reduce the amount of time between the
behavior and results. For example, milestones and sub-goals provide opportunities to
reinforce short-term results. Although
milestones have been a part of project
management for a long time, reinforcement
has not. The real value of having a milestone
or sub-goal is in the opportunity it provides
for reinforcement.

4. When the relevant behaviors are socially sensitive

Problem behaviors at work involving
violations of social etiquette or personal style
cause difficulties for both the performer and
co-workers. These behaviors are difficult for
co-workers because they are offensive or
cause personal embarrassment. They are
difficult for the performers because they often

aren't aware of the problem.

Problems involving inappropriate dress,
talking too much, poor grammar, messy
eating habits, body odor or bad breath are
rarely handled in a constructive way in most
businesses. And whether you realize it or
not, these things often have a significant
effect on the way performers are evaluated.
Peers, customers, and even managers are
unlikely to give feedback on such behaviors.
Often, an employee may be denied an
opportunity, not because of performance, but
because of some aspect of personal groom-
ing, appearance, or personal habit.

If such socially sensitive behaviors are
interfering with results, managers have the responsibility to tell the performer. The performer can't change a problem behavior if he
doesn't know it is a problem. He needs
feedback. Of course, the person must be
able to profit from the feedback, so the
feedback must be pinpointed. Fortunately,
most of these behaviors or habits are easy to
pinpoint. Then, once you communicate the
problem, you must reinforce the appropriate
behaviors.

Although in many cases feedback of this
nature is difficult to give, and indeed often
not given, when it is provided the problem is
usually easy to correct. Sadly, many people
have lost significant opportunities at work,
including promotions, transfers, and even
their jobs, not because they couldn't change,
but because they did not get feedback on
problem behavior and reinforcement for the
behavior change.

5. When poor results are due to causes beyond the performer's control

A final situation in which behavior, rather
than results, should be reinforced is when the
possibility of improving the results is out of
the performer's control. *Sometimes* factors
such as the weather, the economy, or vendors, have a negative impact on performance.
"Sometimes" is emphasized because often
people attribute poor performance to causes
they believe are beyond their control when,
in fact, if they would pinpoint and reinforce

the right behaviors, results would improve dramatically.

With skilled performers, results are usually sufficient to provide adequate feedback and reinforcement to maintain high performance. However, when the results are not forthcoming, due to no fault of the performer, relevant behaviors need to be reinforced to keep them occurring until the results return.

An example of this problem is the effect of a recession on sales. Sales decrease even though salespersons are working harder than usual. If the hard work (behavior) does not result in sales, these behaviors will undergo extinction. During this period reinforcement should be delivered for prospecting, getting appointments, and so on. If results are emphasized in this unfavorable climate, sales will decrease even more than economic conditions warrant. Moreover, when the economy improves, the salespersons won't have the adequate leads and preparation to increase sales quickly.

Another example occurs when inferior raw material or poor running conditions cause poor results. During this period, behaviors must be reinforced to make sure the performers maintain the vigilance and stamina required to maximize the results in spite of the bad material or conditions.

Results as the focus

Pinpointing the relevant behavior is often harder to do than identifying the important result. Moreover, to focus on behavior, you have to actually observe the performer. For the simple reason that results are easier to manage, they typically are overemphasized. However, in certain instances it is more efficient to reinforce results. This does not mean you can forget behaviors, but that you *can get by* with reinforcing results without constantly monitoring behaviors. These instances occur when:

1. Performers are skilled in the behavior

Many people already know the behaviors required to produce a particular result. In

such cases, you can focus reinforcement on results. For example, professional golfers know what they do wrong when they miss the fairway on their drive. They do not need someone to tell them what causes a slice or a hook. They are skilled enough to know what to do to correct the problem by seeing the results. This is in contrast to typical weekend golfers who may not know which of a thousand things they might have done wrong. They need feedback and reinforcement for the right behaviors from some outside source like a fellow player, caddie, or a golf pro.

People who have been doing the same job for a long time or who are skilled at their work are in a similar situation. They know all the behaviors that go into the desired results and therefore all they typically need to improve results is more frequent feedback and reinforcement for those results.

2. Behaviors and results are obviously related

If a result can only be produced by engaging in some obvious behaviors, then reinforcing the result can be efficient and effective. Nothing is gained by focusing on behaviors in situations where the behaviors and results are so obviously related that reinforcement for the result will also reinforce the relevant behaviors.

Highly repetitive tasks usually fall into this category. An example is an assembly-line job where the person does one or a few tasks over and over. If a person has a job of stacking boxes (behavior), you might well reinforce the number of boxes stacked in an hour or a day (result), rather than watch him stack them. Other examples include: orders entered (data processing), railroad cars loaded (shipping), newspapers delivered without a complaint (distribution).

3. Results are improving

When results are improving, that usually means the performers are performing the correct behaviors. Obviously, you want to make sure that results are being obtained through reinforceable behaviors. In addition, the behaviors must be at a high and steady rate. If both conditions exist, you can gain efficiency by giving feedback and reinforcement on results. You can usually do this with highly efficient, experienced performers.

Focus, don't ignore

Figure 12.4 provides a summary of when to focus on behavior and when to focus on results. If, after examining these criteria, you still aren't certain whether to emphasize behavior or results in a particular situation, choose results. If the results don't improve, then change your focus to behavior.

Remember that the key word is focus, not ignore. When you focus on either behavior or results, you must monitor the other. When you completely ignore either, you can expect trouble in the long run. You may get results through undesirable behaviors or have lots of busy people accomplishing nothing. In a situation as simple as "boxes stacked," you need to look in on the

performers from time to time, because they may be doing things that could be unsafe, unhealthy, or otherwise undesirable.

Practically all professional and Olympic athletes have coaches. They need someone to watch them from time to time to see if they can spot "weaknesses" in their game—or opportunities for improving their results. Of course, the good coaches provide plenty of feedback and reinforcement when the trainees make the changes.

While developing the right pinpoint and determining the focus is often time consuming, it is well worth the time. Once you know what you want people to do, you can use this technology to make it happen at a high-and-steady rate.

MANAGING BY WANDERING AROUND (MBWA)

In their best-selling book, *In Search of Excellence*, Peters and Waterman (1982) introduced the concept of MBWA (managing by wandering around). This immediately caught

Figure 12.4

BEHAVORS AND RESULTS—WHICH TO FOCUS ON

Focus on Behavior When	Focus on Results When
1. Current performance is a long way from goal—shaping new employees	1. Performers are skilled and know what behaviors to do
2. The link between the result and behavior is vague	2. Behavior/result link is obvious and clear
3. Result is long delayed—feedback inadequate	3. Results are improving
4. Relative behaviors are socially sensitive	
5. Low results are caused by factors beyond the control of the performer	

the attention of many managers because the authors claimed it was associated with excellence, it made sense, it confirmed the practice of many, and it was easy. Immediately upon reading the book, many managers who had not spent much time in the work area started frequenting the work place, only to create chaos rather than excellence. The reason was they didn't know what to do while they were there.

The manager's presence in the work place may be an antecedent for both punishment and reinforcement. Unfortunately in some cases, it resulted in more punishment to both management and non-management. In such cases the manager used the "wandering" to learn what was going wrong, rather than what was going right.

A more serious problem is that an upper-level manager who wanders around without the front-line supervisor may reinforce or punish the wrong behaviors. This is because of two situations:

1. The manager may not know the proper methods or procedures that are supposed to be followed in the conduct of the job.

Although some managers may have at one time been expert on a particular job, being away from it every day may have resulted in their being ignorant of new methods. This could lead to reinforcing a performance that is not up to date, or punishing one that is.

2. Because the wandering is infrequent, the manager may draw conclusions about the performance from too little data. When going on the floor, a manager might catch a performer sitting down and punish him when he was resting from doing something extraordinary. On the other hand, he might reinforce someone who appears to be working, not knowing that she had been causing problems with co-workers and supervisors all day and only started working when he appeared.

To avoid these problems, wander with a purpose and a supervisor. Most of the wandering around any supervisor should do is among direct reports. While it is reinforcing to many managers to see the front-line activity in the organization, the primary responsibility of a manager is to reinforce direct reports. Upper managers should assist in reinforcing at all levels but usually at the direction of subordinate managers or supervisors. Komaki (1987) discovered that the most effective supervisors and managers spent more time in what she called "job sampling" than the ineffective ones did. You can only deliver positive/immediates when you are in the work area.

Managers who opt to stay in their office can only reinforce results, and not the behaviors that produced them. Because of this, MBWA should be a part of every reinforcement plan. It is not something you do separate from PM; it is an integral part of it.

13

Introduction to Performance Feedback

Performance feedback is information about performance that allows a person to change the performance. The term feedback in this book refers to performance feedback which is a necessary, but not a sufficient, condition for performance change. Feedback must be combined with a consequence if change is to take place. The combination of feedback and positive reinforcement is a very effective approach to improving performance.

People often use the terms "information" and "data" to mean feedback. If information or data does not tell you which behavior to change, it is not feedback. Many organizations have lots of data, but little feedback.

For example, when told that their cholesterol level is 300, some people might respond, "Oh," or "Is that good?" Such responses show that just knowing their cholesterol count does not lead people to change their diet.

To be considered performance feedback, information must serve at least two functions. First, it must tell you where you stand relative to some target or goal. Second, it should tell you what to do to improve.

THE VALUE OF FEEDBACK

Feedback is a natural part of our existence. It is so natural we tend to take it for granted. You can't learn to walk, talk, write, ride a bicycle, drive a car, or use a computer without feedback. In fact, feedback is essential to learning.

Feedback deficiencies are a major contributor to virtually all problems of low performance. Very few, if any, organizations give enough performance feedback.

In his lectures on improving quality, Dr. Edwards Deming repeatedly asks, "How could they know?" He is referring to the sad fact that most performers do not have the information or data they need to do a quality job. Thomas Gilbert (1978), who has worked with organizations for years designing feedback systems, states his experience in industry, business, and schools shows that providing feedback never produces "less than a 20 percent improvement in performance, often a 50 percent change, and sometimes improvements as high as sixfold!"

Managers often overlook inadequate feedback as a cause of poor performance. Frequently, when someone describes a person as "unmotivated," "lazy," "stupid," or "in need of more training," the problem can be traced, in large part, to lack of feedback. A performer in a section of a plant who improved quality by over 300 percent through the use of feedback and reinforcement, said of the improvement, "I've been working here for over 20 years and I never knew there was a problem!"

Feedback is now used extensively in medicine, sports, and schools. Van Houten (1980) devoted an entire book to documenting and describing the effects of feedback on academic performance. Handwriting, arithmetic, spelling, vocabulary and reading skills, along with student attentiveness, increase dramatically with the correct use of feedback.

Numerous studies document the effect of feedback on energy use in the home. Increased feedback consistently reduces energy consumption. For example, in a study by Darley, Seligman, and Becker (1979), households were provided with information about their use of electricity. The authors describe the feedback process as follows:

Each day we worked out a potential consumption rate for each house, noting the temperature range and projecting how much energy the house would use on that kind of day if its residents followed their average patterns of use for the previous six weeks. Then, we computed the percentage of the potential consumption rate actually used.

The actual feedback was quite simple: Several times a week, we placed plastic numerals showing the percentage in a clear lucite holder attached to each family's patio door, where the numbers could easily be seen from the kitchen and family area. A score of 80 percent, for example, meant that actual consumption was 80 percent of predicted consumption, a sign of conservation. A score of 120 percent showed excessive use.

The results were very positive. Over a three-week period, households with the feedback used 16 percent less electricity than did a control group of similar households that were also interested in saving energy but were not given the frequent and visible feedback.

Dr. Judi Komaki and F. Barnett (1977) examined the effects of feedback in a unique setting: a little league football team. To improve play execution, specific desired behaviors of individual team members were pinpointed and the players were given feedback for performing them. The boys involved were five 9- to 10-year-olds who played center and the offensive backfield positions of quarterback, fullback, and right and left halfback. Three very different offensive plays that depended totally on the boys' execution were carefully pinpointed. All the behaviors that were required for each play were written out in detail and summarized into a checklist like the one in Figure 13.1. The pinpointed behavior for one of the plays is also presented in Figure 13.1.

The feedback was delivered in the following manner. After each of the selected plays during the scrimmage, the boys ran over to the coach who immediately showed them the checklist. At a glance, the boys saw what they did correctly and what mistakes they made. The coach praised their correct executions and gave them immediate feedback about their mistakes. Prior to the use of the checklist, the only thing the coach did after a play was yell at the boys for their mistakes.

Results were dramatic. Performance on each of the three plays improved over 10 times! Perfect executions went from 2 of 84 attempted plays to 22 of 89 attempted plays. The quarterback's improvement was especially significant. Before the intervention, he had made the correct decision to throw or hold the ball in only 5 of 23 plays, while with feedback he was correct 26 of 40 times. Prior to feedback, the quarterback never successfully accomplished the "Quarterback Block" in 25 tries. During the feedback phase, he did it correctly 22 of 30 times!

A book by Martin et al (1983) should be required reading for all athletic coaches. In a wide variety of sports and documents, he reports study after study showing improvements of up to 1,000 percent over baseline.

As applied in medical settings, feedback is called "biofeedback"—the process of providing patients with "real-time" data on their physiological functioning. Typical measures used in biofeedback are: heart rate, blood pressure, skin temperature, and muscle tension. As amazing as it seems, people are learning how to control these and other functions heretofore thought uncontrollable without medication. The medical and personal benefits of increasing feedback to patients is enormous. Until recently,

Figure 13.1

DESCRIPTIONS OF STAGES FOR PLAY A, OPTION PLAY

1. QB-Center Exchange
   On the correct count, the center "snaps the ball," i.e., raises the ball between his legs and quickly places the ball in the hands of the quarterback (QB). The QB should have the ball firmly in his hands.

2. QB-RHB Fake
   With the ball in his hands, the QB moves quickly down the line as the right halfback (RHB) goes toward the middle of the line. The QB fakes a handoff to the RHB, i.e., places the ball in the RHB's hands. As the RHB bends over and runs low appearing to have the ball, the QB pulls the ball back and continues going down the line.

3. FB Blocks End
   The fullback (FB) sprints toward the defensive right end, watching his position. Depending on the depth of the end, the FB either blocks or passes him by. If the end penetrates three yards (2.7m) beyond the line of scrimmage, the FB passes him by and turns upfield to block another defensive player. If the end penetrates less than three yards, the FB blocks him away for the QB and drives him out of the area of the play.

4. QB Decision To Pitch or Keep
   After the QB-RHB fake, the QB continues moving down the line, watching the defensive right end. If the end has been passed by the FB, the QB keeps the ball and turns upfield. If the end has been blocked by the FB, the QB pitches, i.e., tosses the ball to the LHB and turns upfield to block.

5. QB Action
   Whatever decision is made, the backs should proceed as described. If the QB decides to keep the ball, he should quickly turn upfield following on the heels of his blockers. The LHB should turn upfield trailing the QB. If the QB decides to pitch, he should pitch the ball to the LHB slightly in front of him and chest height. The LHB should be positioned to the right of and behind the QB keeping his eyes on the QB. Once the LHB catches the ball, he should turn upfield following his blockers.

Sample Checklist for Play A, Option Play			
Behavior		Attempts	
1. QB-Center Exchange	3	3	3
2. QB-RHB Fake	3	3	3
3. FB Blocks End	3	0	3
4. QB Decision To Pitch or Keep	0	0	3
5. QB Action	3	3	3
% Score	80	60	100

QB-Quarterback	3-Done Correctly
RHB-Right Halfback	0-Done Incorrectly
LHB-Left Halfback	
FB-Fullback	

(Adapted from "A Behavioral Approach to Coaching Football: Improving Play Execution of the Offensive Backfield on a Youth Football Team," by J. Komaki and F. Barnett. In Journal of Applied Behavior Analysis, 1977, Vol. 10, 660. Copyright 1971 by the Society of the Experimental Analysis of Behavior, Inc. Reprinted by permission.)

physicians informed patients about their conditions only in the most general terms. Now
the best informed physicians encourage patients to self-monitor their own physical
conditions. Sales of products to aid in self-
monitoring, such as heart-rate monitors, automatic blood-pressure-measuring devices, etc.
are booming. It is easy to see from the wide
range of examples presented that feedback is
important in every phase of life. The need
for feedback doesn't stop when people come
through the office or plant door.

Feedback is often the least expensive and
easiest method people can use to start improving performance. The reason more
people don't turn to increasing feedback as a
solution to performance problems is that they
have tried it in the past and it has not
worked.

Two reasons for this failure are they often
aren't able to differentiate feedback from
information and data, and they don't understand the conditions that make feedback most
effective.

In a comprehensive review of the research
on performance feedback, Balcazar, Hopkins
and Suarez (1985) concluded that:

1. Feedback does not uniformly improve
   performance.
2. Adding rewards and/or goal-setting
   procedures to feedback improves the
   consistency of its effects.
3. Some characteristics of feedback are
   more consistently associated with improved performance than others.

Putting a graph on the wall or having
someone graph performance on some
variable will not guarantee improvement. A
number of factors determine whether feedback will be effective, and when they are
factored into the design of a feedback system,
the performance improvement that follows its
use will surprise even the most experienced
manager. The rest of this chapter will detail
the factors to consider in designing an
effective feedback system.

THE RELATIONSHIP OF FEEDBACK TO ANTECEDENTS AND REINFORCEMENT

Feedback comes in many forms. Our five
senses provide us with constant feedback
from our environment. However, in the work
place we rely primarily on two: seeing and
hearing. We may hear from the boss that our
on-time shipment rate is below last month's.
At the same time we may see a graph showing a decreasing rate of performance over the
last five days. Yet it is possible that neither of
these events will change performance.

We may choose to ignore the feedback and
not use it to improve performance, even
though we could if we wanted to. Feedback
only presents the opportunity to improve
performance. The actual improvement in
performance comes about only if reinforcement is associated with improvement in
performance.

In almost every case where performers
have not been getting systematic feedback on
performance, the addition of feedback results
in immediate improvement. To most people,
it appears that performance improved as a
direct result of the feedback.

One of the problems in assessing the role
of feedback in performance is that the presentation of feedback is usually associated
with some evaluative statement. These
statements, whether positive or negative,
verbal or written, tend to work to increase
performance.

If the comments are positive, performance
increases because of positive reinforcement.
If the comments are negative, performance
increases through negative reinforcement.

The point is, feedback alone does not
change performance; rather, performance
changes because of the consequences directly
associated with it, or those expected in the
future. If there are no consequences associated with the feedback, performance will not
improve, or if it does, the improvement will
only be temporary.

When Balcazar (1985) and colleagues compared studies involving 1) feedback alone,

2) feedback and consequences, 3) feedback and goal setting, and 4) feedback, consequences, and goal setting, they found that feedback alone produced the lowest level of consistent effects.

Feedback is most effective when it is a discriminative stimulus (S^D) for positive reinforcement. In other words, if positive reinforcement is consistently associated with increases in performance, the feedback takes on properties of conditioned reinforcement. That is to say, seeing the improvement is a reinforcer to the performer. From an organizational perspective this is highly desirable because much more reinforcement will occur under these conditions than if all reinforcement is dependent on the presence of a supervisor or manager. Of course, this means there has to be a history of pairing feedback and reinforcement, usually by management, if performers are to take on a part of the reinforcement burden.

In a study of the effect of consequences of individual feedback on behavior, Ilgen, Fisher, and Taylor (1979) stated that the effectiveness of feedback "depends upon the extent to which it functions to lead the individual to anticipate a reward...." They say further: "...the simple conclusion that increased feedback leads to increased motivation..." is questionable. They go on to suggest that feedback and reinforcement are quite different concepts and that increased motivation is attributable to reinforcement, not feedback.

A study by Chapanis (1964) supports that conclusion. He found feedback alone had no effect on performance. Participants in his experiment were asked to do an extremely boring task: punch holes in paper. The amount of feedback varied from group to group. The crucial point in this study was that no consequences were provided for increasing performance. The experimenter in the room acted as if he didn't care whether people did well or poorly. People were paid by the hour, not for their performance. Hence there was no tangible or social reinforcement for improved performance. The

results showed that whether people received feedback or not, their performance did not increase. Therefore, Chapanis concluded feedback without reinforcement does not increase performance.

Feedback is a necessary, but far from a sufficient, condition for maximizing performance.

CHARACTERISTICS OF EFFECTIVE FEEDBACK

Feedback is a seemingly simple concept. However, there are a number of factors that tend to increase or decrease its effectiveness. Ten of them are presented below.

1. Specific information
2. On a performance the person controls
3. Immediate
4. Individualized
5. Self-monitored when possible or, if not, graphed by the person in charge
6. Presented in relation to baseline, subgoals, and final goals
7. Antecedent to reinforcement
8. Positive
9. Easily understood
10. Graphed

1. Give specific how-to information

Specific here means, "Will the performers know exactly what to do to improve performance when they look at the graph?" A graph on department quality may not be feedback to many of the performers because they won't know what to do differently to improve quality when they see the data. But they *will* know if you break out the data by particular aspects of quality, such as number of documents processed without an error, mean number of copies between service calls (copier service technicians), machine run time, number of board-feet sanded per sandpaper belt (furniture plant), or percentage of door weatherstrips installed correctly the first time (auto assembly plant). When planning feedback, it is a good idea to test the performers to see if they know what to do when the data goes up or down.

2. Give feedback on a performance the person can control

There are two aspects to this characteristic. First, the performance must be something the performers can do themselves. While this seems obvious, this principle is often violated. For example, in a furniture plant, employees were charged with reducing the amount of money spent on forklift truck maintenance each month. A graph was put on the wall and everyone set out to do things to reduce the maintenance bill. They were extremely disappointed when the figure for the first month showed an increase over baseline. The problem was that the company repairing their equipment had a price increase that month. The problem was solved when they pinpointed instead "percentage routine maintenance items performed on schedule." The same considerations discussed about control in Chapter Nine on pinpointing are appropriate here.

The other aspect of control to be considered is: does the person have the knowledge and skill to improve the performance? If the person is untrained or poorly trained, feedback will be ineffective, even though the performance is technically under the control of the performer.

3. Give immediate feedback

In repetitive tasks, project work, and other ongoing activity, the general rule on feedback is, the sooner the better. Hourly feedback would give performers more opportunities to change performance than would weekly feedback. Even in a time when computers can process millions of bits of information per second, performance feedback is often in the "dark ages" when it comes to lag-time between the performance and the feedback. Not only is it almost impossible to get daily feedback, many organizations get their monthly data a week or more *after* the measured performance period ends.

Daily feedback is recommended whenever

possible. Weekly is acceptable. Indeed, Balcazar et al (1985) found that weekly feedback was as effective as daily feedback. However, this finding should be interpreted cautiously since over 40 percent of studies reviewed were conducted using feedback without reinforcement. In a study on the prevention of back injuries, Alavosius and Sulzer-Azaroff (in press) found that immediate feedback produced results in two days, whereas weekly feedback required several weeks.

Findings clearly show monthly feedback is rarely associated with consistent improvement. While monthly data may be interesting, and even reinforcing, it should not be the only feedback that performers get.

Where feedback is given to improve the quality of performance (called formative feedback by Tosti and Jackson, 1981), research indicates the best time for the feedback is not immediately after the session or performance, but immediately prior to the next session or performance. Brewer (1989) conducted a study in which trainees were given feedback on their performance in an interviewing training program. Three feedback conditions were examined: immediately before the sessions, immediately after the sessions, or no feedback. The results showed a significantly better performance for the "feedback before" group as compared to the "feedback after" group. See Figure 13.2.

4. Individualize feedback

Feedback is most helpful when it is based on an individual's performance. When you have individual feedback, many other characteristics of effective feedback are easily met. It is more likely to be specific, under the performer's control, self-monitored, immediate, and easily understood.

However, in many instances individual measures do not exist. In such cases, the rule is to provide feedback to the smallest group possible. If three people operate as a team on a particular machine, feedback should be on team performance. If two people work on a project and their individual performance is

Figure 13.2

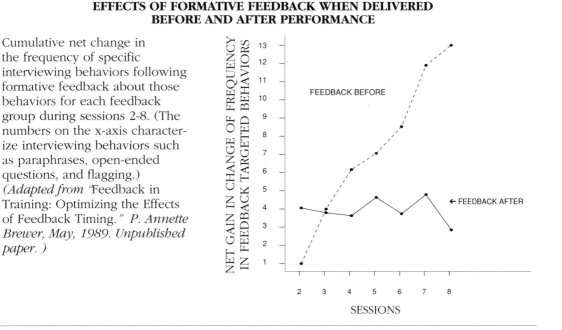

EFFECTS OF FORMATIVE FEEDBACK WHEN DELIVERED BEFORE AND AFTER PERFORMANCE

Cumulative net change in the frequency of specific interviewing behaviors following formative feedback about those behaviors for each feedback group during sessions 2-8. (The numbers on the x-axis characterize interviewing behaviors such as paraphrases, open-ended questions, and flagging.)
(Adapted from "Feedback in Training: Optimizing the Effects of Feedback Timing." P. Annette Brewer, May, 1989. Unpublished paper.)

not measured, give feedback on the project status. When giving feedback for any group, no matter how small, you always run the risk of reinforcing the work of those who are not contributing their fair share. Of course in those situations, you want to focus on the behaviors of the individuals so you will know what you are reinforcing.

Even if you are able to give individual feedback, you should also give group feedback. Team, crew, section, shift, and department feedback is always appropriate. In fact, group feedback increases reinforcement opportunities considerably over those provided by individual feedback. With group feedback, supervisors, managers, peers, and even visitors can become part of the reinforcement system. In other words, always give individual *and* group feedback whenever possible. One word of warning: individual feedback should be given privately. Group feedback is most often posted publicly.

5. Encourage self-monitored performance

When feedback is given on the individual level, it is possible for people to measure their own performance, thereby enabling feedback to be immediate. Immediate feedback allows the person to adjust performance before it deviates too greatly from the desired level. Organizations that use Statistical Process Control (SPC) systems stress this point. Performers constantly monitor the process in order to take action and make adjustments that are necessary to keep the process "in control."

Again immediacy is certain if employees collect the data. If they depend on someone else to provide the feedback, it will not be immediate. Nevertheless, supervisory feedback does seem to have some advantages. The data presented by Balcazar et al (1985) indicates that feedback provided by supervisors or managers produced more consistent results than self-generated feedback. Upon interpretation, the authors point out that:

Feedback provided by supervisors may be more likely to be associated with reinforcement or punishment. Feedback from supervisors could function to prompt the supervisors to provide differential reinforcement. If supervisors are responsible for differentially reinforcing work behavior, putting the feedback in the hands of the supervisor may increase the likelihood that reinforcement is contingent on desired behavior.

However, if self-generated feedback is used by the supervisor as the basis for frequent contingent reinforcement, it should produce even greater effects than supervisor-generated feedback alone.

Self-monitoring is especially valuable for new employees. The sooner they know whether they are right or wrong, the more rapidly they will learn the job. Also, if the supervisor pairs reinforcement with self-monitoring, it sets the performer up for later on-the-job success. It also makes the trainee less dependent on the supervisor for feedback, which helps both be more efficient.

A typical objection to self-monitoring is people will "fake the data." Since they know the boss will be looking at the data they keep, they will record information that makes them look good. If people fake data it means that it has been used primarily to punish them in the past. The experience of many people has been that their bosses have ignored data when it showed average or better performance, and used data as an antecedent to threaten or criticize if performance was below average.

If performers have this history, it is best not to begin to give feedback with self-monitoring. Feedback must first be established as an antecedent to reinforcement. It is often necessary to use a combination of social and tangible reinforcers to break down the negative associations that people have with being measured. Often, when feedback has been established as an antecedent for reinforcement, people ask to keep their own graphs.

When starting people on self-monitoring, it is usually advisable to reinforce accurate recording rather than changes in the performance. Accurate recording is easy to measure and easy to reinforce. This ensures that early experiences with feedback will be associated with positive reinforcement. After accurate recording has been achieved you can move into reinforcing improvements in the data.

6. If not self-monitored, feedback should be delivered by the person in charge

When feedback cannot be self-monitored, it should be delivered by the person in charge. This may be the person's boss, team or group leader, teacher, coach, parent, etc. Feedback should not be graphed or delivered by secretaries, clerks, or any other person not in a functional leadership position. Providing feedback to performers is one of the primary responsibilities of a leader and it cannot be delegated to others. If managers and supervisors are to create successful employees, then they must accept that *providing feedback and reinforcement are the most important functions of a leader.*

There are four reasons why the leader should deliver the performance feedback. First, when the leader takes the time to record and deliver the feedback in person, it sends the message that the information is important. Hence, the feedback is more important than the many other numbers the person may see.

Second, performers are aware the boss knows how they are doing. Since the focus is positive, people are more likely to feel the boss cares about them. Of course, in the process of delivering the feedback, conversation with the boss will often confirm that feeling.

The third reason is that by taking the time to graph the data, the boss will learn more about the data than if someone else does it for her. And fourth, if the boss records the data, she is more likely to reinforce than if the facts and figures are recorded by someone else.

The most compelling reason from a performance standpoint, again, comes from the research survey by Balcazar et al (1985). They say:

> Feedback delivered by supervisors or managers has been more frequently associated with consistent effects than feedback from any other sources for which adequate numbers of experiments have been conducted.

7. *Positive feedback is most effective*
The most frequent kind of feedback people get on their performance is about what they are doing wrong. As a matter of fact, when someone says, "I need to give you some feedback," most people don't expect a discourse on their personality strengths.

Performance data in most organizations is consistent with that philosophy. We count rejects, mistakes, errors, accidents, absenteeism, etc. Of course, most of these pinpoints violate the "Dead Man's Test," (see Chapter Ten) and as such are subject to all the problems associated with such pinpoints.

It is, therefore, much better to give feedback on attendance, percent of yield, percent of orders processed correctly, percent of error-free documents processed, and percent of safe working behaviors.

However, there is another compelling reason to track positively-stated pinpoints. It has to do with positive reinforcement. Feedback on a negatively stated pinpoint is a poor antecedent for positive reinforcement. For example, imagine a boss saying, "Rejects are down 10 percentage points. You aren't doing as badly this week as you were last week." This would not likely be a reinforcing statement. If, instead, the boss said, "Quality has improved by 10 percentage points this week over last week—that's good improvement," people will find that more reinforcing.

A clue as to whether you are violating this guideline is the direction of improvement on the feedback graph. If, in order to indicate improvement, your graph line must go down, you probably have a negatively stated

Figure 13.3

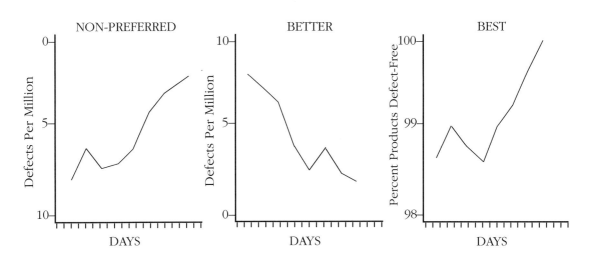

PREFERRED WAY FOR MAKING A GRAPH POSITIVE

pinpoint.

Some people try to solve this problem by inverting the scale. That is, if "zero defects" is our goal, put the zero on the top of the graph. See Figure 13.3. A better alternative is to graph the number or percentage of quality products produced or services delivered.

Another way to avoid this problem is to graph percent improvement over baseline. Therefore, "improvement in waste" would be preferable to "waste reduction." See Figure 13.4. If you cannot think of how to express a particular problem in a positive way, graph the negative and show a decreasing line. When you do this, write on the graph in large letters, "Down is Good."

In any event, you need to be aware of the problem of negatively stated pinpoints and try to avoid them. Also, take special pains not to couple negative statements with attempts at positive reinforcement.

8. Feedback should be goal related

A significant advantage that feedback offers to performers is that it lets them know where they stand in relation to some goal, standard, or other target level. (Goals will be discussed in detail in Chapter Fifteen.) For now, the important point is that feedback with good goals is more consistently associated with

performance improvement than feedback without goals.

Even when managers don't set goals, many performers will set them for themselves when they have proper feedback. Just putting a baseline on the feedback graph will cause many performers to set at least some minimal goal above it. Setting good goals requires considerable knowledge and experience. But when properly used with feedback, the performance improvement that is generated often surprises even the most optimistic of managers.

9. Feedback should be easy to understand

Feedback that is not understood is not feedback by our definition. If performers don't understand the feedback, it is unlikely that they know what to do to make improvements. Even though it may be understandable to the person presenting it, you must make sure that it is understandable to the person receiving it. This is particularly important when giving feedback in the form of composite scores, such as indexes, checklists, and matrices.

It is a good idea, at least in the beginning, for supervisors or managers to present the feedback in person. This way you can see people's responses and can ask if they understand the data. You can also determine if the performers know what to do to improve by asking them to explain it to you, or to someone else in your presence.

Another way to avoid the confusion is to allow the performers to create the feedback.

10. Feedback should be on graphs

Something that people can see in picture form is often better than oral or written descriptions of how well they are performing—"a picture is worth a thousand words." Feedback is best displayed on a graph. Brethower (1972) states:

> Graphic displays of performance measures are exceptionally useful. They are objective; they can show performance

Figure 13.4

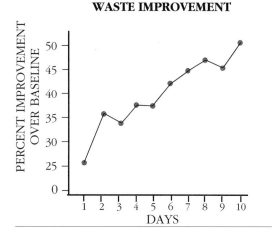

WASTE IMPROVEMENT

The Graph Didn't Work

In the early days of applying Performance Management, we often saw graphs that were weeks out-of-date. When asked why they were not up-to-date, supervisors replied, "The graph quit working." In other words, they put the graph up and, as if by magic, the performance went up, often dramatically. However, after a few weeks it began to decline, and when it did the supervisors' graphing behavior was extinguished. Inevitably, they quit graphing. It became clear in these instances that the presence of graphed data alone was not a reinforcer.

Usually, the appearance of measures in any form in the work place is an antecedent for punishment. Good numbers are taken for granted and poor numbers are the occasion for "corrective action." It is not surprising, therefore, that when performance—individual or group—is graphed, performance increases as a means of avoiding the punishment (negative reinforcement). However, as performance varies, sometimes higher and sometimes lower than normal, and nothing happens in either case, performance typically drifts back to the original level. The conclusion reached by many supervisors at that point is, "The graph quit working."

Graphs don't change performance. Consequences do. More often than not, people are necessary to deliver those consequences. If you think graphs are a substitute for personal interaction with employees, you are in for a disappointment.

Computers will inevitably provide much feedback automatically. Some people use this as a way of either managing more people or spending less time with the present ones. The results of such a strategy are clear—poorer performance than would otherwise be possible with a more knowledgeable and personal application of feedback.

changes over time and they can often be maintained by the person or persons whose performance is being graphed.

In over 20 years of PM applications, graphs have consistently been the most effective device for giving feedback. This is no accident, because when graphs go up, so does reinforcement. In schools and homes, as well as in work settings, when someone graphs performance, that performance is likely to improve because in most cases graphs are an antecedent for reinforcement.

11. Feedback should be an antecedent for reinforcement

This topic, discussed earlier in the chapter, cannot be overemphasized. Feedback presented without reinforcement will, under the best of circumstances, eventually lose its ability to sustain or improve performance. If you don't have a plan for reinforcing improvement *before* you start giving feedback, the probability is you will eventually get only a minimal level of performance.

One final quote from Balcazar et al (1985):

...the evidence suggests that the best bets are to combine feedback that is graphically presented at least once a week with tangible rewards. Eighty percent of the studies with known effects that applied these characteristics were consistently effective regardless of whether goal-setting procedures were additionally used.

This does not mean that tangible reinforcement must be given at least once a week, but simply that feedback when paired with reinforcement, both social and tangible, produces the best effect.

14

Feedback in Graphs

Graphs are the best way to present feedback because they create additional opportunities for reinforcement. In the last chapter we stressed that feedback alone is not a reinforcer. Instead, feedback acts as an antecedent for reinforcement, allowing individuals to reinforce each other and creating possibilities for self-reinforcement. In other words, graphs enhance feedback and reinforcement.

When people view an ascending line on a graph that represents their team's performance, team members usually comment to each other about the performance. Often they report feelings of pride, satisfaction, and achievement. Under these conditions, seeing an improving trend can be a powerful antecedent for reinforcement. And if team improvements are reinforced, it makes the individual feedback even more effective.

Trends are often not easy to see when data is only in tabular form. For example, compare the graphs and the tables in Figure 14.1. Which display makes the easiest and clearest comparison between past and present performance and future goals? Graphs do.

Seeing performance improve and approach a goal is a significant reinforcer for most people, but that improvement is not always visible when information is presented as a list of numbers or in a table.

Since feedback is defined in terms of information that will help the performer know what to do, graphs must provide that information to be effective. In fact, they must contain a number of elements.

THE MECHANICS OF GRAPHING PERFORMANCE FEEDBACK

The following items will usually be included on a graph: 1) labels, 2) baseline, 3) intervention, and 4) goal. Each will be discussed, and illustrated in Figure 14.2.

Feedback is an antecedent for reinforcement

©Ray Helle. Reprinted with permission.

It's just something the kids scratched out but for some reason I feel good when I look at it.

Figure 14.1

A COMPARISON OF THE USE OF TABLES AND GRAPHS IN PRESENTING FEEDBACK

1. Average Weekly Temperature
   in Atlanta, Georgia

March	51
	49
	47
	53
April	67
	65
	70
	66
May	70
	66
	62
	78

2. Percentage Productivity
   Improvements Third Shift

Week	Percent
1	72.9
2	71.1
3	71.2
4	73.2
5	72.3
6	72.3
7	73.45
8	73.58
9	73.9
10	74.39
11	79.5
12	75.18
13	74.6
14	76.1
15	78.5
16	72.8
17	78.3
18	79.2

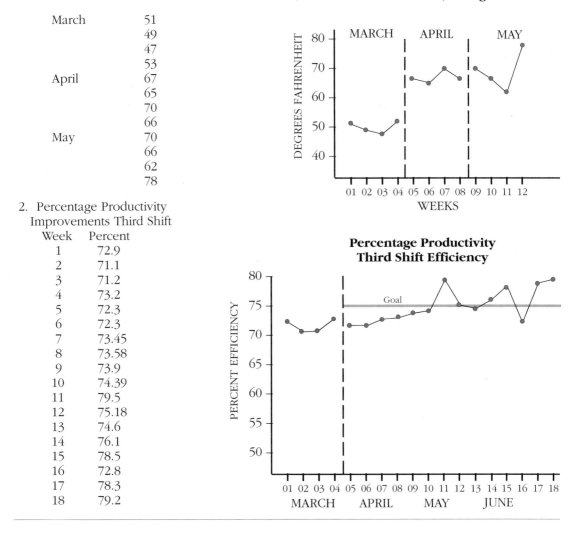

Labels

The graph label **(1)** should be a concise but descriptive statement of the performance being graphed. It is usually centered across the top of the graph.

The vertical axis, sometimes referred to as the y-axis **(2)**, is the measure of the performance being graphed. A label **(3)** of the measure should also be included.

Since you are usually interested in performance over time, the horizontal axis or x-axis **(4)** should denote the time periods. The x-axis label **(5)** will usually be hours, days, weeks, etc.

Baseline

A graph should have a plotted baseline. A baseline **(6)** shows the performance prior to any changes in feedback, reinforcement, or other variables. This allows performers to compare their present performance with their past performance. The baseline can be labeled either "baseline" or the specific time period covered by the baseline, e.g., "1987" or "prior six months."

Generally, representing the baseline data in terms of an average is not appropriate unless it is very stable. An average line may give a very distorted picture of performance. An average conceals trends. Because the same average can represent either an increasing or decreasing trend (see Figure 14.3), it is best to use actual data in the baseline.

Intervention

The intervention **(7)** is defined by the point where you start your performance improvement procedures. A vertical line is usually placed between the last data point in the baseline and the intervention. Any additional changes in the program should be so marked. For example, if you change the feedback interval or the reinforcement schedule, additional intervention lines should indicate those changes **(8)**. The intervention usually will be labeled either "intervention" or will use the procedural description of the intervention such as "Feedback and R+".

Separate the intervention data from the baseline data by a break in the line. When the lines are connected, it inaccurately gives the appearance of change before the intervention.

In addition, when data points are missing for some reason, do not draw a line through the missing week. Break the line **(9)**. This more accurately represents performance data.

Goals

Most graphs should include goals. If the final goal is known and represents significant improvement, sub-goals should be drawn on

Figure 14.2

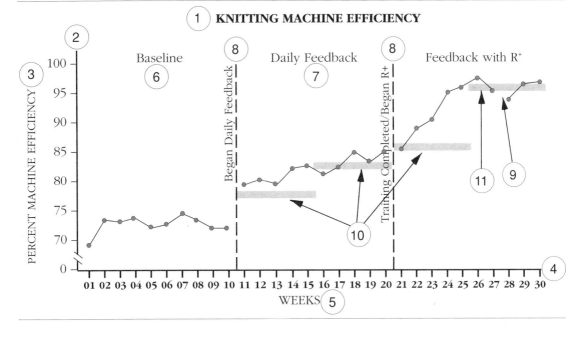

Figure 14.3

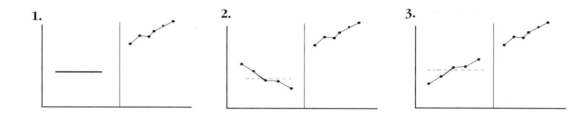

ILLUSTRATION OF PROBLEMS WITH
PERFORMANCE AVERAGE USED AS BASELINE

1. Using an average for baseline makes the intervention results look good.

2. However, when the actual data is plotted, it looks even better.

3. Unfortunately the actual baseline data could look like this, which shows no change in the baseline trend.

the graph **(10)** in addition to the final goal **(11)**. The rules for setting sub-goals are discussed in Chapter Fifteen.

A graph doesn't have to include a goal to provide effective feedback. In fact, if you have a new performance, or one for which you don't have baseline data, you may not know where to set a goal. The graph can still be effective if the highest data point serves as the goal for the next performance period. For example, if you have no baseline data, the first data point would serve as a performance target to improve for the next measurement period.

SPECIAL CHARACTERISTICS OF PUBLICLY DISPLAYED GROUP GRAPHS

Management should not display individual performance graphs publicly. In addition, management should not put pressure on people to post their own performance graphs.

If performers want to display them on their own initiative, it is certainly acceptable. Public posting has advantages in that it

increases reinforcement opportunities, but the key is that the performer must want to do it. The rule for management is: individual graphs should be kept privately; group graphs should be displayed publicly.

While public and individual graphs have many characteristics in common, there are some differences. The differences generally relate to such things as size, location, and appearance. While individual graphs can be constructed according to the rules presented above, to be most effective, group graphs should be constructed with the following characteristics in mind.

Easy to understand

A line graph is the easiest to construct and the easiest to understand. In addition, since most of the graphs in Applied Behavior Analysis are **time-series graphs**—graphs that track the same variable over some period of time—the line graph is most appropriate from the standpoint of analyzing the data.

Bar graphs, pie charts, and various other formats are useful under certain circumstances. For example, when graphing several variables at one point in time, bar graphs are the most appropriate. However, in PM the most frequently used format is the line graph. For more information on when to use various graphic formats and the advantages and disadvantages of each, read Wilkinson (1988).

Another element in making a graph easy to understand is to limit the number of lines on the graph. Although there may be circumstances that dictate several lines, the general guideline is to have only one or two lines on a single graph. When you have more than two, the lines begin to cross and performance is hard to track. If you have more than two variables to plot, make separate graphs.

Easy to see

Make the graph large enough to see and read from a distance (at least 24" x 36"). The average $8^{1/2}$ x 11 page is too small for most publicly-displayed graphs. People should be able to read the graph from a distance without having to come close to study it.

Attractive, neat, and colorful

To be effective antecedents, graphs must attract attention. People must want to look at them. The basic principles of advertising apply here. What gets you to read an advertisement in a magazine or newspaper? Why do you look at it?

If graphs are attractive, neat, and colorful, people will pay more attention than if they are not. In addition, the more creatively the information is displayed, the more effective it will be in attracting attention. Make the graph look different from other things on the wall.

Accessible and convenient

Graphs should be located in places where employees will encounter them in the course of their day-to-day activities. Generally speaking, graphs should be in the work area.

For posting group and team graphs, any place where employees and managers pass daily would usually be suitable. The best

places for this kind of feedback are in common places near entrances, breakrooms, vending machines, work stations, the cafeteria, or even the restrooms. Avoid dark hallways, conference rooms, and private offices.

People should not have to go out of their way to see the graphs. Nor should they have to interrupt someone else's work to see the graphs. That's why the supervisor's office or conference room is not a good place for a group-performance graph that is posted daily.

Varied

To maintain interest in the graph, you should do two things. One is to continue to provide consequences for the performance represented by the graph. The other is to vary its location and appearance. Don't let it become a part of the wallpaper. Moving the graph around and changing the format and appearance helps maintain interest.

Remember that graphs don't change performance. Consequences do. You can have a graph that meets all the above criteria, but performance will not improve until reinforcement occurs. Do not count on the graph to provide reinforcement. If you don't reinforce at least occasionally, you may find that the performers have little interest in the graph and the feedback will be ineffective.

EVALUATING PERFORMANCE CHANGE

Another very important function of graphs is to facilitate data analysis. Since data is often the source of reinforcement, you must be able to interpret the data so you know when to reinforce. The way data is presented can make a difference in whether a performer is reinforced appropriately.

For example, if an average is used in the baseline for the data in Figure 14.4, you would probably not reinforce since the two points are below the average. However, if you had plotted the actual data, you would

Figure 14.4

EXAMPLE OF PLOTTING BASELINE DATA

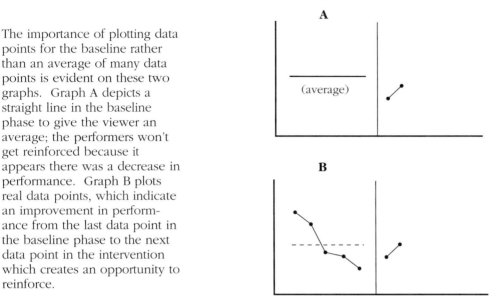

The importance of plotting data points for the baseline rather than an average of many data points is evident on these two graphs. Graph A depicts a straight line in the baseline phase to give the viewer an average; the performers won't get reinforced because it appears there was a decrease in performance. Graph B plots real data points, which indicate an improvement in perform- ance from the last data point in the baseline phase to the next data point in the intervention which creates an opportunity to reinforce.

probably have reinforced since the two data points represent substantial improvement in reversing a downward trend.

One of the problems with using graphs as the basis for reinforcement is that only results are graphed (and only behaviors are rein- forced). Therefore, people delivering the reinforcement on the basis of graphed data are at an immediate disadvantage if they have not seen the behavior occurring at some point. Reinforcing solely on the basis of a graph can lead to serious problems. These problems have been discussed at several points in this book.

Just because you see an increase on a graph does not mean you should reinforce unless you are confident that the person or group has engaged in reinforceable behaviors to get the increase. Deming has heightened management's awareness of the folly of trying to manage without data on the manufacturing system and the necessity of understanding the natural variation in the system.

When attempting to reinforce from graphs

you need to be able to separate human per- formance from system performance. Data can go up just from natural variation in the system or from changes in the system that the performer had no part in bringing about. If you reinforce the changes you see on a graph, not due to a change on the part of the performer, then you don't know what behav- ior actually got reinforced.

It is critically important to maximizing per- formance in organizations that you are able to differentiate changes due to *human* per- formance from *system* performance. In many cases a knowledge of statistics is required. Organizations that don't have Statistical Process Control systems are at a serious competitive disadvantage with those who do.

With PM we are trying to learn how people function most effectively and how to create the conditions in an organization to bring that about. There are many systems in organiza- tions that do not facilitate performance, yet they continue to operate year in and year out. This happens because management is not able to see the effect of these systems on human performance. By being able to isolate the contribution of human performance on the system and the contribution of the system to human performance, you are on the way to being able to create the ideal work place.

Applied behavior analysts use several techniques to evaluate behavior and performance change. Many sophisticated techniques are available, but we will detail only three since they will handle most of the situations you'll encounter. For a more detailed description of these and other methods, read Cooper et al (1987).

The A-B design

The most common way to evaluate behavior change is with the use of an A-B design. An A-B design is the simple comparison of baseline data with intervention data. Figure 14.5 is an A-B design.

While this is easy and often is sufficient to evaluate change and provide reinforcement, it is the least powerful of the three designs. You can increase the power of this procedure by having a good baseline.

The best baseline is one that is long and stable. In practice this means you want enough data to rule out the existence of either an upward or downward trend. There are many statistical tests to determine trends in data. Two tests used by SPC practitioners are: 1) seven consecutive points above the baseline average and, 2) seven consecutive ascending or descending points.

Even if there is a trend in the baseline, it still may be useful. For example, if the trend is in the opposite direction from the goal of the intervention, reversing the trend can be impressive. See Figure 14.5. If the baseline is

Figure 14.5

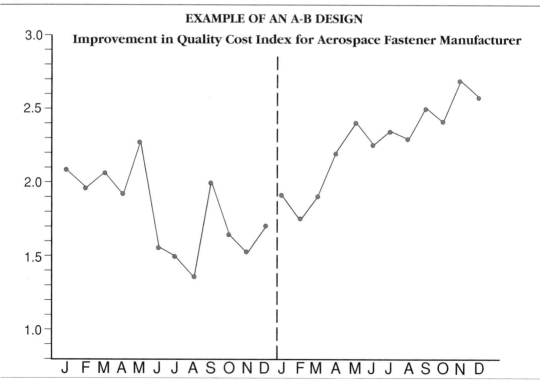

EXAMPLE OF AN A-B DESIGN
Improvement in Quality Cost Index for Aerospace Fastener Manufacturer

in the direction of the goal, the only way you would be able to show an effect would be to accelerate the trend. Figure 14.6 illustrates some good and poor baselines.

A criticism of the A-B design is other factors may change coincidentally with the intervention: "Attendance always improves this time of year," "The humidity changed," "We changed vendors at about that same time," "We are running an easier pattern now." In other words, what happened was due to factors other than the PM intervention. When this criticism is leveled, other more powerful experimental designs must be used.

The A-B-A and A-B-A-B designs

The A-B-A design, often referred to as a reversal design, is the same as the A-B design but with the addition of a third phase which is a return to the baseline condition. Often what this involves is the removal of the feedback or reinforcement that was added in the intervention (B phase). When the third phase is implemented, you would of course expect the data would change in the direction of the baseline, if the intervention was truly what produced the change.

In most of the Applied Behavior Analysis research there is the addition of another phase to the A-B-A procedure. It is the reintroduction of the initial intervention (B phase). For example, if feedback and reinforcement were introduced after collecting baseline data and later stopped, it would be started again in the fourth phase. See Figure 14.7.

These four steps constitute the A-B-A-B design. As Cooper et al (1987) state:

The A-B-A-B reversal design is the most straightforward, powerful, single subject design for demonstrating a functional relation between an environmental manipulation and behavior. When a functional relation is revealed (i.e., an analysis has been achieved) with a reversal design, the data tells how the behavior works.

While A-B-A designs are an important way to verify the effects of a particular PM intervention, they are rarely recommended in business situations.

One reason is that they are not practical. It is unrealistic to expect that a manager who institutes reinforcement as a way to solve a problem will deliberately stop the reinforcement after the performance has improved just to demonstrate a functional relationship between the reinforcement and the change in performance.

Another reason is an ethical consideration. Many people would be reluctant to withhold reinforcement when the recipient is benefiting substantially from it.

Even at that, there are many unintentional reversals that allow us to see clearly the impact of PM interventions. Often a supervisor who has been giving feedback and reinforcement may get sick, be promoted, quit or otherwise be absent, and her replacement does not provide the feedback and reinforcement. People sometimes reach a goal and stop reinforcement because they think it is no longer needed. At other times improvements are so substantial that managers don't believe they could result from such a simple change, and they discontinue reinforcement.

If you capitalize on these naturally occurring reversals, you will learn much about the effect of your various attempts to maximize performance.

Multiple baseline designs

One of the most practical designs is the multiple baseline. Multiple baseline does not require a reversal or rearranging the work force as required in traditional control group designs. All you have to do is stagger the interventions. Since most PM interventions do not start at the same time anyway, multiple baseline is the ideal method for doing behavioral analyses in the work place.

Look at Figure 14.8. Baseline data was collected on the percentage of time employees performed certain behaviors safely. A safety program was then introduced in the

Figure 14.6

EXAMPLES OF GOOD AND POOR BASELINES

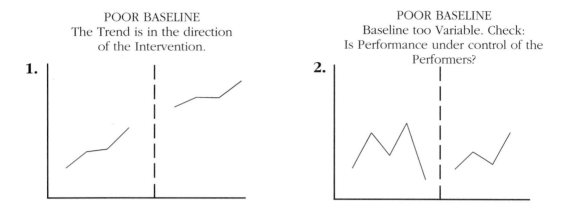

POOR BASELINE
The Trend is in the direction
of the Intervention.

1.

POOR BASELINE
Baseline too Variable. Check:
Is Performance under control of the
Performers?

2.

ACCEPTABLE BASELINE
If the Baseline shows a small but stable trending in the desired direction, it may be
acceptable when the goal of the intervention is to increase the rate of improvement.

3.

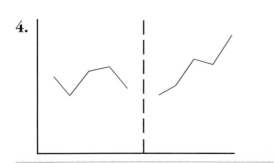

GOOD BASELINE
Stable, No Trend.

4.

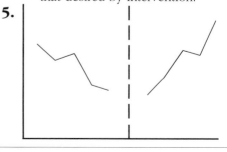

GOOD BASELINE
Decrease due to human performance. Baseline
is acceptable because it is in a trend opposite
that desired by intervention.

5.

Figure 14.7

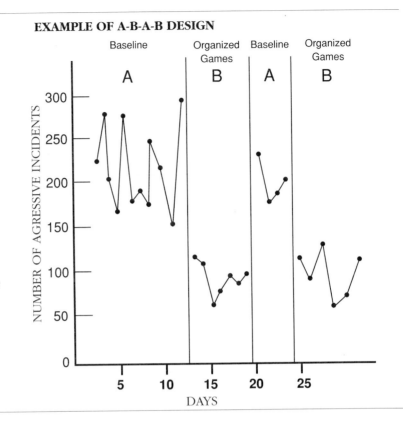

EXAMPLE OF A-B-A-B DESIGN

Frequency of incidents recorded during the 20-minute, morning observation periods on the playground.
(From "Behavioral School Psychology Goes Outdoors: The Effect of Organized Games on Playground Aggression" by H. A. Murphy, N. M. Hutchinson, and J. S. Bailey, 1983, Journal of Applied Behavior Analysis, *16, p. 33, Copyright 1983 by the Society for the Experimental Analysis of Behavior, Inc. Reprinted by permission.)*

wrapping department. At the same time, baseline data continued to be collected in the make-up department. Notice there was immediate improvement in the wrapping department, but there was no change in the make-up department. Twenty sessions later the program was introduced in the make-up department and there was immediate improvement there also.

The beauty of this design is that it allows you to assess change in different behaviors in one person, such as, quality, productivity, waste, etc; or change between individuals; between different groups in the same setting (shifts); or between different groups in different settings (departments, offices or plants).

In order to use the multiple baseline effectively, several conditions must exist.

1. The performances or behaviors must be independent

Don't choose two variables that co-vary. For example, in some settings quality and production co-vary; that is, the better the equipment runs, the better the quality of the product. In other settings, particularly where production is not machine paced, the two variables operate somewhat independently and the multiple baseline would be appropriate.

2. The variables must be measured concurrently

While baselines do not always have to be started at the same time for all variables, there must be some overlap between the intervention on the first variable and the baseline of the later variables. (See Figure

14.8). This allows the comparisons needed between the interventions and baselines of other variables in the same time periods.

3. Any changes in baseline conditions must be documented

In order to make the proper analysis, any changes that might affect performance should be noted. In a number of cases, managers and supervisors have increased reinforcement in a casual way before they started their "formal" application. While it is desirable to increase reinforcement any time, it should be noted when it occurred so as not to confound the analysis.

Some people say that data analysis of this type is for the researchers and not for the real world. They don't realize they are *analyzing* data constantly, they're just not doing it *systematically.* If everybody more systematically evaluated the changes they make in the work place, we would be able to increase the effectiveness of our organizations dramatically because we would spend a lot less time doing things that contribute little or nothing to the enterprise.

Figure 14.8

PERCENTAGE OF ITEMS PERFORMED SAFELY BY EMPLOYEES IN TWO DEPARTMENTS OF A FOOD MANUFACTURING PLANT DURING A 25-WEEK PERIOD

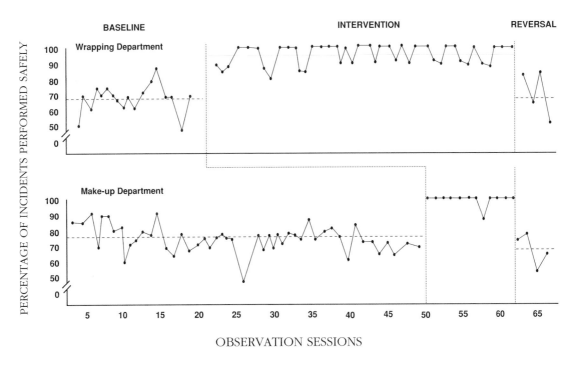

OBSERVATION SESSIONS

(Adapted from "A Behavioral Approach to Occupational Safety: Pinpointing and Reinforcing Safe Performance in a Food Manufacturing Plant" by J. Komaki, K. Barwick, and L. Scott, 1978 *Journal of Applied Psychology, Vol 63,4, pp. 434-445. Reprinted by permission.)*

15

Setting and Attaining Goals

Once you have established the correct pinpoint, selected relevant measures, and set up a feedback graph, you should determine the level of performance you need. Defining a specified, or preset, level of performance to be attained is called **goal setting**.

When the goal is far from the present performance, you will probably want to set sub-goals. **Sub-goals** are goals along the way to some ultimate goal.

An almost universal misconception is that goals alone improve performance, but the research does not support this belief. In an article on the behavioral analysis of goal setting, Fellner and Sulzer-Azaroff (1984) state, "Goal setting alone may be ineffective because the behavior of concern has been inadequately, differentially reinforced in the presence of the goal." In a study comparing financial reinforcers and goal setting, Huber (1985) concluded that "...the setting of goals, regardless of the method, does not evoke greater learning than that achieved when trainees are offered only a base salary." The fact that goals alone do not automatically improve performance can be validated by almost everyone's personal experience. We have all set goals we didn't reach, and some we didn't even try to reach. This is not to suggest that goals are ineffective. Quite the contrary, they can be very effective. However, it is naive to think that just setting a goal will consistently improve performance.

When goal setting is understood and used properly, the results can be substantial. Huber (1986) reports increases as much as 58 percent, and Locke, Feren, McCaleb, Shaw and Denny (1980) found a median performance gain of 40 percent. Pritchard, Jones, Philip and Stuebing (1988) found gains of 75 percent. Let's take a look at the proper use of goals.

THE PROPER USE OF GOALS IN PM

The most important reason for setting goals is to create additional opportunities for reinforcement. Goal attainment should, of course, be the occasion for reinforcement. You can also reinforce progress toward the goal, maintenance of performance at or above goal, and achieving levels of performance above the goal. Having a common goal gives a team a common purpose, something to rally around, something to talk about. Since added reinforcement increases performance, goals are a valuable performance improvement tool.

Goals are antecedents for performance. Therefore, they do not consistently produce improvement unless they are paired with reinforcement. Goals provide the opportunity for reinforcement, but are not necessarily the source of it. People who set goals without planning how they will celebrate success are often disappointed in the results.

When goal attainment has been consistently paired with reinforcement for a period of time, the goal takes on secondary reinforcing characteristics. This means under some conditions, reaching a goal can be reinforcing in and of itself. For this to happen, however, you must first create a history of celebrating goal achievement.

The number of pairings needed to create goals as a reinforcer is highly variable as there are a number of factors to consider. As a general rule, you should always plan reinforcement, either social or a combination of social and tangible, for all goal attainment. For an extensive analysis of the research on goal setting, the reader is referred to Fellner and Sulzer-Azaroff (1984).

Additional benefits of goal setting

Increased reinforcement is the primary way goals benefit individuals. Improved performance is the primary benefit of effective goal setting to organizations. However, there are other benefits.

Goals improve communications because they tell the performers exactly what and how much performance is desired. If their pinpoint is weight loss and the goal is to lose 25 pounds in six months, they know what to work on and when to celebrate. If the pinpoint is error-free documents and the goal is to increase the number of error-free documents processed per month, the employees know exactly what to do and when to celebrate: whenever they exceed the previous high.

The very act of collecting data on performance creates goals. The extensive statistics kept in sports, for example, are easily transformed into goals. But sometimes the proliferation of "records," especially in baseball, approaches the ridiculous. There may soon be a baseball record for "the most bases stolen by a rookie second baseman when his mother was in the stands." Bob Uecker, a baseball comedian, claims the record for "most consecutive games not played." However, the number of records that are tracked do provide much reinforcement to the fans and the players, and the game would be considerably less interesting without them.

For instance, national attention was focused on Pete Rose when he was approaching Joe DiMaggio's record of hitting safely in 56 consecutive games. Attendance increased dramatically at every ballpark in which Rose played, and his record was often the lead story on the "Six O'Clock News".

Most managers only wish they could create in the work place a fraction of the interest and enthusiasm generated by such an event. Yet excitement like that is possible at work if you understand the technology of goal setting.

HOW TO SET GOALS

Good goals

A very important consideration in setting goals is the degree to which the goal is both challenging and attainable. These two elements play a large role in the ultimate success of goal setting.

The criterion of "challenging" refers to how high to set a goal. The criterion of "attainable" refers to how low a goal should be. The best goals meet both criteria.

Making goals challenging

Most people think that high goals are the best goals. But David McClelland, who conducted research on achievement for over 40 years, discovered that taking *moderate* risks is probably the single most descriptive characteristic of high achievers. For an excellent summary of McClelland's research, particularly that which relates to managers, see Luthans (1981).

Most managers are convinced that people will not achieve what is possible unless they set very high goals. This notion has led to the practice of setting stretch goals. A stretch goal is one that is higher than the final goal. For example, if your annual goal is for a 10 percent increase, a stretch goal might be 15 or 20 percent. More often than not, the probability of attaining stretch goals is low.

The primary reason this practice has emerged has been the observation that if you don't keep another goal in front of people, they tend to slow or stop performing when they reach their goal. You probably realize by now that if this happens, performance is being driven by negative reinforcement.

The most common mistake made in goal setting is to set the goal too high. This is, of course, the worst mistake to make since goals that are too high are rarely reached, thereby reducing reinforcement for goal-directed behavior.

In most cases a goal should be set higher than present or baseline performance. When positive reinforcement is being used, people rarely find it reinforcing to attain only past performance levels.

No specific guidelines are available to indicate how far above present performance levels the goal should be set. But, most assuredly, the art of setting a challenging goal is related to the ability to set a goal no higher than people can reach before extinction sets in. The best way to ensure that extinction does not occur is to set attainable goals.

Making goals attainable

Attainable goals are those for which success is highly probable. The more attainable the goal, the more likely performers will reach it. If goal attainment is paired with positive reinforcement, successful performers will want to set higher goals. It is much better to set many small, but highly attainable goals, than one that is overly challenging.

If you make a mistake in goal setting, the best mistake is to set the goal too low. If the goal is set too low, goal attainment is likely. If the achievement is reinforced, the performers will want to achieve more in the future. By setting the goal too low, there is only a temporary loss in efficiency. Once the low goal is reached and the performance reinforced, the rate of performance will increase.

By setting a goal too high, you create a situation in which the effort toward goal attainment is extinguished, even though the effort may have improved over baseline.

This will, of course, decrease motivation in the future.

Shaping

Even if you do your best to set a final goal that seems attainable and challenging, you may still find that it is too hard for some people to reach. In such cases, shaping is necessary. **Shaping** is the process of reinforcing successive approximations toward a goal.

Shaping is usually required when teaching any new response or activity. It is also necessary when working with people who have been unsuccessful at a particular behavior or performance in the past. The performance of new employees and poor performers often requires extensive shaping.

A classical shaping situation can easily be demonstrated in teaching someone the correct way to swing a golf club. Simek and O'Brien (1981) describe the typical advice a novice might receive when trying to learn the golf swing:

> "Keep your head down!" "Keep your left arm straight!" "Take a full turn with your shoulders and a half-turn with your hips!" "Pause briefly at the top of your swing!" "Don't hurry!" "Slide your hips diagonally to the left to start your downswing!" "Now, swiftly slash your hands into the shot!" "No peeking!" "Now remember: follow through in a high graceful finish!"

Since learning golf is such a complex task, if you only told or showed someone how to do it and then only reinforced when it was correct, the student would probably never learn. Indeed many never do. If, however, the task is broken down into simple steps and the students are reinforced every time they make the slightest improvement, they will certainly want to continue practicing or look forward to their next lesson. If, on the other hand, they get no reinforcement and finish the lesson with no sign of improvement (because they still can't hit the ball correctly), they will probably be discouraged and wonder if they have any aptitude for the sport at all.

The success of group participation often depends on how well the leader shapes. If the group is reticent, the leader might reinforce any verbal comment in the beginning, no matter how off-the-wall it might be. Later, as participation increases, the criterion is changed and only comments related to the topic under discussion are reinforced. Finally, only comments that are directly related to the topic receive R+.

In teaching gymnastics, coaches give much physical help in the beginning and gradually remove it until the students perform alone. For example, in teaching a backflip, coaches may place one hand on the back and use the other to flip the child. The child is reinforced for even the smallest improvement until no help is required. At that point, only occasional reinforcement is needed to generate continuous improvement.

Every major corporation in America today preaches the need for continuous improvement. Indeed, Imai (1986) attributes the results being achieved by Japanese industry to the concept of Kaizen. He defines Kaizen as follows:

> Kaizen means improvement. Moreover, Kaizen means ongoing improvement involving everyone, including both managers and workers. The Kaizen philosophy assumes that our way of life—be it our working life, our social life, or our home life—deserves to be constantly improved.

The book *Kaizen* is filled with examples of how the Japanese use this concept in their work. Although Imai does not mention positive reinforcement specifically, it is evident in many of his illustrations. Any one person or organization seeking continuous improvement without an understanding and practice of shaping, will ultimately be unsuccessful in attaining that goal.

Setting sub-goals in shaping

In shaping, the criterion for reinforcement is any improvement, no matter how small. Generally speaking, the smaller the improvement that is reinforced, the *faster* the progress. This occurs because as small improvements are reinforced, behaviors are strengthened and more improvements will inevitably follow. Usually, shaping takes the form of setting sub-goals toward some final goal. In shaping new goal attainment, it is important to remember that the new level should be reinforced several times until it stabilizes, before proceeding to a new sub-goal.

Figure 15.1 shows an example of shaping (using a result). Notice that when a particular level is reached, lower levels are not reinforced. If performance does not improve, you will usually need to break the task into smaller elements and reinforce them before proceeding. At that point you may lower the goal, but usually when a level of performance is reached, you'll know that it is attainable, and you would therefore not reinforce performance below that level.

Attainability is clearly the key criterion in shaping. Having many smaller sub-goals instead of one large goal is not the distinguishing feature of shaping. It is the attainability of the sub-goals and the reinforcement for reaching each that defines shaping. For example, if people are performing at 75 percent efficiency and you set goals at 95 percent, 96 percent, and 97 percent, you are not shaping. The initial goal is too far from current performance.

Shaping involves two distinct activities: 1) setting a sequence of attainable sub-goals, and 2) reinforcing each time a sub-goal is met. Although some tangible reinforcement may be associated with reaching some of the sub-goals, social reinforcement is appropriate for any improvement.

Making shaping work

Successful shaping requires knowledge, skill, and patience: knowledge of the proper

Figure 15.1

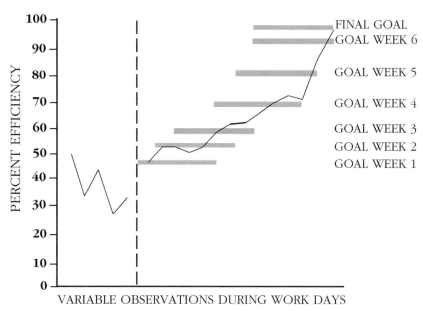

USE OF SUB-GOALS IN SHAPING HIGH PERFORMANCE

behaviors and the sequence of behaviors that constitute the desirable performance; the patience to watch others make mistakes at something you do well; and the skill to positively reinforce even small improvement.

Most of us are not highly skilled at recognizing small improvements in performance and reinforcing them. Yet that is the essential skill for the most efficient and effective managers, teachers, counselors, and coaches. Shaping requires patience but when done properly, it is the most efficient and expedient route to high performance.

Technically, shaping refers to reinforcing any behaviors that resemble the desired behavior in some way. The most obvious situation requiring behavior shaping in business is in skill training. For example, very often the behavior of giving verbal reinforcement requires shaping. If someone who never says anything complimentary about your performance makes a crude attempt at positive reinforcement, you had better reinforce it. It is unreasonable to expect that

a first attempt will be perfect. If crude attempts are reinforced, you will get more of them and have more opportunities to shape toward a more effective style. If crude attempts are punished, you can bet there will be no more attempts of any kind.

Reinforcing results may not seem like behavior shaping. However, since improved levels of efficiency, quality, and so on require people to do things differently, reinforcing small improvements indirectly reinforces changes in behaviors.

Chaining

Most of the complex performances we are concerned about in business involve many behaviors that occur in a series or sequence. Two or more behaviors that lead to reinforcement are called **behavior chains**. When we speak of performance, we are usually talking about a number of behavior chains.

In a chain, each behavior is an antecedent for the next. Even though the final behavior in the chain is the one that gets reinforced, the person learns that the final behavior will not be reinforced unless all the behaviors in the chain have been successfully executed.

For example, in assembling a motor, a person may place Part A in Slot A, put Nut A on Bolt A, and tighten. Then he turns the assembly over and repeats the procedure on the other side. Once that is done he may proceed to place a cover on the assembly and secure it with four screws.

This task can be viewed as three short chains or one long one. Initially, you might reinforce when the person gets the A chain correct. After this success, you would probably increase the requirement for reinforcement to completing both sides. Finally, you would reinforce only for completing the whole assembly correctly.

Chains can be developed in two ways: forward chaining and backward chaining. In **forward chaining** you build the chain by reinforcing the first behavior in the chain and then requiring the first and second behaviors to be performed before reinforcement is delivered. Next, you reinforce only when the first three behaviors in the chain are properly executed. This continues until the chain is completed. This process is often used in teaching children to tie their shoelaces. First, you reinforce pulling the strings tight; then you show them how to cross the laces. The next step might be to have them pull the laces tight and make a cross before reinforcing.

In **backward chaining** you begin with the last behavior in the chain and gradually move to the first. Simek and O'Brien (1981) describe this method in their book on golf. In teaching golf, they start the students putting two feet from the hole and as they master that skill, the students move farther back from the hole. Once they have met the standard for the longest putts, they move off the green and practice the chip shot to criterion before working on the nine iron. The driver is the last shot practiced. This is, of course, in contrast to the way most people are taught golf, but it has been demonstrated

to be more effective and reinforcing than traditional methods. In a study by O'Brien and Simek (1978), the "chaining-mastery" group averaged 17.33 strokes lower than the traditionally trained group.

The overall superiority of backward chaining to forward chaining remains to be demonstrated. However, the advantage of backward chaining is that it puts the performer in contact with the reinforcer earlier. In the golfing example, putting from two feet is likely to be successful sooner than hitting a straight drive from the tee. For this reason, in teaching a skill, if a performance can be chained backward, that is probably the most desirable method to use.

In the motor assembly example, backward chaining would require the instructor to complete all the assembly except putting the cover on. Then it would be given to the student for completion. When that was done to some criterion, the instructor would complete all but the last two steps, and so on until completion.

Backward chaining is especially effective in teaching people complex skills, such as the use of computers, complex dance steps, fancy crafts, and making stand-up presentations.

Although people learn very long chains, they present a greater opportunity for errors and extinction to occur. This is particularly problematic in the safety and quality areas.

If a step in the chain can be omitted and the person still gets reinforced, a new chain is reinforced and the original one weakened. For example, if a mechanic fails to inspect a piece of safety equipment for wear and tear before putting it on, it may still function safely even though it was not checked. If it does, the probability that he will check the next time he puts this equipment on has been reduced, even if only slightly. If someone is supposed to check a product for a certain aspect of quality before assembling it, but doesn't and the product works anyway, the chain has been weakened.

In order to prevent a gradual deterioration of such chains, they must be observed periodically. If they are intact, they should be reinforced. If they are not, they should be corrected.

SOURCES OF INFORMATION AND DATA FOR SETTING GOALS

In setting goals, there are five major sources of helpful information and data. They are:

1. The characteristics of the performance

One source of data to help you come up with attainable goals is to examine the characteristics of the performance. In other words, how do people typically learn or change? How do people learn a new skill or change a bad habit? Many performances have distinct learning curves. In some situations, improvement is fast in the beginning and slow later on. In other situations, there is little obvious change in the beginning, but later improvement is rapid.

As an example, consider the problem of weight loss. Any weight-loss program should contain reinforcement for proper eating behaviors, such as eating the right foods, in the right amounts, and at the right times. However, it should also include a final goal and sub-goals along the way.

Losing weight has a predictable pattern. People usually lose more weight per week in the early weeks of a diet than the later ones, as illustrated in Figure 15.2. This pattern suggests that goals should be larger in the beginning and smaller later on. However, very few people on a diet take this into account when setting weight-loss goals. Straight-line goals of something like two pounds a week are more common. While two pounds may be appropriate for the first week, or maybe even the second, it would rarely be appropriate in the later stages of the diet.

Weight loss has a **negatively accelerated learning curve** in which performance improvement is rapid at the beginning but

slows later. In any task where the learning curve is rapid initially but slows down later, you can set higher goals in the early stages than in the later stages. In most cases these are simple tasks, or tasks in which people catch on quickly, so they take giant steps at first but smaller and smaller ones as they approach the optimal level.

There are other tasks, possibly the more common, where progress is slowest in the beginning with more rapid improvement in the middle stages and slower progress in the final stage. These follow a **positively accelerated learning curve**, often referred to as an **S-shaped learning curve**. With these tasks, goals should be quite low in the beginning, higher in the middle stage and lower in the final stage. Figure 15.3 illustrates this curve.

An example of a task that follows a positively accelerated curve is learning to input computer documents. Suppose you were tracking the number of error-free documents processed per hour. Let's assume that it is a complicated document with many entries. Assume further that the standard for the job is 60 error-free documents per hour.

It is conceivable that the beginning goal should only be six error-free documents per hour. This would depend on the performer's beginning level. After the performer reaches six, the next goal might be eight. Then 10 and 12. However, at that point it might be that he could go from 12 to 20 quite quickly and easily. The next goal might be 30, then 45.

Look at the curve at this point and notice that improvement slows as performance reaches some maximum. Goals should be changed to reflect this. From a level of 45, you might set the next at 50 then to 54, 57, 59, and then to the standard of 60.

2. The performer's past history

Although many tasks involve the "S-shaped" curve, it is not always necessary to set goals in this way. For example, if you have experienced performers, goals may be set very differently. People who have done

Figure 15.2

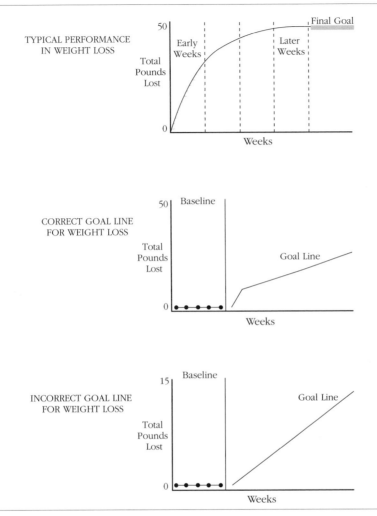

In the example of the computer operator in Figure 15.3,

the same job, or even similar jobs previously, may not only start at a higher goal, but progress at a different rate. In the example of the computer operator in Figure 15.3, a person with a history of similar work might start with a goal of 56 and proceed in increments of only two or three to some final level.

The best way to set goals is to base them on previous performance. By setting them in this way, you should always be able to set them at an attainable level. In doing so, you will increase the chances of success, which will increase motivation to do better in the future.

This is often thought to be a poor way to obtain goal-setting data because the performance may be a long way from where it should be. Even under these conditions it is the preferred, and practically always the fastest, way to achieve maximum performance.

In all cases of shaping, goals should be set, taking into consideration the nature of the performance and the history of the performers.

Figure 15.3

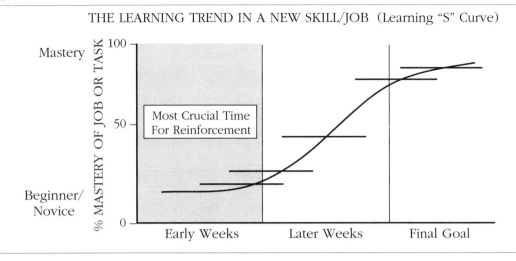

THE LEARNING TREND IN A NEW SKILL/JOB (Learning "S" Curve)

Mastery — % MASTERY OF JOB OR TASK — 100

50

Beginner/ Novice

0

Most Crucial Time For Reinforcement

Early Weeks   Later Weeks   Final Goal

3. The performance of others

The performance of others can be the source of valuable information for proper goal setting. Exemplary performers, both inside and outside the organization, demonstrate levels of performance that are possible. However, a strong word of caution is in order. Do not set up a person or group to compete against the internal exemplars. This is usually destructive. Use the information as a guide to what is possible to aim for in the future. When you say, "B crew did the best last month. What are you, a bunch of wimps?", you have set up revenge as a possible positive reinforcer. B crew may get punished by the other crews, and future failure by B crew may even be promoted and applauded by the other crews.

Using the performance of your external competition is much more productive. If you know how well or poorly your competitor does, it can be very reinforcing to close the gap or increase the distance between "us and them." This is an untapped source of information for setting goals that has tremendous reinforcement potential. More companies are beginning to seek this information, and the phrase "competitive benchmarking" is heard more frequently. While general data about

levels of cost, productivity, and quality are available in many industries, specific facts about performance levels are more difficult to obtain.

If you can't find what a competitor does, locate the "best practice" in a non-competitor. In other words, if you are a distribution manager, look for the best non-competitive distributors with products similar to yours, and ask them to share their data with you.

When using competitive data, be sure you use it as an opportunity for additional positive reinforcement—not negative reinforcement. If the competitor is substantially ahead of your performance, you will need to shape toward the goal. In addition, before setting a goal of exceeding competitor performance, make sure the data is comparable and performance conditions—equipment, material, and processes—are similar.

4. Existing industrially-engineered standards

Probably the most common information used to set goals in business are budgets and industrially-engineered standards. Deming, on the other hand, has basically told managers to throw out standards. This is probably because he has witnessed standards being used as a negative reinforcer rather than a positive reinforcer.

In many organizations, standards are used to set the level "above which you get to keep your job." People who perform below the standard are singled out for punishment. As such, standards are achieved by negative reinforcement. Therefore, few go above them and it is necessary to raise the standard in order to increase performance. Because standards are constantly being raised in this manner, they are resented as goals.

Another equally serious problem is that, generally, standards are defined by the average performer. Thus, the standard represents, at best, only a mediocre level of performance. It would be a proper goal only for those performing below standard. Experience over the last 20 years consistently shows that in PM applications, standards considered adequate for many years are regularly exceeded, often by substantial margins. Standards are useful in setting up goals, only when used as reference points for measuring success.

5. Participation by the performers

Few management techniques are more misunderstood than participative goal setting. Most managers think that participation in goal setting produces a better goal: that is, one that is more likely to be achieved. And it is true that common sense tells you if people are involved in setting a goal, they will be more committed to the goal and will perform better than if they are assigned a goal.

Remember that much research on this subject shows that many variables determine the effectiveness of participation—and that participative goal setting is not necessarily superior to assigned goal setting in goal attainment.

Many studies have found little difference between assigned and participative goal setting. While some studies have shown differences favoring participative goal setting, others show results favoring assigned goals. In their summary of research on goal setting,

Fellner and Sulzer-Azaroff (1984) state, "Despite the inconsistent findings, it can be concluded that self-selected goals will be at least as effective as those externally imposed." Even if participative goal setting isn't superior, it usually doesn't hurt to ask good performers to be involved, and most people find just being asked very reinforcing.

Asking for employees' input, however, is not always advisable. Huber (1986) states, "External goals [meaning assigned goals] are most likely to be effective when individuals lack task experience."

If the performers don't have adequate knowledge or experience with the task, participative goal setting should not be used. Participation can be used effectively in setting goals if the performers are knowledgeable enough to know what is realistically attainable, and then set a goal with a reasonable probability of being reached.

In many cases of participation, individuals and groups will set goals that are unrealistically high. In those cases, the person in charge should lower them. Many think such an act violates the spirit of participation and involvement that organizations are trying to foster today. But it's the leader's responsibility to make sure the team is successful. If he knows that a goal set by the group is unattainable or very unlikely to be attained, it is his duty to lower it. If the team is unsuccessful, or their accomplishments go unreinforced, the members will lose interest in the goal and the team, even if they participated in setting the goal.

A final reminder: Even if performers participate in setting a realistic goal, if there is no reinforcement for attainment, the goal still might not be reached. Huber (1986) notes:

> It is important to remember that the effectiveness of participative goal setting rests on the assumption that information is exchanged between the manager and subordinate which clarifies the nature of the behavioral contingency. Clarification may include information about how to perform the task, deadlines for completion, or

reinforcing consequences. If additional information is not forthcoming, then

participative goal setting might not evoke desired behavior."

16

Applying Performance Management

Hopefully by now you are convinced of the value of Performance Management as a way to manage efficiently and effectively. However, you will only be able to realize its value through systematic application of the methods described in this book.

Successful use of PM to solve a performance problem or to enhance good performance involves a series of specific steps and procedures. Omitting any of the steps significantly reduces the probability of long-term success. Therefore, it's essential to have a plan that includes all these steps and procedures.

A PERFORMANCE IMPROVEMENT PLAN

There are six critical steps in a **Performance Improvement Plan** (PIP). They are as follows:

1. **Pinpoint** the results and the supporting behaviors.
2. Develop a way to **measure** the result.
3. Develop a way to give the performers **feedback**.
4. Develop a positive **reinforcement** plan.
5. **Review** the results periodically.
6. Develop an **antecedent** plan.

Years ago, a plant implemented a very successful PM system and produced some very good bottom-line results. These improvements were noticed by upper management,

and subsequently two managers from a sister plant visited to see what they were hearing so much about. After spending most of the afternoon in the plant, they came into the performance manager's office with this assessment: "Yes, we agree that you are doing some good things, but we're doing the same things." The performance manager, who had some knowledge of management at the other plant, was shocked by this evaluation.

"What do you mean, you are doing the same thing?" he asked.

"Well," replied the visiting manager, "we have had an MBO program for years, and that is pretty much the same as your 'pinpointing.' And you know we have more measures than we can keep up with. We've got so many graphs you can hardly see the walls in the conference room. Now, I will admit that we're not doing much with recognition, but we're basically doing the same thing."

A major flaw exists in this manager's reasoning. Even if they were doing everything but reinforcement, they still were not doing PM because the only reason you do the first three steps is to be able to reinforce properly.

The Performance Improvement Plan (PIP) provides a formal way to apply PM. If the plan is followed, it ensures that all of the elements mentioned previously will be included. Of course, there are forms available to assist in the development of an effective plan. See Figure 16.1. A form alone, however, never solved a performance problem.

Figure 16.1

Performance Improvement Plan (PIP)

Pinpointing

Measurable result _____

Who are the performer(s)? _____

List the behaviors that the performer(s) need(s) to do that will significantly impact the result

_____

_____

_____

_____

Behaviors and Results need to meet the MORCA criteria   *Circle the four most important behaviors*

Data

How will you measure the result?

_____

_____

_____

How will you gather the data?

☐ Existing reports   ☐ BARS

☐ New report   ☐ Checklist

☐ Observation/counting   ☐ Self monitoring

how often? _____

Antecedents

How will you set the performer(s) up for success?

Communications plan: _____

_____

Materials/supplies needed: _____

_____

Obstacles I can remove: _____

_____

Additional training needed: _____

_____

Anything else I can do: _____

_____

Feedback

Sketch graph with legends, baseline data and goal levels (if known)

baseline

☐ Individual and for   ☐ Group

Update by: _____

How often: _____

Location: _____

How often will you discuss this verbally with the performer(s)? _____

Goals

How will you establish the goals?

☐ Performer(s) decide(s)   ☐ With the performers

☐ I will establish   ☐ Organization established

What are the goals going to be?

Desired Result	1st sub	2nd sub	3rd sub

© Copyright 1989 by Aubrey Daniels & Associates. This material may not be reproduced without written permission.

REINFORCEMENT PLAN

Result————————————

SHAPING PLAN FOR BEHAVIORS/ RESULTS *(What Am I Going to R⁺?)*	SOCIAL R⁺/TANGIBLE R⁺/COST	*PIC NFU	SCHD	DATE DELIVERED

*Can only be delivered while the behavior is occurring.

© *Copyright 1989 by Aubrey Daniels & Associates. This material may not be reproduced without written permission.*

The form is of value only if you can develop a more effective plan with it than you could without it. Experience indicates that those who make formal plans, particularly in the beginning stages of applying PM, are most successful at solving their problems.

The next section includes a fuller explanation of the six-step Performance Improvement Plan.

Step One: Pinpoint

The first step in developing a PIP is to determine the pinpoint. As you recall from previous chapters, you always pinpoint both a result and its supporting behaviors. A **supporting behavior** is any ongoing behavior that is essential to producing the desired result. Ongoing means any behavior that is continuously involved in producing a product or delivering a service.

To help yourself pinpoint supporting behaviors, you might ask, "What would the performers have to do to produce the result?" For example, suppose the desired result is to assemble several parts to complete a product of some kind. The result might be stated as "number of units assembled to specifications." Some of the supporting behaviors might be "checking each part for quality before assembly," "cleaning the assembly stand," "checking tools for proper settings," and "posting changes in assembly procedures manual." "Training" would not be considered a supporting behavior for this performance because it is not an ongoing behavior. It is a critical antecedent for the desired result and will be listed under the "Antecedent" section of the plan.

Listing as many supporting behaviors as possible will alert you to reinforce those behaviors occasionally when you see them occur. However, you will want to boil the list down to several of the most critical behaviors which will have the greatest impact on the results. Then plan more systematic and frequent reinforcement for these behaviors.

Step Two: Measure

In completing a PIP you not only should determine how you are going to measure, you also should ascertain how much time and effort is required to obtain the data. Ideally, the measures are already available and automatically recorded. If they are not, then you must balance what is desirable against what is practical. For example, if your measure involves auditing safe behavior on the shop floor, it might be desirable to check everybody at least twice each day. Most people consider this unreasonable. The question that must be answered in this situation then is: "What is the least amount of checking that would still provide us with an adequate sample of safe behavior?"

Where possible, self-recording is not only the least demanding administratively, but it also provides other advantages to the performer, as discussed earlier in this book. Whatever the method chosen, you must make sure that it is a valid and reliable one.

To complete this part of the plan, the following questions must be answered.

1. What is the measure?
2. Who collects the data?
3. How often is the data collected?
4. Is the measure easily understood by the performers?

Step Three: Feedback

Your intervention will probably require that you design a feedback system where none previously existed. Of course you will want to follow the guidelines presented in Chapter Thirteen. However, some additional points to consider in completing a feedback plan are: 1) decide where the group feedback will be posted; and 2) decide who will graph the data.

Step Four: Reinforcement

Although all parts of the plan are important, the reinforcement plan is the most important. Certainly, in the beginning it will take a considerable amount of time, since planning reinforcement is not a frequently practiced skill for most people.

Several elements constitute a good R⁺ plan. First, design your plan so that the performers will receive R⁺ early: the first day is not too soon. Second, use a variety of reinforcers: mix social and tangible. Third, provide many opportunities for R⁺: the more the better. Fourth, *do not escalate* tangible reinforcers. In other words, find things that are reinforcing; do not equate dollar value with reinforcement. If you use some things that cost money, be sure to include some that do not. Fifth, make sure that your plan does not create winners and losers. Sixth, plan some immediate R⁺ for behaviors. This means you will need to spend time with the performers to catch them in the act of doing something good.

Step Five: Review

Plan a time to get with the performers and review progress, deliver group reinforcers earned, and get verbal feedback on how the plan is working. It's a rare plan that works without some changes in the process. Use the meeting to find if performers understand the pinpoint and can help improve it by identifying supporting behaviors other than the ones listed in the plan.

An important part of the plan is to review the reinforcement plan and get feedback on whether the reinforcers you are using are indeed reinforcing. Ask for ideas of other things that might be used. Shape realistic suggestions. Do not set up false expectations as to what might be used in the future.

You should also plan at least two reviews with your boss. The first is to review the plan before it is used. Bosses don't like surprises. Make sure that the pinpoint you have chosen is important to the boss. If it isn't, don't expect any R⁺ from her for improvement in it. Also, make sure she is comfortable with the kinds of reinforcers you have chosen and their cost. This meeting will save you a lot of

grief and increase your reinforcement from up the ladder.

The second review with your boss is to review progress on the pinpoint. If you had prior agreement that the variable is worth improving, this meeting can be very reinforcing. It will also increase the boss's knowledge and interest in what the performers are doing and often brings additional reinforcement from upper management.

All of these reviews should be planned. As a part of your plan you need to set dates for these meetings before you start your implementation.

Step Six: Develop your antecedents

Although antecedents are the first part of an implementation, they are the last to be planned. A major function of the antecedent plan is to get the performers excited about the PIP. Therefore, it cannot be planned until the other parts are completed.

The overall purpose of this section is to set the performers up for success. Make sure that they are trained to do what is required to produce the result, that they understand the measure and the feedback, and that they know the supporting behaviors.

Have a meeting to explain the complete plan. You may want to put up posters or creative graphs in the work place to generate interest. Anything you can think of to increase interest and the chances of success are a part of the antecedent plan. Figure 16.2 is a checklist to aid in the development of effective PIPs.

MANAGING AN ORGANIZATION THE PM WAY

PM is not just a matter of completing PIPs and implementing them. It should ultimately provide us with an effective way of relating to others at work, at home, and at leisure. An ideal way, in fact, of fostering PM skills in the work place is to look for opportunities at

Figure 16.2

CHECKLIST FOR DEVELOPING PIPS

1. **Pinpointing**
   Results:
   - Are the results Measurable, Observable, Reliable?
   - Are they under the performer's control?
   - Is it an active performance?
   Behavior:
   - Meet criteria for result?
   - Describe all of what the performer needs to do?

2. **Data**
   - Can the performance data be collected frequently?
   - Will the data allow you to discriminate small changes in performance?
   - Is data directly related to a measurable result?
   - Will you be gathering data on both behaviors and results?

3. **Feedback**
   - Will the feedback graph be available for the performers to see?
   - Who will keep it up-to-date?

4. **Goals**
   - Did you consider the baseline data?
   - When you established the goals did you involve the performers?
   - Did you consider the past learning history?
   - Have you established the goal level you wish to attain?
   - Have you established sub-goals?

5. **Reinforcement Plan**
   - Have you included R⁺ on a VR or VI schedule?
   - Are there eight or more R⁺ opportunities listed?
   - Are there different tangibles and socials listed?
   - Are the reinforcers non-escalating?
   - Do all the performers have an opportunity to be reinforced?
   - Have you received input from the performers on what the R⁺ will be?
   - Are the most important behaviors identified in the pinpointing section included?
   - Are immediate consequences included?

6. **Antecedents**
   - Does the plan ensure the performers will know what to do?
   - Is there a specific communications plan included?
   - Have all the tools, training, and necessary materials been provided?

7. **Review**
   - Have reviews been scheduled?
   - Are there plans to ensure that meetings will be reinforcing to participants?
   - Have plans been made to reinforce performance after goal is reached?

home to reinforce family members and friends for successes and for moral and spiritual growth. Once in the "search" mode for R+ opportunity at home and at work, you're on the way to a happier, more prolific future.

When used in a systematic way at work, PM should provide the most effective way of managing a business. PM should be just as helpful to the presidents of a business in their jobs as it is for supervisors and machine operators. In order to maximize the opportunity that this technology presents to an organization, everybody must be involved in the process.

Imagine an organization where all employees could describe the mission of the organization, along with its values and operating principles, and tell you precisely the numerical goals for the company, for their department, and for their own jobs. Imagine also that they could show you specifically (possibly by using a graph) what they were doing at any moment to increase the likelihood that the organization would be successful. It may sound like a dream, but an increasing number of organizations are realizing that dream. (*Performance Management Magazine* regularly documents the successes of organizations using this approach.)

The ultimate goal is to make PM a way of life for the company. The responsibilities for feedback and reinforcement are not just for management but for everybody—managers to subordinates, subordinates to managers, peers to peers, employees to customers, and employees to vendors.

There are eight steps to making PM a way of life in an organization:

1. Link PM to the organizational mission

For PM to survive, it must contribute to the accomplishment of the organizational mission. What is the organization trying to do and how can PM help? What are the key results the organization is trying to produce?

Years ago I was sent to talk to the director of a carpet division by the owner of a major textile firm about installing PM in the

division plants. The manager knew I was a psychologist and that I had developed some "motivational program." I waited for over an hour to see him. I was not on the top of his priority list for the day.

At length, he burst into the conference room where I had been instructed to wait, and without introducing himself, plopped down at the opposite end of the conference table, pointed his finger at me, and in rapid-fire speech said, "Can you help me make carpet?" Startled by the abruptness of these events, I stammered, "Yes, sir."

Although he didn't say it, I knew he didn't believe me. He had seen many of these "programs" come and go over the years. Most of them had been directed at morale or performance problems of one kind or another. Even if they produced any effect, none had been lasting, and none had any demonstrable effect on making carpet better, faster, and cheaper—the problems that kept him awake nights and on the carpet (no pun intended) with his boss.

The only reason this manager should spend the time and money required to implement PM in his division is that it *would* make a difference in how well the organization performed against its mission—its reason for being in existence. When managers see a direct contribution to "bottom-line" variables, it is easy to get and maintain their interest in the effective use of PM throughout the organization.

The first step in making PM a way of life in any organization is to determine the results to be affected. In other words, how will the success of the implementation be judged? Which variables are important?

By now you know how to improve performance. The problem is, "Which performance?" The best way to ensure reinforcement from the top of the organization is to improve performance that affects what the top manager is most concerned about.

Once the manager at the top of the organization has identified the desired outcome, it is a rather simple matter to identify the outcomes and behaviors at the other levels of the organization that affect that outcome.

2. Train all levels of management in PM

Some people seem to do many of the elements of PM naturally. Unfortunately, these skills are not natural to everybody. At first glance, giving effective feedback and reinforcement appear to be simple tasks, but as you may have discovered, it is anything but simple. A multitude of factors determine the effectiveness of these procedures and any one of them, if done incorrectly, can undo all the others. Consequently, all managers and supervisors should be trained. Even those who are "naturals" benefit from a systematic understanding and application of these principles and techniques.

Ideally, training should start with the executives. Also, they should know the most about the system. With many training programs, it is sufficient to brief the executives on the program, because they will not have day-to-day responsibilities in it. This is not the case with PM. Every day managers engage in activities and make decisions that will affect the performance of all employees. Therefore, managers should be experts in these principles of behavior.

It is rare that executives receive the most training and are the first to be trained. In spite of this, numerous organizations have been extremely successful with PM by starting lower, sometimes much lower, in the management hierarchy. When lower-level managers and supervisors demonstrate consistent success by using this approach, it almost inevitably attracts upper-management attention. Most of the presidents who have invested the time and energy necessary to become skilled in PM started because subordinates who were using the process consistently got results where others did not.

Ideally, start training as high in the hierarchy as possible and produce results that compel upper managers to get involved. The lack of participation by upper management does not prevent others from getting significant results, but it does take longer to get

results and they are harder to maintain.

3. All those trained should apply what they learned

Classroom training is only an antecedent. The knowledge gained will be applied only if the consequences favor it. To be successful at this level, at least two things should happen. One, the first application should be on a meaningful pinpoint. Two, those who apply PM should be reinforced by their bosses for developing the plan and using it.

Many people make the mistake of starting with a trivial application. You do want to be successful with your first application. However, if the pinpoint is unimportant, you probably won't get much reinforcement even if you are successful. Ultimately you should have a PIP for all your key-result areas.

4. Provide assistance to those applying PM

It takes more than training to become proficient at any skill. In order to become proficient at PM, you will need much reinforced practice.

Organizations often make the mistake of training large numbers of people in PM and then provide no on-the-floor assistance following the training. This is a mistake.

The rule is: Never train more people than you can follow-up with. Trainers get reinforced for training. And often they are reinforced for the number of people trained. But if people come out of training and are unable to apply what they have learned, either because of some knowledge or skill deficiency or because of time or other priorities, the skills will inevitably extinguish.

Ideally, some form of follow-up (one-on-one or small group) should occur within the first week after training. Two weeks is acceptable. After a month, significant deterioration of skills has already occurred.

5. Establish opportunities for all who are involved in PM to discuss their progress

Since the intent of a PIP is to help performers improve through positive reinforcement, it is necessary to talk to them to ensure that the plan is working as intended. The primary forum for this is a periodic meeting with all involved. However, frequent contact between meetings, one-on-one and in small groups, is highly desirable.

In the meetings the leader should focus on reinforcing any results obtained and should prompt reinforcement among peers. Remember, it is a leader's responsibility to set performers up for success. If, as a leader, you have monitored performance between the meetings, not only does this allow you to reinforce on-the-spot, but it also provides a benefit in the meeting because you will be able to point out the specific things you saw people do that contributed to any improvement made between meetings.

You should also prompt the team to discuss the things they did and saw others do that contributed to the improvement. This will generate considerable peer reinforcement and provide antecedents for others to do those things when they return to work.

The meetings are sometimes held weekly but, in any event, should be held at least monthly. If the team is producing significant improvement, its members will not complain about the frequency of the meetings. If they are not improving, you will probably find it necessary to work more closely with individuals and small groups to produce improvement.

6. Hold review meetings for all supervisors and managers

It is necessary when beginning PM in an organization to hold review meetings for all people involved in the formal application. The primary purpose of this meeting is to provide reinforcement for those who are making the effort to use PM in their work. It is not to be a problem-solving meeting.

A secondary purpose of the meeting is to prompt reinforcement among peers. Idea sharing, idea building, and individual and departmental cooperation and assistance are targets for reinforcement. The more reinforcement that occurs during this meeting,

the greater the likelihood that more reinforcement will occur in the work place.

Generally speaking, the first review meeting should be held within a month of the first PM application. This allows people sufficient time to have some results to report. Remember, if at the time of the meeting most people do not have positive results, then they are procrastinating or implementing incorrectly. As a leader, you should monitor behavior during the month to ensure that participants are in fact participating. Don't wait until the end of the month to see what people are doing. Your monitoring and reinforcement will ensure that most of the participants will have a success to relate at the meeting.

The review meetings should be held at every level of the organization. Meetings should be small enough for everyone to present what they are doing without the meeting lasting for over an hour and a half. The best way to do this is to allot each person an equal share of the time, usually no more than five minutes. Reasonably strict adherence to the time limit is necessary. Experience indicates that people who are doing the least, talk the longest. If they are able to ramble about why they are not using the process, some of those who are doing the most are invariably deprived of the opportunity to show their results. That obviously defeats the purpose of the meeting.

The meeting is most successful when people want to come to it. If attendance drops off, or if you find yourself postponing the meetings, they are not serving their purpose and should be analyzed to discover why they are not reinforcing. Then use what you have learned to ensure that they will be reinforcing. Keep in mind, if meetings are truly reinforcing, people will look forward to attending.

7. Involve all employees in Performance Management

Once all management has been trained in and are practicing PM, all employees should be trained in the system. Employee participation is necessary if the system is to reach its full potential.

The amount of reinforcement necessary to sustain a high-performance organization is more than management can provide alone. PM empowers everyone to solve problems without having to appeal to the management hierarchy. When employees understand feedback and reinforcement, they can use it with everybody they come in contact with—peers, supervisors, customers, and vendors. Figures 16.3 and 16.4 show two small examples of employees solving problems by themselves that previously would have been solved only by management. Figure 16.3 shows the results obtained by a lab technician in applying PM to the performance of product designers. By reinforcing the design-

ers for doing a more thorough design before he made molds for them, he was able to achieve a significant reduction in the amount of time he spent in revision.

Figure 16.4 shows the result achieved by nurses who applied feedback and positive reinforcement to doctors who reduced the amount of time patients waited.

All teams should be trained in this technology. By applying it to the team, you can increase its productivity as well as the satisfaction of its members. Teams trained in PM can plan feedback and reinforcement for all those outside of the team who affect the accomplishment of the team mission. Allen (1982) developed a course for integrating PM into traditional team training.

Figure 16.3

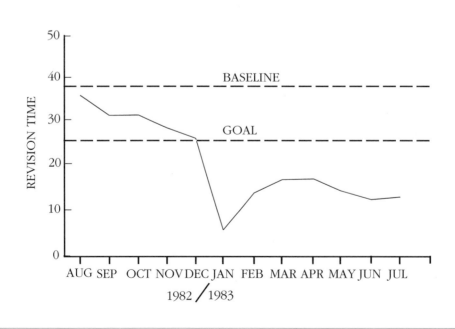

**HPD–RESEARCH AND DEVELOPMENT DEPARTMENT
1982 NEW PRODUCT MODEL REVISIONS**

Figure 16.4

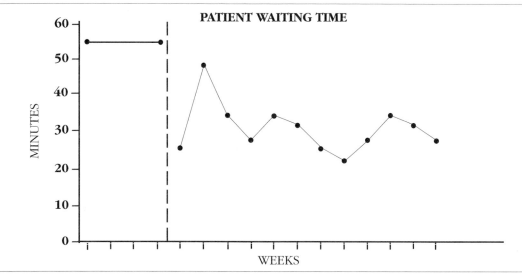

Think of what an organization could accomplish when everybody is systematically working every day to help all those they come in contact with to maximize their performance. The technology of PM makes it possible.

8. Integrate Performance Management into organizational policies and management procedures

Eventually, organizations begin to examine the way they do everything from a PM perspective. The elements of PM should be obvious in the company mission and operating principles and values.

Pay systems, benefit packages, labor contracts, attendance policies, disciplinary policies, performance appraisals, promotion policies, customer relations, vendor performance, sales and marketing, and public relations should all be administered in a manner consistent with the PM processes and procedures described in this book. This not only sends a clear message to the organization about senior management's support of PM, but also shows the value placed on it as a way to manage.

CONCLUDING REMARKS

A Beginning. The very nature of science is a never-ending quest to understand the unexplained. PM is based on scientific research, and new discoveries about behavior are constantly being made. Even with the many recent advances in Applied Behavior Analysis, our understanding of how to design and manage the ideal work place is still very limited.

Even though our knowledge is limited, the effect on organizational performance is substantial. The future is, indeed, exciting because as we learn more, the benefits to organizations and their employees will only increase.

Hopefully, this book will be an antecedent for you to continue your learning. Practicing the principles as you understand them from studying this book and from reading other books, magazines, and research journals on PM will allow you to enrich your own life and the lives of all those with whom you come in contact.

A Vision. Think of a work place in which all employees practice the leave-it-just-a-little-bit-better-than-I-found-it principle. A work place in which everyone tries to improve a little bit every day. A work place in which everyone actively seeks to find ways to help others. One in which everyone is working toward a common goal that benefits all. The practice of the principles described in this book can take us a long way toward such a place.

Future research in Applied Behavior Analysis will provide a more complete understanding of behavior, and Performance Management will benefit from these discoveries. A quote from George Land's book (1973), *Grow or Die*, should be a by-word for all organizations as they head toward business in the next century. He said:

"There can be no completely expressed growth for, as we grow more and more, new ways to grow will always be found. In this tragedy of Man is the lost opportunity when he himself turns away from exploring a new avenue of growth."

As the title of Land's book indicates, all nature is either growing or dying. PM is no exception. If PM is a truly viable approach to an effective work place, there will be many improvements in its practice in the future. We look forward to the years ahead when our new knowledge will result in an even more satisfying and productive world of work.

NOTES

REFERENCES

ALLEN, J. (1982). *Performance Teams: Completing the Feedback Loop.* Tucker, GA: Performance Management Publications, Inc.

AYLLON, T. and KOLKO, D. J. (1982). "Productivity and Schedules of Reinforcement in Business and Industry." From O'Brien, R. M., Dickinson, A. M., and Rosow, M. P. (Eds.), *Industrial Behavior Modification: A Management Handbook.* Chapter Two. New York: Pergamon Press.

AZRIN, N. H. and HOLZ, W. C. (1966). "Punishment." In Honig, W. K. (Ed.) *Operant Behavior: Areas of Research and Application.* New York: Appleton-Century-Crofts.

BAER, D., WOLF, M. and RISLEY, T. (1968). "Some Current Dimensions of Applied Behavior Analysis." *Journal of Applied Behavior Analysis, Vol 20, No. 4.* Lawrence, KS: Society for the Experimental Analysis of Behavior, Inc.

BALCAZAR, F., HOPKINS, F. and SUAREZ, W. (1985). "A Critical Objective View of Performance Feedback." *Journal of Organizational Behavior Management, Vol. 7, Nos. 3/4.* New York: Haworth Press Inc.

BANDURA, A. (1969). *Principles of Behavior Modification.* New York: Holt-Rinehart & Winston.

BRETHOWER, D. M. (1972). *Behavior Analysis in Business and Industry: A Total Performance System.* Kalamazoo, MI: Behaviordelia, Inc.

BREWER, A. (1989). "Feedback in Training: Optimizing the Effects of Feedback Timing." A thesis for The University of the Pacific, Graduate Psychology Program.

CATANIA, A. C. (1984). *Learning.* Second Edition. New Jersey: Prentice-Hall, Inc.

CHAPANIS, A. (1964). "Knowledge of Performance as an Incentive in Repetitive Monotonous Tasks." *Journal of Applied Psychology, Vol. 48, pp 263-267.* Washington, DC : American Psychological Association.

CONNELLAN, T. K. (1978). *How to Improve Human Performance: Behaviorism in Business and Industry.* New York: Harper & Row.

COOPER, J. O., HERON, T. E. and HEWARD, W. L. (1987). *Applied Behavior Analysis.*

Columbus, OH: Merrill Publishing Co.

DARLEY, J. M., SELIGMAN, C. and BECKER, L. J. (1979). "The Lessons of Twin Rivers: Feedback Works." *Psychology Today, Vol. 12, No. 11, pp 16, 23-24.* New York: Ziff-Davis Publishing Co.

DEMING, W. E. (1986). *Out of The Crisis.* Cambridge, MA: MIT Press.

DOWIS, R. (1983). "Alabama Blues: Don't Sing the Blues Anymore." *Performance Management Magazine, Vol. 1, No. 2, pp 3-5.* Tucker, GA: Performance Management Publications.

DUNCAN, P. (1989). "OBM and Success: What's the PIP?" *Journal of Organizational Behavior Management, Vol. 10, No. 1, pp 193-203.* New York: The Haworth Press, Inc.

ELDRIDGE, L., LEMASTERS, S. and SZYPOT, B. (1978). "A Performance Feedback Intervention to Reduce Waste: Performance Data and Participant Responses." *Journal of Organizational Behavior Management, Vol. 1, pp 258-266.* New York: The Haworth Press, Inc.

EPSTEIN, R. (1985). "The Positive Side-Effects of Positive Reinforcement: A commentary on Balsom & Bondy." *Journal Of Applied Behavior Analysis, Vol. 18, No. 1, pp 73-78.* Lawrence, KS: Society for Experimental Analysis of Behavior.

FEIN, M. (1981). *Improshare. An Alternative to Traditional Managing.* Norcross, GA: American Institute of Industrial Engineers.

FELLNER, D. J. and SULZER-AZAROFF, B. (1984). "A Behavioral Analysis of Goal Setting." *Journal of Organizational Behavior Management, Vol. 6, No. 1, pp 33-51.* New York: The Haworth Press, Inc.

FERSTER, C. B. and SKINNER, B. F. (1957). *Schedules of Reinforcement.* New York: Appleton-Century-Crofts.

FREDRICKSON, L. W. (Ed.) (1982). *Handbook of Organizational Behavior Management.* New York: John Wiley & Sons.

GILBERT, T. F. (1978). *Human Competence— Engineering Worthy Performance.* New York: McGraw-Hill.

GOLDRATT, E. M. and COX, J. (1986). *The Goal.* BV Netherlands: Creative Output.

HOLLAND, J. G. (1958). "Human Vigilance." *Science, Vol. 128, pp 61-67.*

HONIG, W. K. (1966). *Operant Behavior: Areas of Research and Application.* New York: Appleton-Century-Crofts.

HUBER, V. L. (1985-86). "The Interplay of Goals and Promises of Pay-for-Performance on Individuals and Group Performance: An Operant Interpretation." *Journal Of Organizational Behavior Management, Vol. 7, Nos. 3/4, FA 1985/ Winter 1985-86.* New York: The Haworth Press, Inc.

ILGEN, D. R., FISHER, C. D. and TAYLOR, M. S. (1979). "Consequences of Individual Feedback on Behavior in Organizations." *Journal of Applied Psychology, Vol. 64, No. 4, pp 361.* Washington, DC : The American Psychology Association.

IMAI, M. (1986). *Kaizen: The Key to Japan's Competitive Success.* New York: Random House.

JOHNSON, G. A. (1975). "The Relative Efficacy of Stimulus vs. Reinforcement Control for Obtaining Stable Performance Change." *Journal of Organizational and Human Performance, Vol. 14, pp 321-341.* New York: Academic Press, Inc.

KAZDIN, A. E. (1975). *Behavior Modification in Applied Settings*. Georgetown, Ontario: The Dorsey Press.

KNAPP, M. L., HOPPER, R. and BELL, R. A., (1984). "Compliments, A Descriptive Taxonomy." *Journal of Communication, Vol. 34, pp 12-31.*

KOMAKI, J. (1986). "Toward Effective Supervision: An Operant Analysis and Comparison of Managers at Work." *Journal of Applied Psychology, Vol. 71, No. 2 , pp 270-279.* Washington, DC : American Psychological Association.

KOMAKI, J. (1977). "Alternative Evaluation Strategies in Work Settings." *Journal of Organizational Behavior Management, Vol. 1, No. 1, pp 53-57.* New York: The Haworth Press, Inc.

KOMAKI, J. and BARNETT, F. (1977). "A Behavioral Approach To Coaching Football: Improving Play Execution of the Offensive Backfield on A Youth Football Team." *Journal of Applied Behavior Analysis, Vol. 10, pp 657-664.* Lawrence, KS: Society for Experimental Analysis of Behavior, Inc.

LAND, G. (1973). *Grow or Die.* New York: Dell Publishing Co.

LIKERT, R. L. (1961). *New Patterns of Management.* New York: McGraw-Hill.

LINDSLEY, O.R. (1965). "From Technical Jargon to Plain English for Application." *Journal of Applied Psychology, Vol. 24, No. 3, pp 449-458.* Lawrence, KS: Society for the Experimental Analysis of Behavior, Inc.

LOCKE, E. A., FEREN, D. B., McCALEB, V. M., SHAW, K. N. and DENNY, A. T. (1980). "The relative effectiveness of four methods of motivating employee performance." In Duncan, K. D., Gruenberg, M. M. and Wallis, P. (Eds.) *Changes in Work Life.* New York: John Wiley & Sons, Ltd.

LUNDIN, R. W. (1969). *Personality: A Behavioral Analysis .* London: The McMillan Co.

LUTHANS, F. (1981). *Organizational Behavior. Third Edition.* New York: McGraw-Hill .

LYONS, T. (1973). "An Application of Contingency Management." Unpublished term paper. "Transitional Contingency Contracting and the Premack Principle in Business." Berthold, H. C., Jr. O'Brien, R. M., Dickenson, A. M. and Rosow, M. P. (Eds.) (1987). *Industrial Behavior Modification.* New York: Pergamon Press.

MADSEN, C. H., Jr. and MADSEN, C. R. (1974). *Teaching and Discipline: Behavior Principles Toward a Positive Approach.* Boston: Allyn & Bacon.

MAGER, R. F. and PIPE, P. (1970). *Analyzing Performance Problems, or "You Really-Oughta-Wanna."* Belmont, CA: Fearon-Pitman Publishers, Inc.

MARTIN, G.L. and HRYCAIKO, D. (Eds.) (1983). *Behavior Modification and Coaching.* Champaign, IL: Charles C. Thomas Publisher.

MASLOW, A. H. (1943). "A Theory of Human Motivation." *Psychological Review,* July, *pp 370-396.*

MILLENSON, J. R. and LESLIE, J. C. (1979). *Principles of Behavioral Analysis.* New York: MacMillan & Co.

MORSE, E. (1988). "Contingent Compensation—Pay for Performance as Pie Comp." *Perfomance Management Magazine, Vol. 6, No. 2, pp 21-31.* Tucker, GA: Performance Management Publications, Inc.

MURPHY, H. A., HUTCHINSON, N. M. and

BAILEY, J. S. (1983). "Behavioral School Psychology Goes Outdoors: The Effect of Organized Games on Playground Aggression." *Journal of Applied Behavior Analysis, Vol. 16, pp 33.* Lawrence, KS: Society for the Experimental Analysis of Behavior.

O'BRIEN, R. M., DICKENSON, A. M. and ROSOW, M. P. (Eds.) (1982). *Industrial Behavior Modification: A Management Handbook.* New York: Pergamon Press.

O'BRIEN, R. M. and SIMEK, T. G. (1978). "A Comparison of Behavioral and Traditional Methods of Teaching Golf." Paper presented at the Toronto meeting of the American Psychological Association, August, 1978.

PETERS, T. J. and WATERMAN, R. H. (1982). *In Search of Excellence.* NewYork: Harper & Row.

POOR RICHARD'S ALMANACK (1979). New York: Bonanza Books.

PREMACK, D. (1959). "Toward Empirical Behavior Laws: I. Positive Reinforcement." *Psychological Review, Vol. 66, pp 219-233.*

PRITCHARD, R. D., JONES, S. D., PHILIP, L. and STUEBING, K. K. (1988). *Journal Of Applied Psychology, Vol. 73, No. 2, pp 337-358.* Washington, DC : American Psychological Association.

RIGGS, J. L. (1986). "Monitoring with a Matrix that Motivates." *Performance Management Magazine, Vol. 4, No. 3.* Tucker, GA: Performance Management Publications, Inc.

SHANNON, W. V. (1974). *They Could Not Trust the King: Nixon, Watergate, and the American People.* New York: Collier Press.

SHEWHART, W. A. (1939). *Statistical Methods from the Standpoint of Quality Control.*

W. E. Deming (Ed.) Washington DC Graduate School, Dept. of Agriculture.

SIMEK , T. C. and O'BRIEN, R. M. (1981). *Total Golf: A Behavioral Approach to Lowering Your Score and Getting More out of Your Game.* New York: Doubleday & Co.

SKINNER, B. F. (1938). *The Behavior of Organisms.* New York: Appleton-Century-Crofts.

SKINNER, B. F. (1953). *Science and Human Behavior.* New York: Appleton-Century-Crofts.

SKINNER, B. F. (1968). *The Technology of Teaching.* Englewood Cliffs, NJ: Prentice-Hall.

SKINNER, B. F. (1969). *Contingencies of Reinforcement. A Theoretical Analysis.* Englewood Cliffs, NJ: Prentice-Hall.

SKINNER, B. F. (1972). *Cumulative Record: A Selection of Papers.* New York: Appleton-Century-Crofts.

SKINNER, B. F. (1976). *About Behaviorism.* New York: Knopf.

STUART, R. B. (1971). "Assessment and Change of the Communication Patterns of Juvenile Delinquents and Their Parents." From: *Advances Of Behavior Therapy.* New York: Academic Press.

SULZER-AZAROFF, B. (1988). Personal Communication.

SULZER-AZAROFF, B. and MAYER, R. G. (1977). *Applying Behavior Analysis Procedures with Children and Youth.* New York: Holt, Rinehart and Winston.

SULZER-AZAROFF, B. and ALAVOSIUS, M P. (in press). "Acquisition and maintenance of Health Care Routines as a Function of

Intensive vs. Intermittent Feedback."
Journal of Applied Behavior Analysis,
Lawrence, KS: Society for the Experimental
Analysis of Behavior.

TOSTI, D. T. and JACKSON, S. F. (May,1981).
"Formative and Summative Feedback."
Paper presented at the Annual Meeting for
the Association for Behavior Analysis.
Milwaukee, WI.

VAN HOUTEN, R. (1980). *Learning Through
Feedback.* New York: Human Sciences
Press.

WEISBERG, P. and WALDROP, P. (1972).
*Journal of Applied Behavior Analysis, Vol.
5, No. 1.* Lawrence, KS: Society for the Experimental Analysis of Behavior.

WILKINSON, L. (1988). *Sygraph: The System
of Graphics.* IL: Systat, Inc.

YANKELOVICH, D. and IMMERWAHR, J.
(1983). *Putting the Work Ethic to Work—A
Public Agenda Report on Restoring
America's Competitive Vitality.* New York:
The Public Agenda Foundation.

GLOSSARY

A-B design. An experimental design in which baseline data is collected (A), which is followed by an intervention (B).

A-B-A design. An experimental design in which a baseline (A) is followed by an intervention (B) which is subsequently withdrawn or stopped, creating a return to baseline conditions (A). Also referred to as a reversal design because the intervention is reversed.

A-B-A-B design. The same as the A-B-A design but the intervention is started again following the return to baseline period.

ABC analysis. A problem-solving process in which the antecedents and consequences currently operating for the desired (correct) and undesired (incorrect) behaviors are identified and classified. This process usually leads to the conclusion that more positive/immediate consequences are needed for the desired or correct performance.

ABC grid. The form used in completing an ABC analysis.

Accuracy. A subcategory of the measurement of quality. In the past, errors were the more frequent measure for this aspect of

quality. Because errors are a measure of something you don't want, accuracy is the better measure of quality performance.

ACORN. An acronym that describes a criterion test developed by Thomas Gilbert for determining a job mission. Any result that might be the job mission is tested against the criteria of: **A**ccomplishment, **C**ontrol, Overall **O**bjective, **R**econcilable, and **N**umbers.

Antecedent. A person, place, thing, or event coming before a behavior that encourages you to perform that behavior. Antecedents only set the stage for behavior or performance; they don't control it.

Backwards chaining. Developing a chain of behaviors by starting with the last behavior in the chain, then proceeding to make a chain of the last two behaviors and continuing to lengthen the chain backwards to the first behavior in such a way that the complete sequence of behaviors can be performed reliably.

Baseline. Data collected before a performance improvement effort that provides a comparison with the intervention data for the purpose of evaluating the effectiveness of your intervention.

Behavior. A pinpoint that describes a person's actions. Behavior is what you see if you observe someone working.

Behavior chains. See Chain.

Behavioral consequences. Events that follow behaviors and change the probability that the behaviors will recur in the future.

Behaviorally Anchored Rating Scale (BARS). A judgment measurement technique in which each number on the scale represents a specific set of observable behaviors.

Bribery. Giving positive reinforcement before the desired behavior or performance. Because it is given before desired behavior, it practically always reinforces inappropriate behaviors.

Certain/Uncertain consequence (C/U). A way of classifying consequences in an ABC analysis. C/U asks the question: How likely is it that the person will receive the consequence?

Chain. A sequence of two or more behaviors occurring in some definite order.

Class. A subcategory of the measurement of quality. Class involves the comparison of one performance to another on the basis of something other than accuracy or errors, e.g., art, academy awards, athletic competitions such as ice-skating and diving.

Cognitive antecedent. Thoughts, feelings and internal images that prompt behavior.

Competitive benchmarking. A method of setting goals that avoids the problem of internal competition. It involves finding the performance level of your competitors and setting goals toward widening or closing the gap between your performance and your competition.

Consequences. See Behavioral conse-

quences.

Contingent. An explicit or implicit arrangement between a behavior and a consequence (usually a positive reinforcer) in which the consequence is available only when the behavior or performance is completed.

Continuous schedule of reinforcement (CRF). A schedule of reinforcement in which every occurrence of the behavior is reinforced.

Correcting. A technique for dealing with unwanted or incorrect performance. It involves providing an unpleasant consequence (punishment) for any instance of unwanted performance and positive reinforcement for the desired or correct performance.

Counting. The preferred measurement technique. Involves simply determining the number of times a performance occurs or how much time it takes.

Dead man's test. A test to determine if you have an active pinpoint. If a dead man can do it perfectly, you have the wrong pinpoint.

Differential Reinforcement of Alternative behavior (DRA). A technique for dealing with unwanted performance. DRA involves removing an existing pleasant consequence for any instance of the unwanted performance (extinction) and positively reinforcing the desired performance.

Differential Reinforcement of Low rates (DRL). A behavior is reinforced only if the frequency falls below a criterion level for a specified period of time. DRL is often used when the behavior is appropriate but its frequency is too high. Example: Disrupting a meeting by telling a joke may be appropriate to put people at ease or break the tension. However, if it happens every five minutes or during every presentation, it would be a problem.

Discriminative stimulus (S^D). An antecedent that has a history of being paired with positive reinforcement. In other words, an S^D indicates a high probability that the behavior associated with it will be reinforced. S^Ds are very effective antecedents.

Extinction (P-). Withholding, or non-delivery, of positive reinforcement for previously reinforced behavior. Extinction decreases performance. One of the four behavioral consequences.

Extinction burst. A sudden, often dramatic increase in behavior that usually occurs soon after extinction begins.

Feedback. Information on past performance which allows people to change their performance.

Feedback graph. Usually a line graph of the performance of an individual or a group. A feedback graph is the best visual device for presenting feedback.

Fixed Interval (FI). An intermittent schedule of reinforcement on which an established amount of time must pass before the behavior of interest is reinforced.

Fixed Ratio (FR). A schedule of reinforcement on which a response is reinforced only after it has been emitted a certain number of times. The ratio describes the number of unreinforced to reinforced responses. A ratio of 9:1 means nine responses would be emitted before the tenth response would be reinforced. This would typically be written as FR10.

Fixed Time (FT). A schedule of reinforcement on which reinforcement is delivered at the end of a specified time whether or not the response has occurred. In other words, reinforcement is not contingent on any performance.

Forward chaining. A chain of behaviors

developed by starting with the first behavior in the chain and proceeding to the next in the chain until the complete sequence of behaviors can be performed reliably.

Four-to-one (4:1) rule. A rule describing a minimum balance between the number of positive reinforcers (4) and punishers (1) that one gives over a period of time. The rule applies to all the reinforcers one gives, not just those to a particular person.

Goal. An antecedent that describes a specified level of performance to be attained. In PM, goals describe the level of performance needed to attain positive reinforcement.

Immediate/Future consequence (I/F). A way of classifying consequences on an ABC analysis. I/F asks the question: Does the consequence occur during or immediately after the behavior or is it delayed, in the future.

Incompatible behavior. Behavior that cannot occur at the same time as the one targeted for change. Example: Sitting down is incompatible with standing up; writing computer code is incompatible with taking long breaks.

Intermittent schedule of reinforcement (INT). Often abbreviated INT, on this schedule not every occurrence of the behavior of interest is reinforced. There are many types of intermittent schedules (see FR, VR, FI, VI).

Intervention. Usually refers to the process of applying Performance Management procedures to a problem or performance improvement opportunity. On a graph, it refers to the point in time when Performance Management was implemented.

Judgment. A major measurement technique that involves more subjective measures than counting, the other major measurement technique. There are four types of judgment measures: rank-opinion, rate-opinion, rank pre-established criteria, and rate pre-established criteria.

MBWA. An acronym for Managing By Wandering (or Walking) Around. Popularized as a management technique by Tom Peters in his book, *In Search of Excellence.*

Measurement. The use of counts or judgments to answer questions relating to the quality, quantity, timeliness, or cost of a performance.

Mission. The single most important result (accomplishment) of a job, team, or organization. (See ACORN.)

Modeling. Imitating the behavior of others. Behaviors that a person sees being positively reinforced tend to be modeled the most.

MOR. An abbreviation for three important characteristics of a pinpoint: Measurable, Observable, Reliable.

Multiple baseline design. An experimental design in which the experimenter attempts to replicate the intervention effects across subjects, settings, or performance variables. The intervention is introduced to each subject, setting, or performance variable in a sequence that allows the evaluation of the intervention against the baseline of succeeding interventions.

Negative/Immediate/Certain consequence (NIC). A category of consequences identified on an ABC analysis that inhibit performance.

Negative reinforcement (R-). The process by which an aversive consequence is escaped or avoided. Negative reinforcement and negative reinforcer are both abbreviated R-.

Negative reinforcer (R-). A consequence that strengthens any behavior that reduces or terminates the consequence. In other words, a negative reinforcer is something people will work (increase their performance) to escape or avoid.

Non-contingent. A term used to describe reinforcement given without regard to performance.

Novelty. A subcategory of the measurement of quality. Refers to performances that are important for their newness or creativity.

Performance. A number, or series, of behaviors directed toward some goal.

Performance feedback. See Feedback.

Performance Improvement Plan (PIP). A written plan for improving performance that includes all the necessary elements for maximizing performance: pinpointing, measurement, feedback, positive reinforcement, and follow-up.

Performance Management. A systematic, data-oriented approach to managing people at work that relies on positive reinforcement as the major way to maximize performance.

Pinpoint. A specific description of performance that refers to any action (behavior) of a person or any outcome (result) he produces.

Pinpointing. The process of defining a pinpoint.

PIP. See Performance Improvement Plan.

PM. See Performance Management.

Point system. A way of combining the measures of many behaviors or performances into a single number or index of performance.

Positive/Immediate/Certain consequence (PIC). A category of consequences identified in an ABC analysis having a powerful influence on performance.

Positive/Negative consequence. A way of classifying consequences on an ABC analysis. Positive refers to reinforcement and negative refers to punishment and extinction.

Positive reinforcement. The process of delivering a positive reinforcer. Also abbreviated R+.

Positive reinforcer (R+). Any consequence that follows a behavior and increases the probability that the behavior will occur more often in the future.

Post-Reinforcement Pause (PRP). The characteristic break in responding following reinforcement on a fixed ratio schedule of reinforcement. The larger the ratio the longer the pause. Following the pause the response rate returns to the high rate associated with the particular ratio.

Premack principle. A method for identifying reinforcers. The Premack principle states that a high probability behavior (one that occurs predictably in a choice situation) may serve as a positive reinforcer for a low probability behavior (one that occurs at a low or zero rate). For example, "When you finish studying (low probability behavior), you can go outside and play (high probability behavior).

Primary reinforcer. A positive reinforcer that is biologically important, such as food, water, warmth and sexual stimulation.

Punisher (P+). A consequence that decreases the frequency of the behavior it follows.

Punishment (P+). A procedure in which a punisher is presented following some behavior or performance.

Quality. A measurement category of the

degree to which a product, service or performance includes specified essential elements. The measurement of quality includes three subcategories: accuracy, class, and novelty.

R+. An abbreviation for positive reinforcer and positive reinforcement.

Rank-opinion. A judgment measurement technique used for measuring the class or novelty of a performance. Groups or individuals are compared on the basis of someone's opinion. For example: "In comparing all the programmers in the section on initiative, I rank Alfie third."

Rank pre-established criteria. A judgment measurement technique used for measuring class or quality of a performance. The performance of a group or individual is ranked with others on specified criteria. Example: "Claude ranked next to last on the Customer Service Survey."

Rate-opinion. A judgment measurement technique often used for measuring the class or novelty of a performance. Performance is scored on an opinion scale. Example: "I would rate your sales presentation as a nine on a 10 point scale."

Rate pre-established criteria. See Behaviorally Anchored Rating Scale.

Ratio strain. A disruption in high rates of performance caused by too little reinforcement or by making large changes in the size of the ratio.

Reinforcement log. A form that enables people to note pertinent information about the reinforcers they give. The form allows an analysis of who is being reinforced and the quantity and variety of reinforcers used.

Reinforcement system. An arrangement for delivering positive reinforcement that doesn't depend solely on a person's efforts. Example:

A point system allows opportunities for reinforcement in the absence of the person responsible for the performance being scored.

Reinforcer survey. A questionnaire or checklist for indicating objects, activities, and events on which one spends, or would like to spend, time and money.

Reinforcer. A consequence that increases the probability of a behavior occurring in the future. There are two types of reinforcers: positive and negative. In this book, for simplicity the word reinforcer means positive reinforcer. Negative reinforcer is denoted completely.

Reliability. Degree to which a measurement system remains consistent regardless of the conditions under which measurement takes place no matter who is measuring.

Result. A pinpoint that refers to an outcome or product of behavior. Synonyms: output, product, outcome, accomplishment.

Resurgence. The reappearance of a previously extinguished behavior.

Review system. A systematic plan for monitoring the progress of a Performance Improvement Plan (PIP). The plan usually includes periodic meetings with bosses and all others involved in the PIP.

Reward. A consequence usually given for some outstanding accomplishment. Since rewards are practically always given long after the accomplishment, they often reinforce behavior other than that involved.

Sampling. A way of collecting data on behavior where every instance of the behavior does not have to be counted. Sampling involves counting behavior at random times and frequently enough to obtain a reliable estimate of the actual frequency.

Sandwich method. An ineffective method of correcting behavior, in which a positive comment or evaluation is followed by criticism which is in turn followed by another positive comment.

Satiation. (Pronounced say'she-a-shun.) A condition created when a reinforcer loses its effectiveness because of overuse.

Scalloped effect. The effect created (on an FI schedule) by the characteristic drop in performance after reinforcement, coupled with the increase in performance that occurs just prior to the next reinforcer. On a cumulative graph this creates a scalloped effect.

Schedule of reinforcement. The response requirements that determine when reinforcement will occur.

Secondary reinforcer. Neutral stimuli that have been paired with primary reinforcers or other established secondary reinforcers to the extent that they take on reinforcing characteristics.

Shaping. A procedure that involves the reinforcement of successive approximations toward some behavioral objective or goal. A very effective method for teaching new behaviors or improving low performance.

Social reinforcers. Reinforcers that involve interaction between people. They may be verbal, written, or physical (hugs and kisses).

Spontaneous recovery. See Resurgence.

SSIP. An acronym for the rules of identifying and delivering reinforcement effectively: Sincere, Specific, Immediate and Personal.

Sub-goal. Goals along the way to some ultimate goal.

Supporting behavior. Any ongoing behavior that is essential to producing a desired result.

Tangible reinforcer. An object or activity that increases a behavior when presented following that behavior. Tangible reinforcers include things such as money, food, privileges and other activities and material items.

Thinning. Changing the schedule of reinforcement so that reinforcement is provided less often.

Time-series graph. A graph that tracks the same variable over a period of time.

Timeliness. A major category of measurement referring to when a performance is completed.

Trend line. A straight line on a graph showing overall direction of the data. The line is drawn in such a way that approximately half the data points lie on either side of the line. Trend lines can also be calculated mathematically for greater precision.

Trust. Measured behaviorally by a high correlation between antecedents and consequences. People who do what they say they will do are trusted; those who do not are not trusted.

Validity. The extent to which a measure measures what is purported to be measured.

Variable Interval (VI). An intermittent schedule of reinforcement on which the time between opportunities for reinforcement vary.

Variable Ratio (VR). An intermittent schedule of reinforcement on which the number of responses or amount of performance required for reinforcement varies.

Variable Time (VT). A schedule of reinforcement on which reinforcement is delivered at varying times with no response requirement. As in fixed time, reinforcement is said to be non-contingent.

WHIP. An acronym for **W**hat you **H**ave **I**n your **P**ossession. It refers to reinforcers that are readily available (a characteristic of effective reinforcers).

NAME INDEX

SUBJECT INDEX

APPENDIX
REINFORCER SURVEY

Name _____ Date _____

SOCIAL	TANGIBLE ($1-$25)	ACTIVITIES
1.	(Favorite Snack)	
2.		
3.		
4.		
5.		
6.		
7.		
8.		
9.		
10.		

I would not enjoy receiving:

_____ _____

_____ _____

It's okay to put this in an "open file":   YES____   NO_____

I like public reinforcement _____   I like planned reinforcement _____

I like private reinforcement _____   I like surprise reinforcement _____

REINFORCER SURVEY

Name:_____   Company:_____

The items in this survey refer to things and experiences that may make you feel good. Check each item in the column which describes how much pleasure you receive from it.

	None at all	A little	A fair amount	Much	Very much
1. Spending time on hobbies (list specific hobbies)					
2. Listening to music (list specific kind)					
3. Attending concerts					
4. Watching sports					
5. Playing sports					
6. Reading					

	None at all	A little	A fair amount	Much	Very much
7. Watching movies					
8. Watching TV					
9. Attending parties					
10. Solving problems					
11. Completing a difficult job					
12. Singing					
13. Dancing					
14. Playing a musical instrument					
15. Shopping					
16. Playing cards					
17. Being around people					
18. Involvement in church/temple					
19. Writing					
20. Organizing a program or refreshments for a meeting					
21. Cooking					
22. Painting					
23. Other					